GREAT
BRITAIN

Liverpool

WALES

Swansea

London

ATLANTIC OCEAN

FRANCE

SPAIN

AFRICA

D0577690

THE CALL OF
ZION

The Story
of the First Welsh
Mormon
Emigration

PUBLICATIONS IN THE COMPANION
RELIGIOUS STUDIES CENTER MONOGRAPH SERIES

NIBLEY ON THE TIMELY AND THE TIMELESS
Classic Essays of Hugh W. Nibley

DEITY AND DEATH
Selected Symposium Papers
edited with an introduction by Spencer J. Palmer

THE GLORY OF GOD IS INTELLIGENCE
Four Lectures on the Role of Intellect in Judaism
by Jacob Neusner

REFLECTIONS ON MORMONISM
Judaeo–Christian Parallels
edited with an introductory essay by Truman G. Madsen

LITERATURE OF BELIEF
Sacred Scripture and Religious Experience
edited with a preface by Neal E. Lambert

THE WORDS OF JOSEPH SMITH
Contemporary Accounts of the Nauvoo Discourses
compiled and edited by Andrew F. Ehat and Lyndon W. Cook

BOOK OF MORMON AUTHORSHIP
New Light on Ancient Origins
edited with an introduction by Noel B. Reynolds

MORMONS AND MUSLIMS
Spiritual Foundations and Modern Manifestations
edited with an introduction by Spencer J. Palmer

THE TEMPLE IN ANTIQUITY
Ancient Records and Modern Perspectives
edited with an introductory essay by Truman G. Madsen

ISAIAH AND THE PROPHETS
Inspired Voices from the Old Testament
edited with an introduction by Monte S. Nyman

SCRIPTURES FOR THE MODERN WORLD
edited by Paul R. Cheesman and C. Wilfred Griggs

THE JOSEPH SMITH TRANSLATION:
THE RESTORATION OF PLAIN AND PRECIOUS THINGS
edited by Monte S. Nyman and Robert L. Millet

APOCRYPHAL WRITINGS AND THE LATTER-DAY SAINTS
edited by C. Wilfred Griggs
with a preface by Noel B. Reynolds

PUBLICATIONS IN THE RELIGIOUS STUDIES CENTER
SPECIALIZED MONOGRAPH SERIES

SUPPORTING SAINTS:
LIFE STORIES OF NINETEENTH-CENTURY MORMONS
edited with an introduction by Donald Q. Cannon and David J. Whittaker

THE CALL OF ZION:
THE STORY OF THE FIRST WELSH MORMON EMIGRATION
written and translated by Ronald D. Dennis

THE CALL OF ZION

The Story
of the First Welsh
Mormon
Emigration

Ronald D. Dennis

Volume Two
in the Religious Studies Center
Specialized Monograph Series

Religious Studies Center
Brigham Young University
Provo, Utah

Produced and Distributed by
BOOKCRAFT, INC.
Salt Lake City, Utah

Printed in the United States of America

Contents

Illustrations

Preface

Monday, 26 February 1849, was a day of great significance in the history of Welsh Mormons. On that day 249 of them set sail in the *Buena Vista* from Waterloo Dock in Liverpool, homeward to their "Zion." Actually, seventy-seven other Welsh converts to Mormonism had paid their passage to travel on the *Buena Vista*; these, however, had to wait until one week later to leave Britain when they left on board the *Hartley*, a ship which contained 161 English and Scottish converts as well.

Although a few Welsh Mormons had gone to America on an individual basis after the introduction of the missionary effort into Wales in 1840, those who sailed on the *Buena Vista* and the *Hartley* constituted the first collective emigration from among the Welsh converts.

The fondest wish of these "first fruits" was that their three thousand brothers and sisters in the faith who remained in Wales would soon join them in the Salt Lake Valley, where they would live in peace and harmony far from the animosity and persecution which they had received from their nonbelieving compatriots. They desperately wanted their sea voyage and their land trek to be perfect in every way so that their success would offer encouragement to the others to follow after them. Thus the letters sent back to Wales by Church leaders were without exception enthusiastic and optimistic, almost to the point of being suspect. Captain Dan Jones, author of most of the letters concerning the migration, made even the funeral held at sea sound attractive. Hardships were minimized and conflicts were brushed aside while the primary focus was placed on the positive, adventurous, and spiritual aspects of the journey.

Jones's letters, together with those of Thomas Jeremy and William Morgan, offer extensive documentation of the crossing of the *Buena Vista* and the *Hartley*, among the best of any crossing of Mormon emigrants from Great Britain; but these letters have been almost totally ignored by Mormon historians. Because the writers penned them in Welsh, the letters and other extensive writings were rendered mute to all but the Welsh-speaking historian, a rare breed in this country.

What began for me as a casual interest in my own Welsh Mormon ancestors eventually developed into a fascination for the history of the Welsh Mormons in general. Overcoming the language obstacle was a far greater task than I had originally thought, but the reward of being able to inject life into the once meaningless pages amply justified the effort.

My objective in this book is to present a detailed account of these "sons of Gomer," inhabitants of the hills of Cambria, from the time they made the decision to seek rest in Zion's chambers until they marched proudly into the Salt Lake Valley.

Appendix A contains an alphabetized list of all 326 Welsh emigrants on board the *Buena Vista* and the *Hartley*.

Appendixes B and C combine passenger list information about the emigrants with information gleaned from numerous other sources.

Appendix D is a series of biographical sketches of many of the emigrants.

Appendix E contains English translations of the complete texts of thirty items originally written in Welsh—twenty-three letters, four poems, and three periodical articles—all dealing directly with the 1849 crossing. A separate table of contents for Appendix E lists the reference number under which the entire text may be found, indicated following the quotation by TD (for Translated Documents). "TD7," for example, would mean that item 7 of Appendix E is the full text of Dan Jones's 28 April 1849 letter to John Davis. Other quotations from Welsh to English from documents for which the entire text is not provided are indicated by the abbreviation *trans*. All translations are mine.

I would like to thank D. L. Davies, Cwmaman, Wales, for offering valuable suggestions. I also wish to express appreciation to Linda Hunter Adams of the College of Humanities Publications Center at BYU for her help and editorial skills.

Gather to Zion

The first Mormon missionaries assigned to Wales were Henry Royle and Frederick Cook, who began to proselyte in North Wales in October 1840. Some months earlier others had been preaching in the English counties which border Wales. These missionaries could well have gone into some of the Welsh villages for a street meeting or two.

The first missionary assigned to the heartland of Wales was William Henshaw. He went directly to cosmopolitan Merthyr Tydfil, a burgeoning town which had recently become the industrial center of Wales. With no knowledge of the Welsh language, Henshaw had to proclaim his message in English and hope some would understand. On 19 February 1843 he baptized his first converts, the William Davis family. During the following three years, Henshaw established several branches in Glamorgan and Monmouth, branches with a membership totaling nearly five hundred members.

In December 1845 Captain Dan Jones was called to preside over all Welsh Mormons. He went down to Merthyr Tydfil after having spent the previous year in an unproductive North Wales. For the next decade this feisty and somewhat flamboyant mariner, having exchanged a ship's deck for a preacher's pulpit, would be the central figure of Welsh Mormondom.

Born in North Wales in 1810, Dan Jones went to sea at age seventeen and for the following ten years spent most of his life away from Wales. Shortly after he married Jane Melling in 1837 he took her to America, where he became an American citizen and operated a steamboat on the Mississippi River. It was while he was captain of the little steamer *Maid of Iowa* that he first heard of the Mormons. Incredulous at the scurrilous stories then being printed in the *Warsaw* (Illinois) *Signal* and elsewhere, Jones sought out the missionaries to obtain

firsthand information. The result was his conversion, and in
January of 1843 he accepted baptism in the icy waters of the
Mississippi. He had not as yet met the Prophet Joseph Smith
but did so just a few months later in April after transporting
a group of British immigrants from St. Louis to Nauvoo. The
friendship that resulted between the Prophet and the Captain
continued right up to Joseph's martyrdom at the Carthage Jail
in Illinois. Jones was the recipient of Joseph's last prophecy,
which was that the Welshman would return to his native land
and fulfill the mission to which he had been called some
months earlier. After three narrow escapes from death during
the next thirty-six hours, Jones proceeded to make preparations to journey back to Britain.

Jones and his wife, Jane, traveling in company with
Wilford Woodruff and Hiram Clark, reached Liverpool in
January of 1845. First assigned to North Wales, Jones labored
nearly all of 1845 but baptized only two or three converts. He
was amazed at William Henshaw's success in South Wales and
was no doubt disappointed at the lack of his own. His reassign-
ment to South Wales, however, would bring forth more
encouraging results. During 1846 there were nearly five
hundred Welsh converts; in 1847 just under one thousand;
and an astounding 1,700 during 1848, the last year of Jones's
first mission.

One of Jones's principal tools in proselyting the Welsh
nation was the printing press. Numerous pamphlets in support
of Mormonism, together with a monthly periodical called
Prophwyd y Jubili (Prophet of the Jubilee) and a 288-page
scriptural commentary—all in Welsh—were published between
1845 and 1848 by this energetic Welshman.

Converting his compatriots, however, represented only one
of his objectives. Getting them "home to Zion" was the
ultimate goal. The location of "Zion" shifted from Nauvoo,
Illinois, to the Rocky Mountains during Jones's first mission,
but enthusiasm for emigrating continued undiminished.

The Perpetual Emigrating Fund, which would assist many
British converts to emigrate, had not as yet been established,
and the cost of the voyage was out of reach for most Welsh

converts, inasmuch as most of them clung to the lowest rungs of the economic ladder. They were encouraged, however, to rely on faith and save what they could; and the Lord would provide.

A ray of hope shone through the clouds of British Mormon poverty when the Joint Stock Company was established. From its inception in 1845, Jones was an ardent supporter and encouraged his flock to purchase all the shares they could afford. Hope was extinguished about a year later when Reuben Hedlock absconded with over £400 of the company's funds, £70 of which had been invested by Welsh Saints. To what extent this fiasco caused investors to abandon Mormonism is difficult to assess, since the *Millennial Star* printed very little about it and the *Prophwyd y Jubili* was totally silent. But William Henshaw, William Phillips, and Dan Jones, the three persons whose names are seen most often as contributors, continued firm in the faith after the loss. Also in the fall of 1846 when the company was terminated by the Church, there were fewer than nine hundred Welsh Mormons. That conversions increased and that the other religious periodicals did not make an issue of the company's failure suggest that repercussions were comparatively small.

The official organ of the Welsh Mormons, *Prophwyd y Jubili*, appeared monthly between July 1846 and December 1848. In nearly every one of the thirty issues there was something about emigrating: such articles as ''The Landing of Sam Brannan in California,'' ''Description of California,''[1] ''News from the Saints in the Wilderness,'' ''Who Is Ready to Start Homeward?,'' a letter from Wilford Woodruff while crossing the plains—all these fanned the flames of emigrating fever. A three-page article entitled ''Twenty-nine Welshmen Lose Their Jobs in Cwmbychan Because They Are Mormons'' added fuel.

In the February 1848 *Prophwyd y Jubili* (29–31), Jones announced that official approval had been given for the Welsh to begin making definite plans for emigrating in a year's time. All were encouraged to pay off their debts, and the wealthy were asked to be generous in assisting the poor to leave ''Babylon'' for the promised land.

In the June 1848 *Prophwyd y Jubili* (92–95), Jones printed Thomas Bullock's account of the trek from Council Bluffs to Utah so future emigrants would have a better idea of what lay in store for them. And in October Jones announced that he, himself, had been granted permission to go with the first shipload of Welsh Saints. Thus he would "get the pleasant company and heavenly teaching of the sons of Zion instead of defending the truth against the malicious tales, false assertions, and the poison and slime of this perverse and obstinate nation" (*Prophwyd y Jubili*, October 1848, 153, trans.).

Also in the October issue appeared a new song, "Hail to California," to be sung by the Welsh as they sailed away (no credit is given to the composer of the song; consequently, one would suppose that the editor, Dan Jones, had written it):

> When pestilence is harvesting the countries—
>   Harvesting man like the grass of the field;
> When its foul breeze blows
>   Laying waste the green earth,
>   California,
> Yonder across the distant seas, for me.
>
> When the sharp shining sword
>   Is bathed in blood;
> Yes, blood—the warm blood of men,
>   In the worst battles ever fought,
>   California—
> Yonder to the Rocky Mountains I shall go.
>
> (*Prophwyd y Jubili*, October 1848, 158. Appendix E, Translated Documents, item 1. Hereafter translated documents will be indicated by TD.)

Two months later in *Seren Gomer* (Star of Gomer), a Baptist periodical, appeared a lengthy parody of "Hail to California" entitled "An Invitation to California." The following two verses are typical of the scornful tone throughout:

> We can get corn without sowing or harrowing,
>   Everyone believe, everyone believe.
> And bread without baking it,
>   Everyone believe,

Houses will grow for us from the earth,
  Lovely and attractive palaces,
Oh, this is an alluring place,
  Everyone believe, everyone believe,
A place where pain or sorrow will not come,
  Everyone believe.

There are fat oxen there,
  This is heaven, this is heaven,
And thousands of fat pigs,
  This is heaven,
Are waiting by the doors,
With the knives in their throats,
Ready, morning and night,
  This is heaven, this is heaven,
There is no one with a sparse table,
  This is heaven.
(*Seren Gomer*, December 1848, 373–74, TD4;
the parody is signed ''A Small Seer.'')

The song that was sung, however, as the Welsh left Liverpool was yet another one, entitled ''The Saints' Farewell'':

Farewell now to everyone;
We shall sail the great ocean,
In complete longing for God's Zion,
For it is better to go to the land
Given to us by our Father;
We have lived captive far too long.
Freedom has come to us in the wake of adversity,
We have been called out of Babel;
At the call, our intention is to go—
To go in spite of the cruel enemy:
Our God, through His great grace,
Will bring us safely to His seemly Zion.
(*Prophwyd y Jubili*, December 1848, 186, TD3; the
song was signed ''J. D.,'' a pseudonym for John
Davis, successor to Dan Jones in the printing office.)

The Reverend H. W. Jones, publisher of *Seren Gomer* and former employer of John Davis, was not enthusiastic at the prospect of so many Welsh men and women—many former

Baptists—turning their backs on their homeland. In his periodical he warned the Welsh Mormons with an ominous prophecy:

> After receiving enough money to get a ship or ships to voyage to California, their Chief–President [Dan Jones] will sail them to Cuba, or some place like it, and will sell them as slaves, every jack one of them. It would serve them right for having such little respect for the book of Christ and giving it up for the books of Mormon. (*Seren Gomer*, October 1848, 305, trans.; the article was signed "Anti-Humbug," identified by John Davis as H. W. Jones.)

Through *Prophwd y Jubili* a call was made for the names and ages of all who intended to emigrate. A deposit of one pound sterling per person had to be paid no later than 31 December to secure passage. Detailed instructions concerning essentials such as food, clothing, trunks, and tools were printed in the November 1848 *Prophwyd y Jubili* (165–69, TD2). The itinerary was described and final counsel concerning indebtedness was given. Over three hundred Welsh Saints declared themselves candidates for the first emigrating party.

The opponents of Mormonism in Wales were incensed at these enticements and claimed that their compatriots were victims of a grand and wicked scheme. Anti-Mormon publications, articles, lectures, and campaigns grew in number and intensity. Over a year before the emigration, Dan Jones assessed the situation in the Merthyr area in a 29 September 1847 letter to Orson Spencer, president of the missionary effort in Great Britain:

> They have exhausted all their ammunition at poor Joseph, and have of late beset poor Captain Jones, "his imp," and "arch impostor of Wales;" and it is truly amusing to witness the exertions of these Nothingarians, in ransacking the vocabulary of Billingsgate itself for titles with which to crown me! Some say, they have proven me even worse than Joe Smith! Others say, "He is not quite so bad, but soon will be!" The scenes here are very like the continental rabbles of Missouri, etc., and still raging worse and hotter daily. You need not be surprised should you hear of Carthage tragedies in Wales, ere long. The whole towns and works hereabouts, containing over 60,000 people, are actually drunken with infatuation, and rage for or against Mormonism. (*Millennial Star*, 15 October 1847, 318–19)

Some of Jones's fellow emigrants also wrote of the severe opposition just prior to their departure from Merthyr Tydfil to Swansea en route to Liverpool:

> The life of our dear Brother Captain Jones was in such danger that his house was attacked almost every night for weeks before his leaving Merthyr, so that his godly life was not safe in sleeping except between guards from among his brethren; and there were scoundrels so inhuman who had been paid to kill him as he left, so that he had to leave secretly the day before. (*Udgorn Seion* [Zion's Trumpet], March 1849, 57, TD5)

From Swansea to Liverpool

The plan for emigrating called for all Welsh Saints to meet in Liverpool by 15 February. Those who lived in North Wales would go as individuals or in small groups; those from South Wales would meet in Swansea on the thirteenth and would make the thirty-four-hour voyage together by steamer. The gathering in Swansea caused a great sensation among the residents and was even described in considerable detail in the local newspaper, *The Cambrian*. The tone is one of amazement intermixed with pity:

> Emigration to California.—The Latter Day Saints.—On Tuesday last, Swansea was quite enlivened in consequence of the arrival of several waggons loaded with luggage, attended by some scores of the "bold peasantry" of Carmarthenshire, and almost an equal number of the inhabitants of Merthyr and the surrounding districts, together with their families. The formidable party were nearly all "Latter Day Saints," and came to this town for the purpose of proceeding to Liverpool in the *Troubador* steamer, where a ship is in readiness to transport them next week to the glittering regions

of California. This goodly company is under the command of a pop-
ular Saint, known as Captain Dan Jones, a hardy traveller, and a
brother of the well-known John Jones, Llangollen, the able disputant
on the subject of "Baptism." He arrived in the town on Tuesday
evening, and seems to enjoy the respect and confidence of his faithful band. He entered the town amidst the gaze of hundreds of spectators, and in the evening he delivered his valedictory address at
the Trades' Hall, to a numerous audience, the majority of whom
were led by curiosity to hear his doctrines, which are quite novel in
this town. Amongst the group were many substantial farmers from
the neighbourhoods of Brechfa and Llanybydder, Carmarthenshire;
and although they were well to do, they disposed of their possessions, to get to California, their New Jerusalem as they deem it,
where their fanaticism teaches them to believe they will escape from
the general destruction and conflagration that is shortly to envelop
this earth. It is due to them, however, to state, that they are far
from being smitten by that mania for gold, the discovery of which
has imparted to the modern El Dorado such notoriety of late. They
seem animated only with the most devout feelings and aspirations,
which seem to flow from no other source (judging from their conver-
sation) than a sincere belief that the End of the World is at hand,
and that their great Captain of Salvation is soon to visit his "bobl yn
ngwlad y Saint" [people in the country of the Saints]. It is their
intention, we are informed, not to visit the gold regions, but the
agricultural districts, where they intend, they say, by helping one
another, to reside in peace and harmony, and to exemplify the truth
of "brotherly love," not in name, but in practice. Amongst the
number who came here were several aged men, varing from 70 to
90 years of age, and "whose hoary locks" not only proclaimed their
"lengthened years," but render it very improbable they will live to
see America; yet so deluded are the poor and simple Saints, that they
believe that every one amongst them, however infirm and old they
may be, will as surely land in California safely, as they started from
Wales. Their faith is most extraordinary. On Wednesday morning,
after being addressed by their leader, all repaired on board in admi-
rable order, and with extraordinary resignation. Their departure was
witnessed by hundreds of spectators, and whilst the steamer gaily
passed down the river, the Saints commenced singing a favourite
hymn. On entering the piers, however, they abruptly stopped singing, and lustily responded to the cheering with which they were
greeted by the inhabitants. (*The Cambrian*, 16 February 1849)

The departure from Swansea was at 9 o'clock Wednesday morning, 14 February 1849; the arrival at Liverpool was the following day at 3:30 P.M. The journey, according to William Phillips, Dan Jones's successor, was shorter than usual by four hours. Phillips accompanied the emigrants during the two-week period prior to their departure from Liverpool, not only to see them off but also to gain firsthand knowledge to share with future emigrants. In the March 1849 *Udgorn Seion* he published a brief account of their experiences.

In a fashion that was standard with other letter writers about the journey, William Phillips accentuated the positive aspects of the emigration and downplayed anything of a contrary or discouraging nature: "Everyone was healthy and content during the entire voyage, except that a little seasickness troubled some" (*Udgorn Seion*, March 1849, 59, TD6). The "little seasickness" was described in somewhat different terms by David D. Bowen, an experienced seaman who was also on board the *Troubador*: "All the passengers with few exceptions was very sick on the passage, by the pitching and rocking of the steamer, and no one on board except Dan Jones and myself could do any help to the sick. Everybody had plenty to take care of them selfs" (Bowen, 19). For the majority of the emigrants, this was their first time aboard a ship; thus, sea legs were slow to develop. But there is no record of any having turned back. This short voyage from Swansea to Liverpool, however, was merely a prelude to fifty days of Atlantic waves en route to New Orleans.

Mid-nineteenth-century Liverpool was a bustling port city, much larger than any the Welsh had seen in Wales. Because so many neophytes passed through Liverpool on their way to parts all over the world, a group of fast-talking "sharpers" cropped up. Many a careless emigrant would find himself relieved of his baggage and his currency by these shrewd dealers. The Welsh, however, were given fair warning by their leader in his printed instructions to them (*Prophwyd y Jubili*, November 1848, 167, TD2). Those on board the *Troubador* received additional help from the ship's captain by his landing at a place where there were no such shysters waiting.

William Phillips reported later that "through listening to their leaders' warning to take care of their possessions, all the Saints kept everything safe so that all the cunning of the predators of the place did them no harm in any way" (*Udgorn Seion*, March 1849, 59, TD6).

Brothers and sisters of the faith were encouraged to assist one another at every opportunity. Just as pioneers crossing the plains of America would plant crops along their way for the benefit of those who followed, the Saints in Liverpool assisted their Welsh comrades, despite a centuries-old suspicion between England and Wales. They had rented the "Music Hall," a large, six-story building which had sufficient rooms for the entire company to take lodging in. At the rate of one shilling sixpence per night per person, the Welsh spent five nights there.

In the harbor, final preparations were being made for the vessel which would transport the company to New Orleans. At 547 tons the *Buena Vista* was among the smaller ships used in Mormon emigration. She measured 141 x 29 x 14.5 feet and had been built just the year before at Newburyport, Massachusetts. Her captain was Ebenezer Linnell.[2]

After five nights in the Music Hall, the Welsh emigrants were instructed to go on board the ship. David D. Bowen and a few other families were already on the ship, no doubt to conserve their money supply. Bowen described the spectacle of the emigrants as they went from one place to another in the town: "All the passingers where [sic] marching along the streets of Liverpool in one body like a regiment of solders. I thought it was the biggest sight that the Liverpool people ever seen by the way they where looking at us" (19).

Three unexpected developments took place once the entire group congregated on board the *Buena Vista*: first, the departure was delayed for another six days for unexplained reasons; second, seventy-seven of those who had counted on sailing on the *Buena Vista* would have to wait another week and sail on the *Hartley* along with 161 English and Scottish converts; third, Welsh-speaking ministers from Liverpool went on board to dissuade the emigrants from going.

Many stories, some very strange, indeed, had been circulated all over Wales about the Mormons. In addition to the prophecy about the sale of the emigrants into slavery in Cuba, there was also a strong rumor that widows from South Wales on board had "prepared clothes to put on their departed husbands in California and shoes to put on their feet" (Phillips, *Udgorn Seion*, March 1849, 60, TD6).

The Reverend Henry Rees and "some of the sectarian preachers of the town" made inquiry concerning this and other information which they had received from their colleagues in South Wales. Dan Jones and William Phillips, spokesmen for the group, replied that it was a "barefaced lie" and offered the following explanation: "There are on the ship some widows who have kept some things of their husbands out of respect, but not to greet them with in California" (Phillips, *Udgorn Seion*, March 1849, 60, TD6).

These reverends failed to convert any of the Mormons to the idea of staying in Great Britain, but it was not for lack of effort. One can readily sense the animosity of the Welsh Mormons toward the ministers by these comments in an article entitled "Last greeting of the emigrating Saints," signed by twenty-five of the departing brethren:

> Many preachers of the different sects, after slandering us and smearing our characters through the Welsh publications and condemning our dear religion from their pulpits, and doing everything they could to disgrace us and to shatter our feelings are even here, when we are on board the ship, and as if they had one foot out of Babylon, they are trying to frighten the Saints about the sea voyage, about the country and about everything which is good, trying to persuade them to everything except that which they should do. (*Udgorn Seion*, March 1849, 58, TD5)

Sacrifices had not been small for many of these emigrants to become Mormons. For them to be disowned by their families, shunned by friends, and persecuted by former ministers and fellow parishioners was not uncommon. They had been constantly graced with such epithets as "deceivers, false prophets, weakheaded and unprincipled liars, idlers, the

dregs of everything which stinks in the nostrils of everyone"
(Davis, 6 October 1848, 3, trans.). The label which really
caused the Mormons to breathe fire was one applied to them
by the Reverend W. R. Davies, Baptist minister from Dowlais;
he called them Latter-day "Satanists." It is little wonder, then,
that the emigrants stood their ground on board the *Buena Vista*
and gave prayers of thanksgiving that they would soon be free
of such pernicious influences as the Welsh reverends.

Even before the ministers went on board, President William
Phillips, there to see everyone off, decided to put the Saints
to the test to see if he could convince some of the more
homesick ones to turn back with him. The answer he generally
received was " 'However much we love you, we cannot love
you so much as to wish to turn back with you. Leave us in
peace; it is forward that all of us want to go' " (*Udgorn Seion*,
March 1849, 60, TD6).

The desire of every missionary had been to baptize entire
families into the Church. Many times, however, only the wife
or the husband would become a believer. Such situations
became particularly divisive when the call came to emigrate.
Accusations were launched that men were deserting their wives
and children by going to Zion without them. And it is true
that there were several men on board who were leaving their
families behind, some with no intention of ever seeing them
again. The emigrants felt justified, however, and placed the
blame on the "Babylonians":

> They were so bad, some of them, that they influenced our own
> families, yes, our dear wives and children! so as to frighten them
> against coming with us! yes, to cause contention between husband
> and wife, between parents and dear children. What worse could
> they have done? They will have much to answer for! (*Udgorn Seion*,
> March 1849, 57, TD5)

The attraction to proceed to Zion was greater than the sense
of duty to stay behind in "Babylon" with intractable wives
and children, and the converts denounced their families as well
as those who had caused their families to refuse to accompany
husbands and fathers:

Yet, no doubt these themselves [the "Babylonians"] will raise their voices highest to condemn a man for leaving his disobedient, peevish and cruel wife behind when she refuses every offer to come. We assure you that there are no men in our midst who have not tried their utmost to get their wives to come with them and their children also. Do not the laws of men and God assure to the husband, as the head of his family, the choice of his country? And if they refuse to follow him, his wife or children are the ones who are leaving him, and it is not he who is leaving them! (*Udgorn Seion*, March 1849, 57, TD5)

Other stories had been spread about wives on board who were emigrating against the wishes of their husbands. Such stories were summarily dismissed by the signers of the "Last greeting" as baseless lies.

William Phillips reported with great enthusiasm the wondrous things which took place on board ship prior to departure: "I saw some of the Saints at times taken sick; but no sooner were hands laid on them than they were restored immediately; and I can bear witness that I have never seen more of the power of God than I saw on the ship" (*Udgorn Seion*, March 1849, 60, TD6). One of these manifestations of divine intervention came when Betsy David, nineteen-year-old daughter of Morgan and Elizabeth David, fell from the top deck to the bottom of the hold. Cut, bruised, and unconscious, she was taken to a hospital. When she regained consciousness the next day, no one thought she would live. But through the blessings and prayers of the elders, she experienced a full recovery and lived for another four decades (Chambers).

The nine children under the age of one were nonpaying passengers. Those between the ages of one and fourteen cost their parents £3 each, and all above the age of fourteen paid £3 12s 6d, a reasonable price considering £5 was not uncommon for such a voyage. The price also included the needed provisions. All the fares having been collected and the ship put into a state of readiness, the only two things left to complete were to organize the emigrants into different sections and set sail.

The 249 persons on board the *Buena Vista* were assigned to be in one of eight sections. An elder was appointed to supervise each section "to see that everyone acted properly and received justice impartially, to foster and nurture love and unity, and especially to see that all kept the places clean and healthful" (Jones, 18 April 1849, 5, TD7). To keep the ship clean, two men were assigned to arise each morning before all the others in their group to wash and dry the deck. Captain Dan Jones, very much at home back on board ship after four years on land, was the president of the emigrating company. He was assisted by the triad of William Morgan, a forty-six-year-old engineer from Merthyr Tydfil; Rice Williams, a forty-five-year-old farmer from Rhymni; and William Davis, a forty-three-year-old tailor from Rhymni. These constituted a "council" which was to organize all temporal and spiritual matters.

After a nine-day wait and after one-fourth of the group had been reassigned to sail a few days later, the *Buena Vista* was ready to be dragged out to sea; two large steamers performed the task. Tears of joy, excitement, and anxiety rolled down the passengers' cheeks. Tears of sadness were in the eyes of William Phillips, Abel Evans, Elieser Edwards, John Davies, David Jeremy, and Daniel Evans, brethren who had come to bid farewell to the emigrants. Tears of disappointment were on the faces of the seventy-seven who had paid to be on the *Buena Vista* but who still had another week of waiting in Liverpool. Dan Jones described the departure:

> On Monday, the 26th of February, about two o'clock in the afternoon, we set sail from the port, and all the Saints, accompanied by the harp, sang "The Saints' Farewell" as we left the dock. Their sweet voices resounded throughout the city, attracting the attention of and causing amazement to thousands of spectators who followed us along the shore as if charmed. (18 April 1849, 6, TD7)[3]

Phillips and the others had purchased oranges to hurl to the outstretched hands of the passengers as the ship was being dragged from the Waterloo Dock. Fresh fruit was expensive in Britain, and the Saints were poor; consequently, appreciation was all the greater. When the ship had gone out of reach for throwing the oranges, handkerchiefs were then waved as a final farewell and "the winds of February . . . turned into summer breezes" (Jones, 18 April 1849, 6, TD7).

Thomas Jeremy became very nostalgic at the prospect of being separated, perhaps permanently, from his brethren in the gospel:

> Oh, how lovely was the association I had with some of these brethren on numerous occasions in Wales. Sometimes the day was too short for us to talk about the things pertaining to the kingdom of God, and we would frequently take the night as an extention to it. And sleep would stand in the distance from us while others would be abundantly comfortable in its grasp. At that time it came to my mind, "When will I see them again?" I imagined hearing something in answer that it would not be long before seeing them over in Zion. And at that I took courage. (18 April 1849, 21, TD8)

The opposition back in Wales had by no means ceased with the departure of this first group of Welsh Saints. In fact, the departure was used as a reason for further agitation. The date of 27 February 1849, just one day after the *Buena Vista* had left Liverpool, was applied to a letter sent to John Davis, editor of *Udgorn Seion*. Signed "Capt. Dan Jones," it contained some rather startling declarations:

> My dear brother in the Lord—I am pleased to be able to inform you that we have landed safely in New Orleans, after a short and comfortable voyage. There is evident care in our behalf, clear proof to the world of the truthfulness of our faith, in spite of so much talk against it by the numerous false religions of the world; and perhaps this letter also will come to your hand rather miraculously; if so, proclaim it before the public, and proclaim in Gath and Ashkelon about the providential care of our Heavenly Father over us. We are going from here to Nauvoo, on the banks of the Mississippi River, in the State of Illinois, and from there to Council Bluffs in the State of Missouri. An angel showed to you in a dream the directions; inform everyone of this also. Tell all the brethren that we are well and comfortable, and convincing the world as we go forward; our numbers will be thousands by the time we reach the end of our journey, and before long we shall overthrow all the kingdoms of the earth, and we shall live one thousand two hundred and sixty years after that happens. I do not have time to write

much to you, for I have much to do. I am yours affectionately, Your father in the Lord, Capt. Dan Jones. (Davis, Preface, iii–iv, trans.)

One could disregard, perhaps, the placing of Council Bluffs in Missouri, but to have the immigrants go first to Nauvoo en route to Council Bluffs three years after the Saints' exodus from Nauvoo was more than Davis could accept. In addition, he noticed the emblem of the Odd Fellows on the stationery and declared the letter a clumsy forgery. He printed it in his foreword to the pamphlet containing Jones's and Jeremy's "authentic" accounts of the *Buena Vista* crossing (TD7, TD8), as a further caution to the already cautious Welsh Saints to beware of the continued efforts to hamper the progress of Mormonism.

On Board the *Buena Vista*

Many of the Welsh Saints were so poor that even after liquidating all their meager assets they still did not have sufficient money to pay the fare of £3 12s 6d for each member of their families. This amount is equivalent to about $18 or perhaps $100 by today's standards. And although that may sound quite reasonable, one must bear in mind that over one-third of a laborer's annual wages was required to transport himself, his wife, and a few children across the Atlantic. Once he reached New Orleans he would have to pay another ten shillings per person to go by steamer upstream to St. Louis. Yet another £1 sterling each would be required for the steamer from St. Louis to Council Bluffs. And the immigrant would need to purchase food for his family while on the Mississippi and Missouri rivers. Once he arrived in Council Bluffs he would face the expense of buying a wagon and oxen plus more provisions for the thousand-mile, three-month journey to the Great Salt Lake Valley. All these considerations in addition to the prospect of about eight months with no income made emigrating a sobering challenge.

The Perpetual Emigrating Fund was established later in 1849 and would be used by many Welsh Mormons. But those on board the *Buena Vista* and the *Hartley* had to use other means. Some intended from the outset to proceed only as far as Council Bluffs, where they would work and save until they could buy themselves a "fitout" to continue westward. Some had just enough to go the full distance. And some made arrangements to earn their way by going as maid or servant to a family that could afford to pay for their services. Elizabeth Lewis, a wealthy convert from Kidwelly, states in a brief autobiographical sketch that she paid passage across the ocean of forty persons and provided expenses of thirty-two persons from Council Bluffs to Salt Lake City (Tullidge, 461–62). Not all of these were maids or servants; there appears to have been an agreement of eventual reimbursement with some.

Of the 249 passengers on the *Buena Vista*, 52 percent (130) were male and 48 percent (119) were female. Table 1 shows the distribution of age groups:

TABLE 1

Age Distribution of *Buena Vista* Passengers

Age	Total	Percentage
0–10	59	23.7
11–17	36	14.5
18–30	71	28.5
31–50	62	24.9
51 +	21	8.4
	249	100.0

Most of the 249 were part of complete or partial family units as shown by table 2:

TABLE 2
Family Units among *Buena Vista* Passengers

	Total	Percentage
Part of a complete family unit (husband, wife, and children [if any])	179	71.9
Part of an incomplete family unit (father or mother and children)	37	14.8
No apparent family attachment	33	13.3
	249	100.0

Nearly 87 percent were emigrating as part of a complete or an incomplete family unit. Eleven of the thirty-three with no apparent family attachment were listed as servants or maids, thus putting them under the supervision of a family head. Only twenty-two individuals on board were "on their own."

A wide variety of occupations was listed under the column "Occupation, Trade or Profession." Family members usually received a ditto mark in this column under the occupation indicated for the family head.[4] An occasional "widow" or "son" was written in this space, and for Sarah Davis and Eliza Williams, the two who died on board the *Buena Vista*, the New Orleans clerk entered "deceased." All the other passengers, in varying numbers, had earned their way in life by performing one of the following occupations:

Blacksmith	Lime burner	Puddler
Butcher	Locksmith	Saddler
Carpenter	Maid	Servant
Clerk	Mason	Schoolmaster
Collier	Milliner	Schoolteacher
Dressmaker	Miner	Shoemaker
Engineer	Moulder	Stone cutter
Farmer	Nailer	Tailor
Joiner	Pattern maker	Wheelright
Laborer	Plasterer	Whitesmith

Only a few of these occupations required classroom training or literacy. Most of the Welsh, including women, were literate, however, thanks to the "circulating schools" from the previous century. These schools consisted of brief training in reading skills from various nonconformist ministers who traveled the countryside out of an intense desire to get people to read the Bible.[5] Their idea was to teach small groups of individuals who in turn would instruct others in their newfound skill. Little attention was given to writing, since the major thrust had to do with reading. Consequently, many of the Welsh could read or quote the scriptures, while at the same time being totally incapable of writing their names. Formal schooling of any kind in the early nineteenth century was deemed a luxury enjoyed only by the well-to-do. Children of the working class nearly always stayed within that class. Occasionally a young lad would be apprenticed to learn a trade and thus was able to rise a notch or two above his father's level, but social mobility was very unusual. The idea of becoming a landowner staggered the imagination. Since this prospect was held out to converts, one would have to assume that it constituted at least part of their motivation for joining the Church and going to the Rocky Mountains.[6]

Initial enthusiasm for the adventure combined with devotion to their newly acquired beliefs perhaps kept some of the emigrants from turning back at Liverpool. Only a few had ever been out to sea before, and had they possessed a clear concept of what was involved in not walking on terra firma for seven weeks, they might well have had second thoughts. Although described in idyllic terms by the letter writers, a crossing of the Atlantic was fraught with numerous inconveniences and hardships which would try the patience of even the most stalwart. Not that the Welsh were strangers to hardship— they had had long years of experience. But the hardships encountered on board a ship were of a variety most had never before dealt with.

Cramped conditions would become a way of life for the next fifty days:

Four to six persons were packed into berths of wooden slats
measuring six feet square. Two people might share a berth six feet
long and three feet wide. The berths were arranged along both
sides of the ship in double or triple tiers. The passenger would
sleep with his feet towards the center aisle, where provisions for
the voyage, hand luggage, and items too fragile for the hold would
be stored. Tin utensils and other light items would hang on the
sides of the berths and the beams above. The hatches had to be
closed during storms, but it might be wet below even in less violent
weather, particularly if the cargo consisted of iron rails, which might
cause greater rolling. The berths were sometimes made of green
wood and would creak horrendously as the ship rolled. In a storm,
temporary berths were known to come tumbling down. (Pratt, 5)

Jim Warner, an emigrant on board another ship, complained:

Their is not room in the beds only for 2. We must mind our heads
when we crawl in our "dogkennels" for you must go [in] head-
first and out the same or you will knock your head against the top.
A botom hamock is the best. . . . We have to get lamp and oil.
The place is very dark. We can't see to read only by the small light
that comes in the door. . . . The single folks have a curtain, goes
over 8 births. We go to dress and undress. (Warner)[7]

Under these conditions privacy was an unknown luxury.
Nowhere on the ship could two people really be by themselves,
no doubt a genuine concern to Caleb and Catherine Parry,
who were married on the day of departure. Fortunately, the
Buena Vista passengers had church and country in common
and were nearly all attached to a family. These circumstances
combined to diminish somewhat the shortage of personal space
during the fifty days of togetherness.

Stench and sanitation were ever-present challenges,
especially at the outset when seasickness was rampant.
William Clayton on board the *North America* in 1840
observed: "The wind blew hard the vessel rock and many were
sick all night. This was a new scene. Such sickness, vomiting,
groaning and bad smells I never witnessed before and added
to this the closeness of the births [berths] almost suffocated
us for want of air" (Clayton, 173). Even the best of modern-
day imaginations strain at conjuring up such scenes.

Seven weeks of being without fresh foods or means of refrigeration made preparation of appetizing meals particularly difficult. The law specified that each passenger over the age of twelve months be furnished with the following items:

Good navy bread	33 lbs.
Rice	10 lbs.
Oatmeal	10 lbs.
Wheat flour	10 lbs.
Peas and beans	10 lbs.
Potatoes	35 lbs.
Vinegar	1 pint
Fresh water	60 gals.
Good salted pork	10 lbs.
Sufficient supply of fuel for cooking	

(*Prophwyd y Jubili*, October 1848, 151, trans.)

Lest these quantities should prove inadequate during the voyage, Dan Jones recommended they be supplemented for all over the age of fourteen with the following provisions:

10 pounds of hard bread at 3 pence a pound
2 pounds of rice at 3 pence a pound
4 pounds of sugar at 3½ pence a pound
¼ pound of tea at 2 shillings a pound
2 pounds of coffee at 6 pence a pound
4 pounds of treacle at 2½ pence a pound
4 pounds of raisins or currants at 4½ pence a pound
3 pounds of butter at 1 shilling a pound
3 pounds of cheese at 8 pence a pound

At the quantity-buying prices in Liverpool these provisions would cost the emigrants about 13 shillings. Captain Jones gave a further suggestion about food: "To those who can prepare oat bread, good butter of their own, cheese, preserves, pickles, or other things they may desire, it will be very good for them to take such things with them from home" (*Prophwyd y Jubili*, November 1848, 166, TD2). These were words of wisdom from "an old tar," as Jones often called himself, who had spent many years on the sea, and the variety such additional commodities would provide was no doubt a welcome relief after a steady diet of the rather unexciting staples provided by the shipping line.

All these supplies were kept at the back of the ship in a storeroom which was dubbed "The Company Shop." Jones and his three assistants—William Morgan, Rice Williams, and William Davis—were assigned the important task of apportioning allotments to each family. The family or groups of families then prepared and cooked the food by using the cooking facilities in shifts.

Aside from the normal problems germane to being restricted to the microcosm of a sailing vessel for several weeks, much of the time passed rather uneventfully. On board the *Horizon* in 1856 was John Jaques, who described passenger life in the following manner:

> Sea-sailing is very pleasant at times. I could sit for hours on the forecastle, and watch our noble vessel dashing through the briny waves, and lashing them into an innumerable variety of fantastic forms of spray and foam. But then, who can possibly like to be continually rocked about. . . . Who admires treading on a platform that seems the plaything of an everlasting earthquake? I have no great taste for these things. I can make myself, with a little exertion, tolerably comfortable at sea, whenever it is advisable for me to go there, but when I have the privilege of choosing, I like to be where I can enjoy myself more naturally. . . . The idea of waiting, day after day, on the idle wind is bad enough, but the reality is much worse. It makes one feel like getting out and pushing behind. Then the wind comes with a bit of a vengeance, as if to make up for lost time, just as people hurry when they have been loitering on the way. Then the willing ship dashes through the waters like a mad thing, at the rate of a dozen miles or more an hour. We tack to the right and tack to the left, and, after sailing so heartily for 200 or 300 miles, the captain takes an observation and finds that we are 20 miles worse for all our trouble, or perhaps we are in about the same place as when becalmed. (*Millennial Star*, 30 August 1856, 553–57)

One of the biggest challenges Dan Jones had to deal with during the crossing was the contention which developed between a small group of passengers who eventually apostatized and the bulk of the more committed. He placed the blame on an uninvited passenger:

Also the devilish foe, himself, asserted his right with Neptune (the god of the sea) to journey with us, though his company was not so sweet; nevertheless, it was hard work to cast him overboard because of his cleverness. And not infrequently in hard times he would turn himself into an angel of light and as such would occasionally hide in the pocket of an officer. Of everyone who may be left behind in Babylon let this one be the last! He is a poor sailor, a troublemaker, and a worse guide than Ahithophel. Not to the swine, not to the sea, but to some of the Babylonians he escapes at times. And the next time that I cross the sea with a group of the Saints to Zion the other two kinds can stay home! (Jones, 18 April 1849, 13, TD7)

The day before leaving Liverpool, this unwelcome meddler had already marred the Sunday meetings held on board the *Buena Vista* by possessing one of the sisters "until she was driven out of her senses, causing her to scream and utter inhuman things and frightening curses" (Jones, 18 April 1849, 5, TD7). But after a blessing, the sister was calmed and peace restored.

Hardly any escaped the almost immediate onset of sea-sickness. The evening of the first night at sea saw all go willingly to their beds after prayer services. But for most, sleep was not to be had, rather they would divide their time between vomiting and agonizing. Though the wind was not stormy and the sea was not rough, just the normal rocking and swaying of the ship was sufficient to create the image of a violent tempest to this lot of landlubbers. Jones and a few others who had their sea legs from previous experience spent the night rendering what assistance and comfort they could to the sufferers. And, although Jones makes no specific reference to such a thing in his letter, the assistance no doubt meant countless clean-ups for and around those whose debilitated condition did not allow them to conduct their regurgitations over the guardrail on deck—a task certainly not to be envied!

The next morning after such a memorable night no one had even the least desire to move out of bed, much less to expend the gargantuan effort required to go on deck and breathe the healthful air, as Captain Jones was insisting they do. Assisted by Daniel Daniels and William Jenkins, Jones prepared some gruel from oat flour. This was better to stay in the shrunken stomachs than anything else, but hardly anyone gave any more than a groan for Jones's efforts. Thomas Jeremy reported that Jones would jokingly threaten to get the pulley down from the deck and put ropes around the recalcitrants to pull them to the top (18 April 1849, 22, TD8). Not wanting to sound negative, Jeremy declared that the sickness had actually been a benefit to the emigrants by cleansing their stomachs!

Jeremy's infant daughter, Mary, was not sick during the entire journey, although some had predicted back in Wales that she was likely to die at sea, because she had not been weaned. However, emigrants were counseled to refrain from weaning their small children just before embarking for fear the adjustment from mother's milk to ship's food would be more than a little constitution could abide.

When the vomiting was reduced to mere agonizing, Dan Jones was allowed a little more time to himself, during which he accomplished much of his pondering and writing. Thus, he began to compose the letter he would eventually send John Davis from New Orleans.[8] He reflected on the scenes he had recently left in Wales as the *Buena Vista* sailed southward between the coasts of Ireland and Wales. Four days previous to his departure from Merthyr Tydfil to meet with the emigrating Saints in Swansea, his wife Jane had given birth to their daughter Claudia; at this time Claudia was their only child, as several others had died previously, including two in Wales during his first mission. In view of the situation Jones deemed it wise to entrust Jane and Claudia to the care of fellow Saints in Merthyr Tydfil until he could return for them after delivering all safely to the Salt Lake Valley. Jane did not applaud this plan, but she could do little about it until after her confinement. Two weeks after the *Buena Vista* left Liverpool, however, Jane had made her way to the same place and booked passage on the *Emblem*, a sailing vessel which would take her and her daughter to New Orleans. From there she would take the steamer up to Council Bluffs and rejoin her husband for the trek to Zion.

But as far as Jones knew at the time, he would not see Jane and Claudia for another two or three years or more. This prospect, together with the threats on his life while back in Merthyr Tydfil, caused him to become a bit nostalgic and reflective in his letter:

> And is it a fact or just a dream that I have escaped on the water from the midst of my Welsh brothers with my life by the skin of my teeth? If so, why? If not, why all the persecution, the slander, and the false accusations I suffered for years from the press and the pulpits? Why did my residence have to be guarded for weeks? Why was my life safe only among guards? Why did I have to flee in secret before the time? Why was I not able to bid farewell to my dear wife and my baby? (18 April 1849, 8, TD7)

Just about the time that the passengers were getting accustomed to being in a constant state of motion, all were surprised and saddened at the unexpected passing of Sarah Davies from Liverpool. Although she was sixty years of age and in poor health at the outset, her desire to accompany her husband and daughter was greater than her fear of being buried at sea. The ship became a house of mourning. A prayer meeting was held that evening (6 March), and plans were made for the funeral. At two o'clock the next afternoon burial services were held on the deck. Jones preached the funeral sermon in which he endeavored to answer the question "How are the dead raised up and with what body do they come?" Jones described the event in his account of the crossing:

> After the sermon, the coffin was placed on a large plank, the ship was stopped, and after the Saints had sung a hymn the sailors raised the inward end of the plank so that the coffin slipped down the other end to the salty deep, which, because of the weight of the stones which were placed in the coffin to sink it, opened up to swallow its precious treasure and to keep it safe until the day when the command shall be given for the "sea to yield up the dead which are in it." . . . After the sea had closed its jaws on its morsel, and after our little ship had stood for us to be able to

behold this majestic sight for a few minutes, her sails were filled with breezes and she galloped across the waves as if nothing had ever happened. (18 April 1849, 11, TD7)

Jones's sermon became the topic of discussion for almost every meeting held during the rest of the voyage. Much fear and many "misconceptions" existed among the group about being buried at sea. In addition to speaking about the resurrection in general, Jones endeavored in his sermons to dispel fears and clarify mistaken ideas. With his oft-exercised gift for rhetoric he depicted a sea burial as something to be preferred over the customary ground burials:

> Some think they would float on the surface, a prey to the fish. Even if it were so, it is no worse than rotting in the cold gravel and being food for grave worms; but the fish do not have those who are buried in the sea; the purpose for putting weights with the body is so that it will sink down quickly and lower in the ocean than the fish ever go and lower than they can live. And there it will float in peaceful salt water, which will keep it from decomposing or rotting forever. Yes, until the day of their rising, when the "sea will boil," they will be kept better than the best of the Egyptians were kept through embalming. (18 April 1849, 11, TD7)

Throughout his letter Jones availed himself of every opportunity to reemphasize that the emigrants were being guided by divine powers. One of these opportunities arose on 16 March after eighteen days at sea. Because the wind had been so strong against the ship, Jones called a special prayer meeting so that all might pray for fair wind. Characteristic of the fervent attitude which he had displayed ever since his baptism in the Mississippi River six years before, Jones announced he felt like going on deck and not returning until the fair wind was granted. When he had put his foot on the first rung of the ladder, one of the brethren asked him what he wanted most. He replied he would most like to hear the mate on the deck shouting, "Haul in the weather braces!" (the order to set the sails across the ship, an order which meant fair wind). With obvious contentment Jones announced to his compatriots back in Wales: "And before I had moved my foot,

I, and the others who had heard my wish, heard the mate above
our heads shouting loudly, *'Haul in the weather braces!'*—
yea, word for word as I had said'' (18 April 1849, 12, TD7).
The fair wind came; the grateful Saints gave thanks. Gradually
the passengers developed more and more expertise in travers-
ing the rocking deck, although they frequently observed that
one of their legs was longer than the other or that the other
was shorter. At times, however, the strong winds made it
impossible for anyone to lie or stand in place. Jones compared
the ship to a door on its hinge which continually swayed those
who were reclined. "But as for those standing," he wrote,
"it was throwing them along the deck with the boxes and their
crockery as recklessly and without warning as the wild horse
throws its unskilled rider across the hedge and leaves him
there. But without any pity when the rider got up, the ship
would throw him somewhere else until he crawled home"
(18 April 1849, 10, TD7).

Often, however, the wind was fair and the weather was
lovely so that it was "almost like Wales in June." Jones
describes the activities that would take place whenever sheer
survival was not the focus:

> It is beautiful to see the children playing across the deck and
> entertaining their parents. Some singing here, others talking or
> reading there; some walking arm-in-arm while others prepare foods
> of as many kinds almost as could be obtained in any cookshop.
> The musicians did their best to beautify the atmosphere. Also the
> harp with its pleasant sounds alone in the evening entertained us
> as it sang farewell to the king of the day as he lowered his red head
> into the western sea. (18 April 1849, 12, TD7)

One other activity, engaged in for the first time by many,
Jones mentions a bit apologetically and by first holding up
a revered Old Testament prophet as precedent:

> No wonder that scenes less wondrous than this excited the heels
> of David of old to the point that he even took off his garment
> in the temple—and for what? Hush! shall we reply? What is the
> use of hiding the fact; did he not do this in order to dance? Yes,
> yes, and there was hardly anyone in our midst, except for an

occasional dry sectarian, who did not prefer to imitate him rather than to find fault. At least it would be hard to deny that it was so here at times, and it did not even cause a storm. (18 April 1849, 12–13, TD7)

On 7 April, after thirty-nine days at sea, the emigrants sighted land. The little ship had arrived at the Bahamas and the Welsh passengers were jubilant. Because this area was one of the most dangerous places in the world for navigation, a number of small ships called "wreckers" sailed around continually waiting for the opportunity to profit from the misfortune of other ships. The wreckers were well acquainted with the dangers presented by the many islands and would offer their services for a handsome fee to the ships which became lost in the maze. And often, much like today's dishonest mechanic who creates problems with an engine so he can repair it, the wreckers would send deceptive signals to lead ships into difficulty so they could go to their assistance. The *Buena Vista* passed through the area without any such assistance.

Cuba was not far to the south. Its proximity brought to mind the "ridiculous and loathesome prophecy" which had appeared in the *Seren Gomer* that Dan Jones would sell his followers into slavery. All on the deck scornfully discussed the absurdity of such a prediction. Jones observed:

> That correspondent has immortalized his foolishness with poor taste and has brought Cuba more notoriety than anything else. This now serves to bring to the recollection of the emigrants the lies and false accusations which were said and published about them and their dear religion by their fellow nation until it loosened their love, knot by knot, even from the country of their birth. And instead of thinking of turning back, it prompted them to turn their faces not toward the east but into the sunset for freedom to worship God, and for those rights of which they were deprived by "zealous Christians" of their own country! Yes, the constant prayer of everyone throughout the ship is, "Blow, east wind, blow us fiercely to the western ocean." (18 April 1849, 17, TD7)

Something which marred the crossing was the council's having to excommunicate William Jones and his wife, Marian, both nineteen. The young couple had been at odds with other passengers and especially with the religious leaders on board from quite early on in the voyage. They did not manifest the proper commitment to the teachings of their new religion to satisfy Jones and other members of the council (William Morgan, Rice Williams, and William Davis). It is quite possible that the two recalcitrants had used the Church and the emigration plan simply as a vehicle to transport them to America, as such things were not uncommon. Perhaps their intentions initially had been pure. In any event, they stayed with the Saints until they all reached St. Louis on 1 May, fifteen days after their excommunication for causing "much worry to the Saints through their false accusations to the captain, disgracing . . . [their] religion, etc." (Jones, 18 April 1849, 20, TD7). Upon landing at St. Louis, William and Marian, along with several others, left without uttering a word to Jones.

William and Marian Jones were deprived of their membership in the Church just two days prior to arriving at New Orleans. The infraction which precipitated this action by the council occurred 5 April during the Thursday night "Saints' Meeting." It was on this occasion that the Saints first "put the gifts into practice." Exactly what this phrase was meant to imply is not clear, but it appears to have reference to a special kind of communication with divine powers. Jones describes the collusion and the collision which ensued:

> Great was the commotion this caused up and down the ship amongst the Babylonians![9] They clustered along with the officers of the ship at the entrance of our place and listened in amazement. We wondered greatly what had caused this; then we perceived that "Achan"[10] was in our midst—that two or three of the Saints who had transgressed were there with them, translating for them and causing them to believe evil things about us, so that the officers of the ship and the captain also were more bitter toward us then than ever before, and I had a hard time calming him down.

Jones laments the confusion caused by traitors in their midst:

> To our dismay their interference obliged us to cease practicing the gifts in the middle of the meeting, but not before we had

received great comfort through them and learned some things about you, yourselves, there in Wales, etc. We were informed that the party of those who failed in their designs on me as I was about to leave Wales is plotting revenge on my dear fellow officers who were left behind me; but they will not succeed. (18 April 1849, 17, TD7)

One further event which caused sorrow among the emigrants was the passing of Eliza Williams, age seventy-seven, just six days before the *Buena Vista* landed at New Orleans. She had been ill several days prior to her demise. After fifty-five years with the Methodists, she rejoiced on her deathbed at the honor of dying a Mormon and bore strong testimony to the truthfulness of Mormonism. Sister Williams's funeral was similar to the one held five weeks earlier for Sarah Davis. A few days before reaching New Orleans, Jones recorded:

> More water was apportioned out for washing, as we have plenty on board to last for another month. And I cannot liken this bustling scene with the sisters all around the deck doing their washing any better than to the scenes I remember seeing by the hot waters of the iron furnaces in Merthyr on washday! . . . More food was offered from the "company store," but everyone had such an abundance that they did not come to get it. They said that all their sacks and vessels were full so that they had no room to hold any more. And many said that they had never before had such a variety or abundance of food in their lives. And I maintain that anyone who is not happy with this food should be shut in the oven for a while, like the lap dog of the gentle lady. (18 April 1849, 18, TD7)

Thomas Jeremy's wife Sarah was reported by her descendants to have had a somewhat less enthusiastic attitude concerning the food and water situation at the end of the Atlantic crossing:

> After seven weeks aboard the *Buena Vista*, they ran out of oatmeal, bread and water and had to eat hardtack and drink water full of slime, called "ropey water." (Sarah Jeremy, 8)

Numerous emotions welled within the breasts of the sojourners as they neared New Orleans: relief at the prospect of ending their fifty-day voyage on the Atlantic; joy in anticipation of being on land once again; frustration at having had such poor relations with the small group of cabin passengers (five men and two women in their twenties and one thirteen-year-old girl), one of whom had succeeded in "bemusing and confusing" one of Elizabeth Lewis's maids; anger toward the small group of disenchanted Mormons who had fought against the faithful; gratitude toward the captain and crew, despite the strained relationship with them, for their having brought them safely to the journey's end; and doubtless much nostalgia rife with homesickness as the Saints contemplated their virtually irreversible decision to begin a new life in a new land with, for most, a new language.

On the morning of 16 April two steamers went toward the *Buena Vista* in a frantic race to reach the ship first so as to be the one selected to tow her into New Orleans. The winner was given a large rope which was then used to lead the *Buena Vista* into the mouth of the Mississippi and then to the New Orleans docks.

The weary emigrants arrived at their destination the next day. The long sea voyage was finished. Two rivers, however, had to be ascended and the plains had to be traversed before their final destination was reached.

Crossing of the *Hartley*

About the time the *Buena Vista* emigrants were recuperating from their bout with seasickness, seventy-seven other Welsh Saints back in Liverpool were just about to set sail on board the *Hartley*. These had fully intended to journey across the Atlantic with their compatriots, but when it was determined that the number of paying passengers exceeded the number of accommodations on the modest-sized *Buena Vista*, one-fourth of them had to be reassigned ships. After having waited in Liverpool eleven days, already a week beyond what was originally anticipated, those selected to extend their wait for yet another week were disappointed and displeased. Some had even been sleeping on board the *Buena Vista* when they had been asked to leave. What criteria were used to determine ship assignments is not clear.

The *Hartley*
(used by permission of Peabody Museum of Salem)

David D. Bowen recorded his disgruntlement: "All our friends and acquaintances left in the Buna Vesta with Dan Jones, and we were left among strangers, to sail in another ship, and our ship was not reddy to sail for good many day yet" (19). Bowen had left Llanelli, South Wales, with his wife and two children in company with three other families. Two of these went with the first group, and two remained behind to sail with the second.

Not only did the reassignments result in separations from friends and a costly delay in a strange city, they also caused the Welsh, many of them non-English-speaking, to be thrown in with the English, Scots, and a few Irish, none of whom understood Welsh. Although all 161 of the non-Welsh passengers were also converts to Mormonism, David D. Bowen said that in their midst were "some of the meanest people" he had ever seen (21), although he did not give any illustrations of their "meanness."

Considered as a separate group, the seventy-seven Welsh on board the *Hartley* were similar in composition to those on the *Buena Vista*. Slightly fewer than half were male (35 of the 77, or 45 percent); slightly more than half were female (42 of the 77, or 55 percent). The age group distribution is shown in table 3:

TABLE 3
Age Distribution of *Hartley* Passengers

Age	Total	Percentage
0–10	20	26.0
11–17	12	15.6
18–30	24	31.2
31–50	16	20.8
51 +	5	6.4
	77	100.0

Combining the two groups, the *Buena Vista* and the *Hartley*, results in the following figures:

TABLE 4
Age Distribution of *Buena Vista* and *Hartley* Passengers

Age	Total	Percentage
0–10	79	24.3
11–17	48	14.7
18–30	95	29.1
31–50	78	23.9
51 +	26	8.0
	326	100.0

And like those on the *Buena Vista*, most of the *Hartley*
passengers were part of a complete or partial family unit:

TABLE 5
Family Units among *Hartley* Passengers

	Total	Percentage
Part of a complete family unit (husband, wife, and children [if any])	63	81.8
Part of an incomplete family unit (father or mother and children)	9	11.7
No apparent family attachment	5	6.5
	77	100.0

Combining figures for the *Buena Vista* and the *Hartley* shows:

TABLE 6
Family Units among *Buena Vista* and *Hartley* passengers

	Total	Percentage
Part of a complete family unit (husband, wife, and children [if any])	242	74.2
Part of an incomplete family unit (father or mother and children)	46	14.1
No apparent family attachment	38	11.7
	326	100.0

David D. Bowen, because of his experience on the seas, was appointed cook for all the *Hartley* passengers. But for the first few days not many took an interest in sitting up to the table. Gradually business picked up and eventually got quite brisk. It was a "very disagreeable situation," as Bowen described it (20), but the one shilling he was supposed to receive from every passenger, as promised him by Orson Pratt in Liverpool, offered sufficient incentive to keep him in the kitchen. Either the passengers had not been informed about the cook's salary or they simply chose to ignore it, for when the ship arrived at New Orleans only two passengers rewarded Bowen for his services: Cadwalader Owens with 75 cents and David Peters with 25 cents. After preparing food for over two hundred people three times a day for over seven weeks, Bowen felt cheated. He stayed with the Church and the group, however.

William Hulme, president of the Saints on board the *Hartley*, reported a voyage that had "been more like a pleasure excursion" (185). The weather had been so pleasant and the sea and the wind so gentle that only one or two rough days had been experienced during the crossing. They reached the Bahamas on the thirty-fifth day, five days fewer than had been required for the *Buena Vista*. At that point, however, some calms and contrary winds delayed their progress. Consequently, the *Hartley* docked at New Orleans on 28 April 1849, fifty-four days after leaving Liverpool.

The only blemish to an otherwise placid sea-journey was the passing of Elizabeth, infant daughter of Joseph and Mary Stringer. She died of the croup just nine days before the ship arrived at New Orleans. Her body was placed in a tin coffin made of tea canisters; this makeshift coffin was then placed in a wooden one. The burial services were held at New Orleans.

In contrast to the strained relations between the 249 *Buena Vista* Saints and their captain, the *Hartley* company got on famously with Stephen Cammet, their captain. Things had been so pleasant that the leaders of the company drew up a letter of appreciation to Captain Cammet for "the kind, humane, and generous treatment, and the watchful care" which he had demonstrated in their behalf during the passage (Hulme, 186). And four of the sailors had so greatly admired the Mormons that they cast their lot with them and were baptized immediately on arriving at New Orleans. These were John Everett, Alfred Percy, George Percy, and Davis Wilson, all in their twenties.

Two births occurred on board the *Hartley*: a son was born to Joseph and Hannah Hale from Liverpool, and a daughter, Jane Hartley Eames, to Nathaniel and Sarah Eames.[11]

From the *Buena Vista* to the *Constitution*— New Orleans to St. Louis

When the *Buena Vista* was dragged into New Orleans it was the first time for nearly all the passengers to behold the majestic Mississippi. One for whom it was something of a homecoming was their leader, Captain Dan Jones, who several years earlier had plied the *Maid of Iowa* on the river. This time, however, instead of transporting someone else's converts upstream on his boat, he had to rely on someone else's steamer to perform the task for his flock of faithfuls.

When Jones's group docked at New Orleans, they discovered that they had caught up with the Saints on board the *Ashland*, a ship which had left Liverpool on 6 February 1849, nearly three weeks ahead of the *Buena Vista*. And since the two groups were headed in the same direction, Jones hired a steamer which both shared.

"New Orleans," by Frederick Piercy

Engravings by Frederick Piercy reprinted from James Linforth, ed., *Route from Liverpool to the Great Salt Lake Valley* (Liverpool: Franklin D. Richards, 1855).

At the rate of $2.25 (about ten shillings) per person, the captain of the *Constitution* agreed to transport the combined group of nearly 450 passengers a distance of 1,100 miles up the Mississippi to St. Louis. He even agreed to pull alongside the *Buena Vista* in order to take the goods aboard his boat, and thus spared Jones's group the expense of having their belongings moved from one vessel to the other.

The exact date of departure from New Orleans is not clear from the few sources which even mention the event. Because of the cholera in that city it was considered unwise to linger; thus, one would assume that after two or three days the company was on its way once again. There was a separation of eleven days between the arrival of the *Buena Vista* at New Orleans and the arrival of the *Constitution* at St. Louis. The brief voyage was apparently uneventful, for Dan Jones had little to say about it in the 30 April 1849 letter he wrote to William Phillips from St. Louis. A young child of Rees and Jane Price died of consumption on board the *Constitution*, and a baby boy was born to Samuel and Ann Leigh just two days before reaching St. Louis. From among the English Saints who had joined with the Welsh in New Orleans, three died of the deadly cholera. Jones emphasized how fortunate they were to lose so few: "The cholera is very bad in New Orleans, and many are dying on the steamboats along the rivers, especially the immigrants. On one ship which went before us there were forty-two who died from cholera; on their other journey, nineteen, etc. But they were not Saints." Jones wrote of the surprise of the officers of the *Constitution* and quoted them as saying each morning: " 'Are there none of you dead yet?' " (*Udgorn Seion*, June 1849, 122, TD9).

Although everyone feared the cholera, the Saints thought that their faith combined with the will of the Lord that they arrive safe at their destination would make them essentially immune. Jones pointed out that the ones who had suffered so terribly were not Mormons. The writer for the *Cambrian* back in Swansea had marveled at how confident the Latter-day Saints were of reaching the end of their journey completely intact, even the old and the infirm. And it was with obvious relief that Jones happily reported to William Phillips from St. Louis: "The Welsh Saints have come alive and healthy up to this point" (*Udgorn Seion*, June 1849, 122, TD9).

The lone exception was Jenkin Williams, a twenty-year-old engineer from Aberdare, who died within a few hours after arriving at St. Louis. However, Dan Jones was still optimistic as he informed President Phillips of the boy's death: "[He] was a good and faithful lad the whole voyage, except that he went contrary to the counsels which were given, and he hid the cholera as long as he could by taking his own way to treat it through brandy. . . . A few minutes before he died, he left a remarkably good testimony after him and said that he was completely happy as he faced death" (*Udgorn Seion*, June 1849, 122, TD9).

And even though Mary Rees had a stillborn son the same day as Jones wrote his report to the Saints in Wales, he repeated his earlier comment about the general condition: "Everyone is healthy today and heartened and rejoicing in their privilege and desirous to move forward" (*Udgorn Seion*, June 1849, 122, TD9).

St. Louis was the place to purchase flour, meat and other groceries, and everything necessary for the trek to "California," which would be initiated from Council Bluffs, the place where the immigrants gathered. Clothes, firearms, stoves, and even iron to make wagons were included in the buying spree. Jones was delighted that they could hold public meetings at any time they wished. When he had been in St. Louis in 1843 and 1844, "it was worth the life of a man to say that he was a Mormon" (*Udgorn Seion*, June 1849, 123, TD9).

The *Highland Mary*, the steamer which Jones contracted to transport the Saints up the Missouri River to Council Bluffs, had just barely returned from an earlier voyage to Council Bluffs.[12] Terms were still quite reasonable although a bit more expensive than passage on the *Constitution*. There was no charge for children aged three and younger; children between four and fourteen went for half price; all passengers fifteen and older paid the full fare of sixteen shillings eight pence. Each was entitled to one hundred pounds luggage at no extra

40

"St. Louis," by Frederick Piercy

charge: two shillings was the charge for each additional hundred pounds. The cost for making the journey up to this point had turned out to be about what Jones had calculated in his counsel to the emigrants in *Prophwyd y Jubili* five months earlier.

It was May Day 1849, and the *Ashland* Saints and the *Buena Vista* Saints were eager to complete the last leg of their sea-journey to Council Bluffs. The *Highland Mary* had pulled alongside the *Constitution*, and the goods were once again transported from one vessel to another at no expense to the passengers. Preparations were nearly complete, and the departure from St. Louis was set for the following day.

A few passengers, however, desired to seek other company at this point. Jones bitterly remarked in his letter to William Phillips that "Benj. Jones and his whole family except his wife became blemished from unfaithfulness. They went away along the road to destruction at a gallop today. David Giles and David Jones and his wife went with them, completely unknown to me. I shall take greater care next time to refrain from bringing any but the faithful Saints with me" (*Udgorn Seion*, June 1849, 123, TD9). It was Benjamin Jones's son, William, and his daughter-in-law, Marian, who had been excommunicated while on board the *Buena Vista* just two weeks earlier. Benjamin Jones, in addition to his wife, Jane, had yet another son, Thomas, and daughter-in-law, Eliza, and grandson, John, traveling with him. Presumably all seven members of the family, including Jane despite her faithfulness, parted company in St. Louis with their traveling companions and were joined by three others. And, although Dan Jones did not give any further information concerning them, it is very possible that St. Louis had been their destination all along and that they were simply taking advantage of cheaper fares by joining the Church in Wales and traveling with the Mormons. If such were the case, they were certainly not the first to use this money-saving approach for reaching America.

The cholera had spread to St. Louis and had claimed many victims by this time. The second Welshman to die of this dread disease was Benjamin Francis, a forty-six-year-old blacksmith from Llanybydder. His death occurred the morning of 1 May. Jones referred to him as a "dear and faithful elder" and observed: "It would be difficult to find any more faithful than he in his life, and he died happy. His wife and children will come along with us" (*Udgorn Seion*, June 1849, 123, TD9). Benjamin and Margaret Francis had left Wales with four children; the widow Margaret Francis arrived at Council Bluffs in mid-May with only one child and unspeakable sorrow.

Cholera on the Missouri River

Cholera morbus is a highly infectious bacterial disease which is transmitted by polluted food or water; its symptoms are severe diarrhea, vomiting, dehydration, and collapse.

Virtually nothing was known in the mid-nineteenth century about prevention or about treatment of an individual once he or she had contracted the dread disease. Orson Spencer, president of the company of Saints on board the *Zetland*, which arrived at New Orleans two weeks before the *Buena Vista*, told of his experience with the cholera on the Mississippi:

> It was confidently said by officers of this steam boat, that at least fifty of so large a company would die on our passage to St. Louis. We are now within fifty miles of St. Louis, without any apprehension of another death unless a Gentile doctor on board kills them with his favorite dose of 20 grains calomel, laudanum, camphor, and brandy. This dose was given to our deceased brother and sister, contrary to my wishes, . . . and to many others who died immediately within a few hours! Several Saints I rescued from this dose who were as mortally seized, and they now live. (*Millennial Star*, 15 June 1849, 184)

The numerous suggested treatments call to mind modern-day quackery in dealing with arthritis and cancer:

> [Some] felt that the fumes in the air . . . carried the disease. As a result great campaigns were waged in which sulphur was burned for the purposes of purification. Lime was spread on the streets and all kinds of remedies were proposed. The newspaper advertisements proclaimed anti-cholera medicines of all kinds. Blood-letting was advocated and one doctor burned the soles of his patients' feet. Another raised blisters on his sufferers' abdomens. One lucky doctor found most success in washing down medicines in small doses with "lots of water." (Clifford L. Ashton, 65)

Had they listened to this last doctor and followed his advice about drinking plenty of water, fewer lives would have been lost. The medicine he prescribed was of little benefit; rather it was the water which saved the victim from dehydration. A twentieth-century physician commented:

> The prime essential in the treatment of any case of cholera is that it be regarded as a medical emergency. . . . It cannot be too strongly emphasized that the replacement of fluids and electrolytes (salts and potassium) is the most urgent necessity, and all other methods of treatment should be subordinated to it. (Elsom, 1411)

Brother Benjamin Clapp, a Church member, was advising the Saints not to drink any water if they were stricken with cholera—a most unfortunate bit of counsel. One who chose not to heed Clapp's advice was nine-year-old Thomas Jeremy. He "crawled out of his bunk and drank the water off of some oatmeal that one of the ladies had put on the stove to cook and by so doing, his life was spared" (Sarah Jeremy, 8).

Dan Jones had some advice of his own, which he dispensed to the Saints. In St. Louis he wrote to William Phillips that the members of his company had reached that point alive and healthy "through being careful to observe the rules of cleanliness, to refrain from drinking the water of the river without letting it settle, putting alum or oat flour in it—through being faithful and godly—through refraining from eating fruits, meats, etc." (*Udgorn Seion*, June 1849, 122, TD9).

Regardless of how well intended all the advice and remedies were, the reality was that in a twenty-three-day period between 28 April and 21 May, forty-four of the original 249 *Buena Vista* passengers fell victim to the cholera epidemic. One by one their names were recorded by Thomas Jeremy in his pocket-sized journal. One can only attempt to imagine his terror, especially on 6 and 7 May when the ink spelled out the names of his three young daughters, two of them buried in the same small coffin. And he was no doubt near utter despair when just four days later he wrote: "Thomas, my son, and Hanah, my daughter, are sick" (11 May 1849, trans.). These two children, however, recovered.

David and Mary Phillips had begun their journey with four children; part way up the Missouri River they were left with just one child after burying the other three in a three-day period. And so it was with Margaret Francis, who was widowed on 30 April; on 8 May she stood at the shallow, hastily dug grave of her third child to be buried in as many days. Samuel Leigh, whose wife had presented him with a new son just before reaching St. Louis, looked on helpless nine days later as both were taken from him. Very few families were left intact as the cholera swept along its path of devastation, claiming one-fifth of the Welsh Mormons aboard the ill-fated *Highland Mary*. Age was no factor in the selection process—victims ranged from newborn infants to ninety-two-year-old Evan Jones.

The otherwise uncomplicated journey from St. Louis to Council Bluffs was lengthened by several days to allow time nearly every day for graves to be dug along the shore. Only on three days of the fifteen-day passage did Thomas Jeremy not have to record new names in his journal.[13] Dan Jones's pen fell totally silent for the next two months.

Noah Jones, at the passing of his wife, Esther, expressed his grief in verse:

> My dear friends in the environs of Wales,
> Kindly hear my lament in verse;
> Lamenting still am I in sorrow
> Over the loss of my dear Esther,
> Whom I loved as my own soul

While she was mine;
But God called for my maiden;
Only He knows why;
She had to depart, though against my will.
Not one care came to my family
While crossing the ocean,
And on the Mississippi we were full of comfort,
Until we went to the town of St. Louis.
After we got there the enemy came,
With his spears filled with poison;
He cut the strongest from among us,
And did not ask permission of anyone,
Rather did he cut the finest as if the worst.

Five died by his sword,
No powers were able to withstand him.
They were buried, albeit sadly,
And then we left the town of St. Louis.
The third day of May it was,
When we left the city,
And all were glad to take their leave,
In a steamboat named "Mary."
To Council Bluffs we wished to pull.

The next day was the fourth,
Two died, and heavy is the news;
And on the fifth, seven were buried;
Today some who were seen are seen no more;
The sixth day came to meet me,
I shall forever remember that day,
For I had to leave my dear bride,
And put myself in great tribulation,
Blinded by the strength of the blow.

I called two elders to come to me;
They came according to my summons;
I was anointed with holy oil,
According to the commandment of the apostle;
And they prayed
To the One who dwells in the heavens,
And He did not delay in hearing them,
I was made whole under their hands;
As long as I live I shall remember my God.
(Noah Jones, 1–2, trans.)

William Appleby, who was on the Missouri River during
the same time period as the Welsh immigrants, recorded in
his journal a graphic portrayal of the scenes left in the wake
of the cholera:

> And to add to the horrid spectacle were the graves, side by side—
> beds and pillows half burned up—pieces of tents, broken cups,
> bowls, pillows, mattresses, etc., lined as it were the banks of the
> river, near the boat; while blankets, mattresses, beds, etc., on which
> the sick had died came floating down the river; while in town,
> nothing could be seen scarcely but carts and hearses loaded with
> rough coffins (chiefly). Physicians riding to and fro—citizens con-
> gregated together—some locking up their houses, and fleeing into
> the country, and fear and consternation depicted on every
> countenance, mingled with the groans of the sick and dying from
> the hotels, churches and houses, all added to the general and
> prevailing gloom. (Appleby, 1)

For fear of becoming infected themselves, the Saints in
Council Bluffs wanted no part of the new arrivals. Isaac Nash,
having recently buried his brother and his grandmother along
the Missouri, recorded in his journal:

> When we arrived at St. Joseph, the Captain of the boat, by
> the name of Scott, declared he would not take us any further. But
> the authorities of St. Joe made him take us away from there. We
> arrived at Council Bluffs in a sorry condition. Nobody would come
> near us. We were put out on the banks of the river with our dead
> and suffering. Apostle George A. Smith, hearing of our arrival
> and of the sad condition we were in, came down to the river
> banks. . . . Brother Smith sent word to the people that if they
> would not take us in and give us shelter, the Lord would turn a
> scourge upon them. It was not long before teams and wagons came
> down and all were taken care of. (Nash, 6)

Dan Jones may have written to John Davis and William
Phillips about the cholera and its devastation, but very little
ever appeared in print in *Udgorn Seion*. This brief comment,
made in a letter written eight weeks after the arrival at Council
Bluffs (13 July 1849), was printed: ''The cholera imposed
heavy losses on our small army along the rivers, especially

on the accursed waters of the Missouri; yet, the effect was small in comparison to that on other people throughout the neighboring boats and towns" (*Udgorn Seion*, September 1849, 180, TD10). And as Jones neared Salt Lake City three months later, he expressed concern in his letter of 12 October 1849 to William Phillips that Welsh Mormons would remain in Wales after hearing of the effects of the cholera. In addition to offering encouragement to the reluctant Saints, Jones called up the ultimate philosophy in such matters as expressed by Job: " 'The Lord giveth and the Lord taketh away; blessed be the name of the Lord' " (*Udgorn Seion*, April 1850, 108, TD13).

New Orleans to Council Bluffs— the *Hartley* Group

Waiting at New Orleans for the arrival of the *Hartley* was Lucius Scoville, who was there on assignment for the Church to assist the immigrants. Also he was there at the request of Thomas D. Brown. On board were sixty-six boxes which Brown had asked Scoville to see through customs, preferably without having to pay duty. In case that was not possible, Brown had sent $400. Scoville assisted the *Hartley* passengers through customs and succeeded in getting his assigned sixty-six boxes through duty free.

William Hulme, president of the 238 *Hartley* Saints, went back on board the ship to make a final check for any items which may have been left behind. He found one small box containing a writing desk and fixtures. He put the box under his arm and left the boat. He was promptly arrested for smuggling and put in jail to await his trial four days hence. The box was taken to the customhouse, where Lucius Scoville was transacting business. Scoville recognized it as one of the sixty-six and learned that Hulme had been put in prison with bail posted at $750. The *Mameluke*, the steamer which Scoville had arranged to transport the immigrants upriver to St. Louis, was loaded and ready to leave that evening, the third of May, at 7 o'clock. Hulme, who had been a professor of music back in England, was now behind bars of a different kind, and his two teenage daughters were waiting for him at the docks. Scoville did about the only thing he could do; he arranged for a lawyer to go the next morning to the jail, post Hulme's bail and try to clear him of the charges. The lawyer, as Scoville learned later, did just as promised. The *Mameluke*, however, departed on schedule, one passenger short. Hulme was able to rejoin the others shortly thereafter.

The only other happening in New Orleans which David D. Bowen recorded in his journal was that John Hughes Williams, president of the Welsh Saints on board the *Hartley*, got drunk. Although Bowen did not mention any repercussions, the imprisonment of one of their leaders and the inebriety of the other must have caused the immigrating Saints considerable concern. Their minds, however, would soon be fixed on a far more pressing matter—the cholera.

The New Orleans–St. Louis journey of the *Hartley* Saints coincided almost exactly with the St. Louis–Council Bluffs journey of their *Buena Vista* compatriots. And the toll exacted by the cholera epidemic was equally disastrous. On 12 May after a nine-day voyage, the *Mameluke* steamer arrived at St. Louis. Lucius Scoville wrote in his journal: "We had buried 30 Saints and 4 deck hands between New Orleans and St. Louis" (8 June 1849, 2). Ten of the dead were from among the Welsh—five children and five adults from four different families.

At St. Louis another steamboat, the *Lightfoot*, was contracted to take the company up the Missouri River to Council

Bluffs. According to Scoville, only 110 passengers boarded on
14 May. Apparently, nearly half of the original 238 remained
in St. Louis. The *Lightfoot* left St. Louis at 1:00 A.M. on
15 May and stopped a few miles upstream at the mouth of
the Missouri River to bury the seven immigrants who had died
while at St. Louis. Two days later at Jefferson City twenty-five
more passengers were taken on board, all that was left of
Brothers Farnum and Appleby's company who had been on
the *Monroe* (Scoville, 8 June 1849, 4). And at St. Joseph
another fifteen persons boarded the *Lightfoot*, these from
Brother Jesse Haven's company.

By 30 May when the *Lightfoot* reached Iowa Point, twenty
more persons had died from the cholera, the chief pilot and
the fireman among them. The river was high and the current
was so strong that the steamer could not progress any further.
For want of a pilot to take the group the forty-five remaining
miles upstream to Council Bluffs, the boat lay idle for several
days. Finally, Captain Brooks, whom Appleby labeled "a base
swindler without any refinement, more fit for a wood raft than
Captain of a steamboat" (Appleby, 1), decided to go back
downstream about seventy-five miles to Savannah Landing.
There he "put all the passengers and their freight ashore"
(Appleby, 1) and hired another steamer, the *St. Croix*, to take
the hapless immigrants the rest of the way to Council Bluffs.
There they arrived on 8 June after a frustrating and sorrow-
filled twenty-five-day journey, which even the *Buena Vista*
group with all their difficulties had accomplished in fifteen
days.

When the *Lightfoot* backtracked to Savannah Landing,
there was one Welshman who determined that he had had
enough. Having buried his wife and four-year-old son just a
few miles upriver from St. Louis, Thomas Davies decided to
take his remaining eight children and remain in northwestern
Missouri. Nineteen-year-old Thomas, Jr., however, went contrary to his father's wishes and stayed with the main body of
the Saints.

When thirteen-year-old Nathaniel Eames stepped off the
St. Croix at Council Bluffs he had been an orphan for nearly

a month. In a five-day period just before the *Lightfoot* reached St. Louis, Nathaniel had lost his father, his stepmother, his five-year-old half brother and two little half sisters. One of the little girls had been named Jane Hartley Eames, having been born on board the *Hartley* just two months before. At the end of the journey the William Owens family consisted of just three children; a complete family of parents and seven children had left Liverpool three months earlier. Of the seventy-seven Welsh passengers on the *Hartley* at least twenty died between Liverpool and Council Bluffs. There may have been more among those who remained at St. Louis; no record has been located.

David D. Bowen, the unpaid cook for the *Hartley* passengers, was one who stayed in St. Louis. Both his wife, Mary, and his mother-in-law, Elizabeth David, were extremely ill. He took them to a hospital in St. Louis where his mother-in-law was admitted as a cholera patient. Mary Bowen was refused admittance, however, because her illness was something other than cholera. Bowen then left his mother-in-law at the Charity Hospital with her youngest daughter, six-year-old Rachel, whereupon he took his wife about three miles further to the City Hospital. He left her there "with a lot of strengers that shee never seen before" and went back to the *Mameluke*, the steamer which had brought them from New Orleans. "There," wrote Bowen, "I had to nurse my little babe eight months old all night without her mother. We had a very miserable night of it."

The next day did not bring any better fortune:

> When I arrived there [at the Charity Hospital] to my astonishment shee [his mother-in-law] was dead and beried before I got there. I did not see her atall and little girl Rachel was there like a little stranger. I then went to the other hospital where my wife was. There I found her very weak & feble. She said that she had nothing to take while shee was in there but water and shee begged on me to take her out from such a miserable place. I compleyed with her desire. I took her out. I had to carry her on my back most of the way from the hospital to the boat through the City of St. Louis. (Bowen, 12 May 1849, 21)

When they reached the boat, David and Mary found two of Mary's younger sisters sick with cholera.

The next morning Morgan David, Bowen's father-in-law, went out to the country to look for a place to live. He found a small branch of the Church located at Dry Hill, about six miles from St. Louis. Some kind brothers in the gospel, Thomas Green and William Stone, accompanied him back to the *Mameluke* with a team and wagon. There they retrieved Morgan David's family and David Bowen's and transported them with their belongings back to Dry Hill. That night all nine guests, three of them extremely ill, stayed at the home of Brother Green. His landlord, a Mr. Garsaide, gave orders that the newcomers be sent away for fear they would bring the cholera to the coal diggings at Dry Hill. His orders were ignored.

The next day Bowen and his father-in-law purchased a little cabin for fifteen dollars. In a short time all were healthy except for Mary Bowen, whose condition worsened with the passing of each day. On 23 May, Bowen recorded: "With day light this morning shee was very bad and about 4 o clock shee set on the box and leaned her head back on the wall, shee died in an instant without uttering a word" (23 May 1849, 22). A month later Bowen's infant daughter died; she was buried in the same grave with her mother.

Council Bluffs—
Off the Water at Last

Rejoicing was made difficult by the unfathomable sorrow which enshrouded the Welsh immigrants as they dragged

"Council Bluffs Ferry," by Frederick Piercy

themselves, literally, into the city of Council Bluffs. Many times while still in Wales and also during the crossing, they had reviewed with great anticipation what they would do when they reached Council Bluffs. Here was where the *Buena Vista* 249 would reunite with the *Hartley* 77 plus the babies that Ann Leigh, Mary Rees, Sarah Eames, and Letitia Thomas were likely to bring forth by then. Here was where the Welsh speakers would be surrounded by English speakers and where the former would need to begin studying their new language in earnest. Here was where some would begin immediate preparation to make the trek farther westward and where others would search out employment and begin their nest eggs toward their opportunity to complete the journey to the Salt Lake Valley. And here was where the constant swaying and rocking caused by the Atlantic, the Mississippi, and the Missouri would cease.

Many, however, were absent from the anticipated reunion. Nineteen had abandoned their belief in Mormonism and were searching for brighter horizons in St. Louis and in northwestern Missouri. Sixty-seven had died at various points along the way.[14] A number of the *Hartley* Welsh had remained at St. Louis to care for their sick. As for the expectant mothers, only two of the four, Mary Rees and Letitia Thomas, would live to see Council Bluffs. And just one of the babies would survive; little Hannah Maria Thomas, born 13 May 1849, was just four days old when her parents carried her ashore to Council Bluffs. Her maternal grandfather, Dan Davis, had been buried along the shores of the Missouri four days before Hannah Maria's birth.

The need for preparations to get underway and for employment to be found loomed large. Recuperation and mourning were cruelly curtailed by the abrupt reality of the situation.

Insufficient housing was a chronic condition in this way station for the westbound Saints, but space was provided where there really was none by jamming several persons in the already overcrowded rooms. And when no cholera epidemic ensued in that area, fear was replaced by frontier hospitality and kindness.

Council Bluffs was becoming rather cosmopolitan with its English, Norwegians, and now a large band of Welsh. Interpreters were kept busy, as they provided the only way of communicating for many. The need for the Welsh to learn English was diminished by their banding together and by forming a Welsh-speaking branch of the Church, the first in that part of the world.[15] However, communication even between persons of the same language was often hampered by the sometimes frantic atmosphere of excitement.

Those who planned to cross the plains that season needed to arrange for wagons and teams if they expected to make it to Salt Lake City before the cold weather and the snow came upon them. Because of the great influx of immigrants, employment opportunities in the immediate vicinity were not plentiful; consequently, wives and families were often left in Council Bluffs while the men went as far as St. Louis to get work. Tempers were short as people agonized over their recent loss of loved ones and worried about what the future would bring. And, although the situation had become quite irreversible at this point, there were some who wished they had never left the comforts of home and family back in the old country.

Isaac and Eliza Nash together with Morgan and Margaret Hughes had been befriended by Father King at Council Point, not far from the river. Isaac's and Eliza's passages had been paid by Elizabeth Lewis from Kidwelly, South Wales, in exchange for a service which Isaac had performed for her—he had helped persuade her husband to sign papers allowing the sale to Lewis's brother of a rather large inheritance. The money was then used to assist a number of people to emigrate (Nash, 5–6). Isaac had understood that Sister Lewis had agreed to pay for him and his wife all the way to the Rocky Mountains, but Sister Lewis informed him upon reaching Council Bluffs that he was then on his own. Nash, a blacksmith by trade, obtained work with a Brother Ovett at Council Point. Shortly thereafter, Captain Jones requested Nash's services in ironing some wagons. Nash refused, wishing to honor his contract with Brother Ovett. The argument that ensued was solved only with the intervention of Apostle George A. Smith. Nash was to iron the wagons, shoe the horses, and do other work for the company; Jones was to allow Nash the use of a team and wagon filled with provisions until he reached Salt Lake City. In addition, Elder Smith purchased a set of blacksmith tools in St. Louis which he promised to Nash upon arriving at the end of the journey.

Misunderstandings arose also between Elizabeth Lewis and Phoebe Evans, a seventeen-year-old girl who served Sister Lewis as her maid in exchange for passage. Phoebe became so exasperated at demands made on her that she finally packed her belongings and went to live with her sister, Margaret Hughes, also a *Buena Vista* passenger. Dan Jones soon arrived at the house and declared that because Phoebe had not fulfilled her part of the agreement with Sister Lewis he would have to take her clothes and auction them off as restitution. And, according to David D. Bowen, who the following year married Phoebe Evans, the clothes were taken and sold (January 1850, 24).

Eight weeks were required for preparations to be completed for those who would continue directly on to the Salt Lake Valley. During this time approximately 200 Welsh were living in and around Council Bluffs. For the most part they banded together and offered mutual assistance. A special branch of the Church was set up to accommodate other Welsh Saints who would follow. William Morgan made coming to Council Bluffs sound very attractive in his letter dated 2 September 1849 to President Phillips back in Wales:

> This will be to the advantage of the monoglot Welshmen who follow; for there will be people of the same language and from the same country, and most likely many who will know them and have been associated with each other many times, to welcome them to this new country; for there are only Englishmen here for several hundreds of miles—and we, a small handful of Welsh in their midst, brothers and sisters, enjoying our freedom like the birds, with no one to say a word against us, but all of them very friendly. (*Udgorn Seion*, November 1849, 218, TD11)

Dan Jones had arranged for the Welsh who remained in Council Bluffs to have their lands adjoining; he then purchased a land claim of about 150 acres near the Welsh holdings and gave it to William Morgan to administer as a gift to the Welsh. Morgan reported an element of prosperity among the Welsh Saints: "Some in this company who had not a penny when they landed here have cattle and sheep now; in fact, I know of no family in this country who has not a cow or two" (*Udgorn Seion*, November 1849, 219, TD11). He offered encouragement to his brothers and sisters still in Wales to come and join in the abundance.

From Council Bluffs to Salt Lake City—1849

By 13 July a large segment of the Welsh was on the trail to "the Eden," "new Canaan," and "chief paradise of the world" (phrases from the song "Hail to California," TD1). They had covered about eighteen miles of the thousand-mile, 108-day trek and were headed to the nearby Elk Horn River, the gathering place for the George A. Smith Company.

Of the 370 persons in the Smith Company, the Welsh numbered eighty-four, or just over one-fifth:

From the *Buena Vista*	69
From the *Hartley*	12
From the *Emblem*	2
Native-born American	1
	84

The *Emblem*, a ship which left Liverpool two weeks after the *Buena Vista*, carried Jane and Claudia Jones,

Captain Dan Jones's wife and infant daughter. The "native-born American" was little Hannah Maria Thomas, the lone breath of hope midst the miasma of cholera along the Missouri. Most of the eighty-four had buried family members prior to embarking on the overland journey. Had all the families remained intact, twenty-eight more Welsh Saints would likely have gone to the Salt Lake Valley in 1849.

Of the total, forty-one were male and forty-three were female. When seen according to age groups, the pattern is not unlike that of the original 326, despite the cholera, the defections, and the division:

TABLE 7
Age Distribution of the Welsh in the Smith Company

Age	Total	Percentage
0–10	20	23.8
11–17	12	14.3
18–30	29	34.5
31–50	18	21.4
51 +	5	6.0
	84	100.0

The cholera altered the ratio of complete to incomplete family units significantly; the percentage of those with no apparent family attachment was a bit higher:

TABLE 8
Family Units among the Welsh in the Smith Company

	Total	Percentage
Part of a complete family unit (husband, wife, and children [if any])	39	46.4
Part of an incomplete family unit (father or mother and children)	30	35.7
No apparent family attachment	15	17.9
	84	100.0

Dan Jones continued to be the spiritual leader of the Welsh; however, for purposes of temporal organization, the Welsh were divided into three groups, each of which was under the leadership of a "Captain of Ten," a person who was responsible for about ten wagons. Daniel Daniels and Thomas Jeremy, both from the *Buena Vista*, were two of these captains, and Lysander Gee, an American, was the other. In addition to Gee's family there was one other family, that of Robert Berrett, which traveled with the Welsh. Albert Bowen and Ricy Jones, two other Welsh lads who had arrived at Council Bluffs some time prior to the *Buena Vista* immigrants, were also with the group.

The following rules and regulations, used previously by other "Camps of Israel," were adopted:

1.   Each "Ten" was to travel ahead alternately according to numbers.

2.   All lost property was to be brought to the Captain of Fifties' quarters.

3.   All dogs were to be tied up at dark to prevent annoyance of the guard.

4.   No man was to be allowed to leave the camp by himself or without the consent of his captain.

5.   The Captains of Ten were to instruct their men to attend to their family prayers at the sounding of the horn.

6.   The Captain of Fifty was to see that the guards were placed around the camp at half past eight o'clock each night to relieve the captain of the herd, whose duty it was at the sound of the horn in the morning, with the men and boys exempt from guard duty, to take charge of the herd until the night guard was again posted.

7.   The sounding of the horn in the morning was to be the signal for the camp to arise and attend to the duties of the morning.

8.   The camp was to be ready to start each morning at half past seven o'clock.

9.   Implicit obedience to the officers was required of every man in the camp.

10. Each man owning horses or mules was required to take them into the corral at sundown and secure them.

11. Each teamster, without fail, when the herd was driven in at night, was to see that his team was on hand or in the herd.

12. Every member of the camp was to be at his quarters at nine o'clock and the guard was to cry the correct time without making any unnecessary noise (Appleby, 1–2).

The statistics of the camp, recorded by William I. Appleby, clerk, were as follows (2):

Ducks	23	Ponies	3
Turkeys	4	Oxen	477
Crows	1	Cows	214
Doves	2	Loose	
Guns	131	Cattle	35
Pistols	27	Sheep	105
Wagons	118	Pigs	12
Souls	370	Chickens	81
Horses	20	Cats	13
Mules	1	Dogs	20

Driving a team of oxen yoked to pull a covered wagon was something totally foreign to many of the Welsh. John Johnson Davies, a pioneer who crossed a few years later, described the difficulties the Welsh in his group had with this new challenge:

> After breakfast was over, we got the cattle together and tried to yoke them up. I can assure you that this was quite a task for us, and after we got them hitched to the wagon, we started out. Now comes the circus, and it was a good one! The Captain was watching us and telling us what to do. He told us to take the whip and use it, and say "whoa Duke, gee Brandy" and so on! Now the fun commenced. Then we went after them pretty lively. When the cattle went "gee" too much we would run to the off side, yelling at them "whoa!" and bunting them with the stock of the whip. Then they would go "haw" too much and we were puffing and sweating. (160)

With respect to how well the Welsh in his group managed, Dan Jones wrote to William Phillips on 12 October 1849:

The Welsh are holding up under the difficulties of this journey, and are learning to drive oxen better than my expectations, and are winning praise from all the other camps of the Saints for their organization, their virtue and their skill, and especially for their singing. (*Udgorn Seion*, April 1850, 108, TD13)

Singing, something which was far more natural for the Welsh than driving a team of oxen, became the trademark of the Welsh as they gathered around their camp fires at night. William Morgan accompanied them the first few days of the journey and commented with pride to William Phillips and John Davis:

> As we sang the first part of the verse . . . we saw the English and the Norwegians and everyone, I would think with their heads out of their wagons. With the second part the wagons were empty in an instant and their inhabitants running toward us as if they were charmed. . . . Some asked me where they had learned and who was their teacher? I said that the hills of Wales were the schoolhouse, and the Spirit of God was the teacher. Their response was, "Well, indeed, it is wonderful; we never heard such good singing before." (19 July 1850, 6, TD21)

Most likely John Parry directed the singing. After reaching the Valley, he was asked by Brigham Young to organize a choir with his compatriots as the nucleus. His choir gained in fame over the years and evolved into what is now known as the Mormon Tabernacle Choir.

Another talent the Welsh were noted for was poetry. Numbered among the Welsh in the George A. Smith Company was William Lewis, a poet who had won several prizes for his verses in the old country. The muses inspired him to compose the following poem during the trek westward:

Verses

Some of the sectarians insist,—that to sell us
    In shame, like animals,
Across the sea, our leaders would do:
Such was the group's cry.

"The Captain," they say, "enticed,—in the area
  Of Merthyr a huge number of Wales's children,
That they might be sold,—
Yes, a shipful from among the host."

Oh! blind men, poor souls,—if they continue
  In their course of an angry disposition,
When the judgment and the plague come upon them,
Their false tales will be as the wind.

Our Moses and mighty chief—he is Jones,
  Our supreme and heavenly teacher;
Full of the energy of holy wisdom
To lead us into the land of praise.
                                    (Lewis, 12, TD22)

The first three hundred miles of the journey was through
mud and mire, brought about by the frequent rainstorms. The
task of the neophyte teamsters offered daily discouragement
as the wheels inched forward with great reluctance. The heavy
sand which was encountered next was a change, but not much
of a rest. On the positive side, however, were two factors: as
far as Laramie the grazing was abundant and the loss of cattle
was minimal.

The company was following in the tracks of groups of gold
diggers who had crossed the previous year. The bones of
hundreds of cattle which lay along the path served as a
reminder that the animals should receive only the best treatment and that the traveling should be paced according to their
capacity.

After gaining two months' experience and completing
about two-thirds of the journey, these pioneers wished to
impart their new knowledge to others who would travel the
same path later on. At this point George A. Smith, Ezra T.
Benson, and Dan Jones sent an informative letter back to
William Morgan in Council Bluffs with a request that Morgan
translate it into Welsh and send it on to John Davis, who was
then to publish it in the *Udgorn Seion*. Morgan complied with
their request; Davis, however, judged the instructions of such

importance that he published them as a separate pamphlet, together with William Morgan's letter containing additional suggestions. William Lewis's verses were also included in the twelve-page pamphlet.

After reading through the long list of Christian virtues which Brothers Smith, Benson, and Jones recommended to all in the forepart of their letter, one would suspect that love and harmony did not always prevail among the pioneers. Following these initial observations, they presented many suggestions of a pragmatic nature: the oxen should be between five and ten years old; wagon wheels should be six inches larger than normal for keeping supplies dry while crossing rivers; wagon loads should not exceed two thousand pounds with three yoke of oxen; spare parts for the wagons should be brought along; animals should not be expected to cover more than sixty miles each week; "Russian duck" canvas should be purchased in Liverpool as the best covers for the wagons; provisions should be obtained in New Orleans or in St. Louis instead of relying on the merchants of Council Bluffs, who had disappointed others with unfulfilled promises; the service of a few good American teamsters who were gentle with animals should be enlisted.

An item which received special emphasis concerned the use of strong drinks:

> Our brothers come from a distant country where liquor is scarce and hard for anyone to get except for the wealthy, and so they are seldom used by the poor. But when they come to America where liquor is so cheap, and they not being accustomed to the drunkening effect, they are very likely to make too much use of it, to their own harm and great loss. For that reason, we counsel everyone under your care to abstain completely, and refrain from making use of it, only except when necessary in the case of illness. (Jones, 21 September 1849, 4–5, TD12)

One must allow for a bit of exaggeration on Jones's part in this rosy depiction.

In his letter, William Morgan gave a number of recommendations which complemented those given by Brothers Smith,

Benson, and Jones. Morgan directed himself specifically to the farmers and gave them American prices of items such as iron ploughs, iron harrows, files for sharpening saws, scythe handles, hay spikes, wheel rim iron, milk pitchers, pottery, billhooks, axes, tongs, fire shovels, bellows, knives, forks, and spoons. He ended by reiterating the counsel which had been given previously by Dan Jones for individuals to either break engagements or get married before leaving Wales.

When the company was about three hundred miles east of their destination, they were met by a group of teamsters, wagons, and about sixty yoke of oxen which had been sent by Brigham Young from Salt Lake City. Such assistance was gratefully welcomed by the travel-weary Saints and gave them new life with which to complete the last leg of their seemingly interminable journey.

A major setback came during the first week of October as they approached the summit of the South Pass with the Wind River chain of mountains on the north. At this seven-thousand-foot elevation the snow and the wind suddenly became severe and the temperature dropped, forcing the travelers to make a hasty encampment without being able to form their wagons into the customary corral. George A. Smith and William Appleby described the ordeal in their 18 October 1849 letter to Orson Hyde:

> We turned our cattle loose, and drove them into the willows near by, to do the best they could, and share their fate; and such a storm of wind and snow as we experienced, we think was never superseded in Pottawatamie. For thirty-six hours, it continued to howl around us unceasingly, blowing nearly a hurricane, drifting the snow in every direction, and freezing fast to whatever it touched. Being unable to keep fires, (except a few who had stoves in their wagons,) we had to be content without them, and do the best we could. Many were the mother and infant that was obliged to be in bed under their frail covering that sheltered them from the pitiless blast, to keep them from perishing with nothing perhaps, but a piece of dry bread, or a few crackers to subsist upon, while the winds spent their fury upon our camp of canvass, covering

it with a mass of ice, the snow drifting around us in some places to the depth of three or four feet. (*Millennial Star*, 15 April 1850, 126)

First thoughts when the storm abated, after it was verified that no human life was lost, were of the animals: "As we wended our way down the stream among the willows; indeed it was a sorrowful sight to behold our perished cattle, one after another, cold and stiff, lying in the snow banks food for wolves, ravens, catamounts, magpies, etc., that inhabit these mountainous regions in countless numbers, and live on prey" (*Millennial Star*, 15 April 1850, 126). They found that upwards of sixty head of cattle in George A. Smith's camp, as well as in the two camps immediately ahead, had perished. Some others died within a few days from the effects of the storm while still others were some time in recovering. Notwithstanding the loss, the pioneers rejoiced that it had not been worse.

During the entire journey, George A. Smith reported that "not a solitary death . . . occurred of man, woman, or child (*Millennial Star*, 15 April 1850, 127). One birth, however, did occur—that of little Robert Dan Parry, born 15 October, thirty miles east of Fort Bridger, to the widow Ann Parry. Ann's husband had died on the Missouri River. Also there was a marriage—that of William Clarke, widowed while on the Mississippi, and Eliza Thomas, a servant girl to the Jeremy family. They were married on 14 September by Isaac Clarke, president of the company (Appleby Journal, 14 September 1849).

Upon arriving at Little Mountain shortly after the storm, the Welsh gathered for a meeting at which an extraordinary proposal was presented. According to Isaac Nash, Dan Jones told the Welshmen that they needed to stick together as a nation, inasmuch as they had been discriminated against. The wagons, animals, onions and potatoes sent by Brigham Young, Jones explained, had come primarily for Brother Smith and the Americans and would not have been sent at all had the company been entirely Welsh. Because of this perceived unfair treatment, Jones proposed they all go across the Jordan River and settle there as an independent nation with Elizabeth Lewis as their queen.[16] All who were willing to declare their independence and become subject to their new queen were asked to raise their hands. All hands went up except for those of Isaac Nash and Edward (Ned) Williams. When asked why he had not raised his hand, Nash replied that he had had enough of the Welsh and was going to try Americans for a while. When Jones threatened that Nash would be cut off "from the Book of the Nation and never be restored," Nash went and reported the entire incident to George A. Smith, who accompanied Nash immediately back to the meeting. Jones was still speaking when they arrived. Brother Smith, when invited to address the Welsh who had just upheld Jones's unique proposal, made a very conciliatory speech to the "rebels." He said that the wagons, animals, potatoes and onions had been intended for them as much as for anyone else and that there was no need for them to become an independent nation (Nash, 8). Apparently Smith's appeal for unity was successful, as there is no record of any further attempts to set up an independent Welsh nation across the Jordan River. Feelings, however, between Jones and Nash were considerably strained after the incident.

In the Valley

On 26 October 1849, after 108 days on the trail, the Welsh arrived at their "land of promise." Eight months had elasped since they had stretched out their arms for the oranges thrown by their brethren on the Waterloo Dock. One-fourth of the original 326 were now with the main body of the Church and had achieved the goal of all faithful Welsh Mormons.

The first night in the Valley they camped on the northeast of the old Emigration Road, where they were visited by Brigham Young, a familiar face only to Dan Jones. All were excited to be in the presence of the one who had beckoned them there and who now addressed them in a language for which most required interpretation. President Young gave them a warm welcome and requested the mechanics to stay in the city and the farmers to go to a plot of land near the Jordan River about four miles west of the city.

Only seven declared themselves mechanics: John Parry, Caleb and Catherine Parry, William and Eliza Clark, Isaac and Eliza Nash. John and Caleb were stonemasons, William a tinsmith, and Isaac a blacksmith. These all remained at the campground while the others traveled the few remaining miles to receive their parcels of land to farm. To own land had long been the dream of the Welsh, most of whom had been tenant farmers or laborers in Wales. And had they stayed in Wales, it is unlikely that any would ever have become independent landowners. The attraction of actually owning land was so strong as to cause Daniel Leigh, William Lewis, and Daniel Daniels at this point to declare themselves farmers, whereas their occupations in Wales had been joiner, mason, and stonecutter.

Because of the separation of mechanics and farmers, Isaac Nash and his wife were left without a wagon to sleep in. Nash described their first night in the Valley: "About dark that night it began to rain. We were without fire, bedding and food. At ten o'clock a man came to us and wanted to know why we were staying here in the rain. We told him our situation. He suggested that we use a little shanty which he had not far off. It contained a fireplace and we made a fire, cooked some food he gave us, and began to feel comfortable" (9). The hospitable man was Elijah Gifford. By extending assistance to Isaac and Eliza Nash, he was carrying out the instructions which Brigham Young had given to all residents of the Valley—to succor the newcomers.

With the beginning of winter only a short time away, housing became a pressing concern to newly arrived immigrants. Thomas Jeremy and his family lived in their wagon for the first month and then in a rented room in the city for four months before they were able to complete construction of a home on South Temple and 6th West. Built with willows and plastered inside and out, the home was called "The Willow Basket."

Each of the Welsh families received a city lot of one-and-one-fourth acres in addition to some land for farming about four or five miles west of the city. Many of the Welsh built their homes in the same vicinity, and the area was soon called "New Wales." The land had been mapped out into "blocks," each of which measured about ten acres. The Welsh occupied the greater part of three of these blocks. Coming from a land of hills and vales, these "sons of Gomer" were no doubt elated to live and farm on the flat lands of the Salt Lake Valley.

In his letter written the following April, Thomas Jeremy joyfully announced that there was plenty of room for thousands of his compatriots to come and settle in "New Wales." The statistics concerning the fruitfulness of the land offered great encouragement to the Saints in Wales: "Mr. Halliday planted one bushel of wheat, called 'touse wheat,' and got from it about 183 bushels; another planted one bushel of potatoes and got 330 bushels. It is said that you can get from barley obtained from California about 100 bushels from planting one. Perhaps this account is too good for some Welsh to believe, but yet, that will not make it any less true" (*Udgorn Seion*, October 1850, 283, TD19). According to Jeremy, wages in the Valley were considerably higher than in Wales. Laborers were paid $1.50 per day; carpenters received $2.00; masons earned $2.50; and a tailor could earn from $6.00 to $10.00 for making someone a coat. Jeremy reported: "Some of the Welsh brothers here earn from $3 to $4 per day by digging by the job. The Americans are not used to digging. So you see how easy it is to live here" (*Udgorn Seion*, October 1850, 283, TD19).

Elizabeth Lewis, the benefactress of over one-third of the newly arrived Welsh, also offered encouragement to her fellow Saints in the old country:

Though it [the Salt Lake Valley] is not perfect heaven, nor is
everyone in it perfect, yet I am not sorry for having come here,
and the evils which were prophesied to me back there about this
place and its inhabitants have not been fulfilled; and I believe that
it is my duty to my Good Lord and His cause to send my witness
back, for the sake of those who have not had this experience as
I have had, and so they can take heart also to come here. (10 April
1850, 6, TD16)

Sister Lewis compared herself to the Queen of Sheba in that
she had not been told "half the good things about this place
and its inhabitants." She wrote of the joy she felt in being
able to hear from various Church leaders and to mingle in peace
and harmony with other Saints in the Valley.

I have not seen a drunken person in this place or anyone
quarrelling with another; I have only heard of someone threatening to take another to court, except that he was too ashamed to
be the first one in the place to do that.[17] I have yet to hear an
oath or swearing on the street; not one murder or theft that I know
of in the place, nor have I seen any immorality. . . . There is no
one here begging or any poor here. The men who came here the
same time as I did are such freeholders that it is difficult for me
to get anyone to work my small farm. (10 April 1850, 7, TD16)

As was the custom, the Welsh were rebaptized after
reaching the Valley in order for them "to renew their covenants
and seal their faithfulness to the Lord God of Israel" (Jones,
20 November 1849, 2, TD14). Permission was obtained from
President Young to establish a Welsh branch of the Church
and to hold worship services in the Welsh language. Thomas
Jeremy was appointed president of this unique branch with
Daniel Daniels and Rice Williams as his counselors. The Welsh
branch was the first of several foreign-language branches
established in Salt Lake City to accommodate various ethnic
groups which settled there.

The 1850 Census shows that the Welsh were in two groups
plus a few which were scattered in several places. The greater
part of them chose to settle in "New Wales." Sixty-four of
the eighty-four who crossed with the George A. Smith

Company were there together until the fall of 1850; at this time fifteen went to settle in Manti: Dan, Jane, and Claudia Jones; Elizabeth Lewis, who by this time had married Dan Jones, and her six children; Rees Thomas and Mary Evans, who were married by then; Sarah Davis; Owen Owens; and little David Davis, orphaned when his mother, Margaret, died on the Missouri.

Isaac Nash and Caleb Parry and their wives were in other parts of Salt Lake City. Many of the others had married and settled with the families of their spouses. Mary Davis, with her marriage to James Switzler, was among the first to marry a non-Welshman. Such marriages undermined the preservation of the Welsh language and culture. Although many children of the Welsh pioneers learned the Welsh language and customs as they grew up, such things became less and less common with each succeeding generation.

From Council Bluffs to the Salt Lake Valley—1852

Life for the 113 Welsh converts in Council Bluffs and for several others who had remained at St. Louis offered numerous difficulties and challenges. Most had not gone ahead with the George A. Smith Company and their compatriots simply because their resources were exhausted by the time they completed the Atlantic crossing and the ascension of the two rivers. A few who may have had the wherewithal to continue on to the Valley that same year had been requested to stay behind and preside over the other *Buena Vista* and *Hartley* emigrants.

With an organized body of Welsh Saints in Council Bluffs, future immigrants of the same language would have a warm welcome, in addition to instruction and guidance as to how they could complete their journey to the Valley. Housing would be provided, employment information would be given, and assistance in getting "fitouts" would be available.

William Morgan was selected to preside over the Welsh branch of the Church in Council Bluffs. Morgan wrote several letters to the brethren in Wales to give them the benefit of his experience and to encourage all the Saints in the old country to begin preparations immediately for emigration. He also sent them copies of the *Frontier Guardian*, the newspaper published by the Mormons in Council Bluffs. In return, Morgan was to receive an ample supply of *Udgorn Seion*, the periodical which succeeded *Prophwyd y Jubili* and which contained news of Mormons in Wales.

Morgan was a liberal dispenser of counsel and advice as to how to make the sea voyage more enjoyable than the one he had had. In a letter dated 25 December 1849, he wrote to President Phillips: "We advise everyone who will be emigrating to take care that their boxes are strong, made of dry wood; some have suffered losses because their boxes were not dry, and so their clothes have become mouldy. Potatoes on the ocean would be very desirable, and herrings, oat flour, bacon, dried beef, pepper, mustard, salt, pickles, onions and oranges" (*Udgorn Seion*, February 1850, 52, TD15).

He also recommended they bring some brandy, as it was "beneficial to warm the stomach" when the weather was cold and when the sea was rough.

Many gold diggers headed for California were expected to pass through Council Bluffs in the spring of 1850. Some of the Saints had made considerable profit by selling provisions to them; Morgan saw no reason why the next company of Welsh should not take advantage of such an opportunity as well, and he promised to send further information as to what items the emigrants should purchase in Britain for selling in America.[18]

Morgan reported performing two marriages among the Welsh by the end of 1849: Mary Jones to John Williams, and

Alice Richards to Edward Evans. Alexander Owens had died from yellow fever; William Phillips was to inform Owens's wife in Twynrodyn (a suburb of Merthyr Tydfil). Cholera, according to Morgan, was no longer a problem in St. Louis and had not reached Council Bluffs.[19]

Some were able to obtain jobs in the Council Bluffs area. Others were forced to travel all the way back to St. Louis to find work. In October 1849 John Hughes Williams, Rees Price, Morgan Hughes, Noah Jones, and William Lewis[20] all returned to St. Louis in hopes of getting employment in the coal diggings at Gravois, a place in the vicinity of St. Louis. There they met David D. Bowen and Morgan David, who had stopped off at St. Louis back in April because of the illnesses of their wives and children.

Bowen, a widower by this time, was informed by Rees Price of one Phoebe Evans in Council Bluffs, a seventeen-year-old Welsh girl whom Bowen should consider marrying. The following spring Bowen took Price's advice and traveled to the "Bluffs" where he courted and then wed young Phoebe Evans. Their return to St. Louis resulted in a very cool reception on the part of Morgan Hughes, Phoebe's brother-in-law, because Bowen had not obtained his permission for the marriage. And Morgan David's daughters, sisters-in-law to Bowen, were bitter toward Phoebe, possibly because they (at least two of them) were just as old and just as eligible as she.

During the next two years, Bowen worked and saved towards making the overland journey to the Salt Lake Valley. At times he earned as much as twenty-five dollars per week; at times the amount was far less. And on two occasions for periods of several weeks he was totally incapacitated by illness and had no income at all. Others of his fellow Welsh Saints were faced with similar circumstances.

By June of 1852 most of the remaining *Buena Vista* and *Hartley* immigrants were fitted out and ready to begin their journey to the Rocky Mountains. Disease, misfortune, and defection had reduced their numbers. In the winter of 1850 there had been much illness among the Saints at Council Bluffs. William Treharne was among the fatalities.[21]

Noah Jones, the poet, died of Bright's disease in the fall of 1851. His dying wish was that his orphaned fourteen-year-old daughter, Mary, be allowed to cross the plains with the Welsh Saints the following year. In 1852 the explosion of the steamer *Saluda* killed William Rowland and two of his children.

During the three years which William Morgan and his fellow Welsh converts remained at Council Bluffs, they were joined by other Welsh Mormons from various parts of Wales. Those who could afford to continue immediately to the Valley did so; most, however, stayed in Council Bluffs until 1852 when the bulk of the remaining Welsh Saints traversed the plains together.

There were nine wagons of Mormons who traveled from Gravois to Council Bluffs to join with the others for the crossing. Among these was David D. Bowen, who had made enough money by January 1852 to purchase two yoke of oxen and a wagon "on shares" with Thomas Vargo for the purpose of going to the Salt Lake Valley. This small band met together at St. Louis on 6 April 1852 and began their journey across the State of Missouri and up to Council Bluffs. They stayed together as far as Lexington, where Bowen and Vargo struck out on their own with their "shared" wagon. At St. Joseph a misunderstanding occurred between the two, and they decided to part company. Each received one yoke of oxen, a cow, and half the wagon. Bowen sold his share of the wagon to Vargo, put his wife and child on a steamer from St. Louis, and proceeded to finish the remainder of the journey to Council Bluffs on foot with his three animals. Once he reached Council Bluffs in mid-May he made an agreement with an older gentleman by the name of Daniel Shearer. Bowen agreed to haul him and his luggage to Salt Lake City in exchange for the wagon which Shearer owned. Then Bowen worked at unloading steamboats and hauling wood until the main body was prepared to depart about one month later.

By 21 June the Welsh had gathered near Winter Quarters, where they were visited by Apostle Ezra T. Benson. They needed an interpreter to translate Benson's instructions as to how they were to be organized for the crossing. William Morgan was appointed Captain of Fifty (the Welsh with a few English and French made up fifty wagons). His counselors were William Davis and Rees Jones Williams, Davis's son-in-law. Three days later they crossed the Missouri and camped at Winter Quarters for another three days.

On the morning of 28 June, as the company finally got under way, Bowen lamented: "I had a deal of trouble with my cattle for they was not broken, but very whiled [wild] and young. The day we started from winter quarters was very hot. I leboured so hard with the cattle and sweat so much that I had the headache that bad I was all most blind all day" (28 June 1852). In the afternoon William Davis showed his lack of experience at driving a team by running his wagon into another one and breaking his axletree. There was a delay until the following day while repairs were made.

Morgan reported that five buffaloes were killed during the crossing; he described the taste as similar to Welsh beef. It was his custom to ride ahead of the camp to determine the trail and places suitable for stopping.

On one occasion Morgan found himself in the midst of several hundred Sioux and was greeted by one who appeared to be a chief: " 'How do, Mormon good.' " Morgan was then taken to the Indian camp about a mile-and-a-half away, where he was invited to sit down and smoke a "pipe of peace" with the chiefs. Morgan compared this unique custom to the handing around of the shilling jug in the taverns of Wales for each to take a drink (*Udgorn Seion*, 27 August 1853, 145, TD30).

On the whole, the journey for the 1852 Welsh pioneers was considerably more pleasant than it had been for those who crossed in 1849. At the outset William Morgan reported cheerily in a letter dated 22 June 1852: "All the Saints are in good health, each one with his canvas tent as white as snow. . . . Much milk in our camp is thrown out as casually as is the bathwater used by three or four Merthyr colliers. We have more than we can use, and there is no one close by in need of it" (*Udgorn Seion*, 7 August 1852, 259–60, TD28). On 20 September 1852, near the end of the journey, Morgan wrote that the weather had been "unusually moderate"

(*Udgorn Seion*, 8 January 1853, 32, TD29). They had experienced no rainstorms and no snow, even when they went through the mountain pass which had buried the 1849 pioneers in snow. Four Welshmen, however, died before they reached the Valley. One of these was the nine-year-old son of the widow Martha Howells. Morgan describes the happening:

> We administered to him through the ordinances of the Church of Jesus Christ, according to the scriptures, and the next night he was strolling around the camp. He fell sick again in a day or two, and Bro. Taylor and myself administered to him again, but he died in spite of everything and everyone. (*Udgorn Seion*, 8 January 1853, 32, TD29)

When the company reached Fort Laramie, they crossed to the south side of the Platte River. The unusually high water of the river made crossing difficult, and many things were lost as a consequence. A few days later they arrived at Deer Creek, where they stayed for several days. Here David D. Bowen had difficulty with Brother Shearer:

> Here I had a quarrell with old Sherar in consequence of his wagon which he promise me for hauling him and his luggage to Salt Lake City. He said that he did not calculate to give me the wagon. We had to get other men to settle between us. He promise again to give me the wagon or I was going to leave him and his wagon there. I listen to his fair promises and haul him along again. (29 September 1852, 30)

A number of cattle died at Devil's Gate a short time later. It was there the company divided into several parties. David D. Bowen's "Ten" traveled alone the rest of the way to the Valley. On 23 September, they reached the mouth of Emigration Canyon, where they were visited by Bishop Lorenzo D. Young, Brigham Young's brother. His main message, according to Bowen, was to "mind Number One," the first principle in the Valley. Two days later they went down into Salt Lake City, arriving in the early afternoon. Bowen's wagon partner once again decided that he would not part with his wagon. Bishop Joseph D. Noble, asked to arbitrate in the matter, decided that Bowen and Shearer should each have half, but

"Devil's Gate," by Frederick Piercy

Shearer was unwilling to sell his half or to buy Bowen's half. Finally Bowen sold his half to a man from San Pete in exchange for twenty dollars in lumber.

When the main body of the Welsh was about eighty miles from the Salt Lake Valley, they had a reunion with their beloved Captain Jones. Jones, together with Thomas Jeremy and Daniel Daniels, had been called by Brigham Young to return to Wales on another mission. More than three years had elapsed since the 1849 group had left Council Bluffs, and emotions were strong as the 1852 group welcomed Jones into their midst. Morgan described the reunion in a letter dated 20 September 1852: "After shaking hands, embracing, weeping and kissing, we went to the bank of the river where he [Dan Jones] had left his horse, having traveled from twenty to thirty miles during the night ahead of his company in order to meet us. We decided to spend a day in his friendship, to converse with each other about things pertaining to the

"Great Salt Lake City in 1853," by Frederick Piercy

kingdom of our God. Oh, brethren, how sweet the words poured over his lips" (*Udgorn Seion*, 8 January 1853, 33, TD29).

Later in the day, Thomas Jeremy and Daniel Daniels arrived at the Welsh gathering and drank deeply from old friendships as they joined in the camaraderie. Jones gave Morgan a letter which he was to present to Bishop Edward Hunter just as soon as he arrived with his company in the Valley. Morgan was so moved by the letter that he quoted a segment of it in his own letter dated 25 June 1853 to Phillips and Davis back in Wales:

> "Esteemed Bishop Hunter.—Many of my compatriots are coming across in the 13th Company; I do not know their condition; perhaps their money and their provisions are scarce. If so, when they reach the Valley, I shall be grateful to you for furnishing them their needs, through the hand of Brother Morgans [sic], and I shall pay you in Manti, San Pete Valley." (*Udgorn Seion*, 27 August 1853, 147, TD30)

A few days later several other Welsh brethren arrived in the camp. These had traveled over thirty miles from Salt Lake City with a load of "watermelons, mushmelons, potatoes, pickle cucumbers, grapes, etc." These delicacies came as a welcome treat to those who had spent three months on the trail. Two days later, just before the camp reached Little Mountain, they found "a multitude of the brethren" (Morgan, *Udgorn Seion*, 27 August 1853, 144, TD30) awaiting them with wagons of fruit and vegetables from the Valley. Among the group were John Parry, Caleb Parry, Daniel Leigh, Owen Roberts, and Cadwalader Owens. Delighted at having their ranks swelled with the newcomers, these 1849 pioneers extended a sincere and loving welcome to their compatriots.

Morgan was pleased at how the crossing had gone: "Although the journey was long, I considered it nothing but enjoyment every step of the way" (*Udgorn Seion*, 27 August 1853, 146, TD30). He gave equally positive comments concerning everything and everyone in the Valley and predicted that the Salt Lake Temple would be completed three years hence.[22]

Conclusion

Several thousand more Welsh Saints journeyed to the Salt Lake Valley during the next decade. They usually came in clusters rather than in companies, with the 560 "sons of Gomer" on board the *Samuel Curling* in 1856 constituting a notable exception. Many of them settled in the same geographical areas—Malad, a city in southern Idaho, and Spanish Fork, a city fifty-five miles south of Salt Lake City, were initially Welsh communities. The first and second generation Cambrians were conscientious in the preservation of the language and in the observance of periodic Welsh celebrations. By the turn of the century there were many Joneses, Davises, and Williamses who spoke with great pride of their Welsh ancestry. They had to do so, however, in English.

Notes

1. "California" was the name applied to all Western America, including the region now known as Utah.

2. In Welsh Mormon folklore there is a faith-promoting but apocryphal story about the "sinking of the *Buena Vista*." "The boat was a leaky one that the English said, 'Let them have it and it will go down with all the damned Mormons on board.' But Jones, being seaworthy and wise, repaired the ship and, with prayers each day for safety, they came across the ocean, unloaded everything upon the docks (much of it water soaked and spoiled . . .) and the ship sank in the harbor" (*Heart Throbs*, 2:4).

3. One is led to wonder at Jones's estimate of the number of onlookers. The emphatic use of hyperbole is not unusual in Jones's writings.

4. See appendixes for further information on the passengers.

5. The Welsh "protestants" were in opposition not only to the Catholic church but to the Anglican church as well. Consequently, they

referred to themselves as "nonconformists," or those who refused to conform to the religious policies of King Henry VIII.

6. Writers often attribute a "college education" to Captain Dan Jones, but such a distinction is utterly impossible for him to have had, given the circumstances of his laboring-class background. He had gone to sea by age seventeen and somehow had acquired a high degree of polish in speaking and writing. Had he been university trained in nineteenth-century Wales, however, he would have taken his place as a "gentleman" and would never have soiled his hands with such things as anchors and riggings.

7. Warner's spelling has been maintained.

8. Jones had intended the letter to be published in *Udgorn Seion* (Zion's Trumpet); because of its length, however (nearly 10,000 words), Davis combined it with Thomas Jeremy's smaller letter (about 1,800 words) and a foreword of his own and published a twenty-four-page pamphlet which he entitled *Hanes ymfudiad y Saint i Galifornia* (An account of the Saints' emigration to California).

9. In Wales the term *Babylonians* was used by Mormons to refer to all other Welsh citizens; used here it refers to the eight non-Mormon cabin passengers.

10. This is a reference to Achan in the Old Testament, who because of his disobedience causes much consternation among the Israelites following the seige of Jericho (see Joshua 7).

11. William Hulme mentions only the first baby in his letter. See David Peters's records for information on the second.

12. See Ashton, 66, for a detailed explanation concerning the two steamers.

13. Jeremy used Welsh in his early journals; however, knowing that his descendants would probably not speak Welsh, he kept his later journals in English, his second language.

14. These figures could be considerably higher. If accurate records of this period were kept, they have yet to surface.

15. Many, such as Lowry Peters (H34), who lived another fifty-one years, would go to their graves as speakers of Welsh only.

16. Elizabeth Lewis was called the "Welsh Queen" for many years afterwards. Some thought that she actually was a Welsh queen; few knew, however, how the title had arisen.

17. Numerous court cases were held in Salt Lake City prior to Elizabeth Lewis's letter. The "someone" she heard threatening to take another to court could have been Dan Jones. On 22 April 1850, Jones was awarded $239.17 from Edward Williams, a debt which was due Captain Jones, according to Hosea Stout, who was Jones's lawyer, "for assistance in helping him [Williams] from Wales" (Stout, 2:367). How Jones, after four years as a missionary in Wales, was able to proffer assistance to Williams, and how Williams, a collier before emigrating, obtained the wherewithal after just six months in the Salt Lake Valley to pay the settlement to Jones are certainly legitimate, if not answerable, questions. The fact that Jones married the wealthy Elizabeth Lewis two weeks after arriving in the valley may provide some clarification to the first question. Elizabeth said of Jones in her letter to John Davis: "Capt. Jones . . . has not been the evil man that they prophesied about him. . . . He has not received nor has he tried to get any of my money, and I have not heard that anyone of the company has been the loser of one penny because of him" (10 April 1850, 8, TD16).

18. No letter containing such information ever appeared in the *Udgorn Seion*.

19. While the Welsh Saints were being decimated by the cholera along the Mississippi and Missouri rivers in mid-1849, the same disease had reached epidemic proportions in the Merthyr Tydfil area. One of its victims was the Reverend W. R. Davies, the person who had coined the epithet Latter-day "Satanists."

20. There were three men by the name of William Lewis among the emigrants. The one who stayed in Council Bluffs instead of continuing directly on to Utah was number 70 on the *Buena Vista* passenger list.

21. His daughter Jane had also been sick for several days when she heard of her father's death. She was administered to by Brother Abel Evans, whereupon she arose immediately and rode six miles on horseback to attend her father's funeral (see Ashton, 79).

22. The actual completion of the Salt Lake Temple was not until nearly four decades later.

Appendixes

Appendix A
Alphabetized List of
Buena Vista and *Hartley* Welsh Passengers

The numbers are keyed to appendixes B and C. Those with *H* indicate *Hartley* passengers; all others are *Buena Vista* passengers.

BOWEN,	Anne	H21	DAVIS,	Margt	209	
	David	H73		Mary	94	
	Mary	H19		Mary Jane	H64	
	Morgan	H20		Mary Oubery	224	
*CHILDS,	David	215		Morgan	H12	
CLARK,	Francis	H41		Phoebe	H63	
	William	H40		Rachal	233	
DANIELS,	Dan	128		Rachel	H18	
	David	131		Sarah	90	
	Mary	129		Sarah	93	
	Thomas	130		Sarah	223	
DAVIS,	Ann	92		Sophia	H72	
	Anne	H15		Stephen	H71	
	Catherine	H42		Thomas	85	
	Dan	89		Thomas	H62	
	Dan	91		Thomas	H65	
	David	86		William	6	
	David	183		Wm	83	
	David	210		Wm	232	
	Dinna	95	EAMES,	Elenor	H56	
	Edmund	H70		John	H55	
	Eliza	40		Nathaniel	H52	
	Eliza	88		Nathaniel	H54	
	Eliza	H13		Sarah	H53	
	Eliza	H14	EDWARDS,	Edward	237	
	Eliza	H66		Edward	239	
	Eliza Lee	84		Eliza	238	
	Elizabeth	5		Jno	240	
	Emma	H17		Mary	241	
	George	H68		Peter	H36	
	Griffith	211	EVANS,	Chas	H61	
	Hannah	H16		David	172	
	Henry	87		David	201	
	Hugh	222		Edward	206	
	Jane	H67		Evan	208	
	Margaret	H69		Even	199	
	Margret	52		Janet	200	

EVANS,	Margt	203		JONES,	David	220
	Mary	207			Eliza	190
	Morgan	205			Emma	221
	Rachel	204			Ester	197
	William	202			Esther	14
EVENS,	Charlot	50			Even Jos	196
	Edw	179			Evens	120
	Mary	171			Henry	64
	Pheabe	51			Hugh	H58
EYNON,	Charlotte	H32			Jacob	3
	Elizabeth	H29			Jane	65
	James	H28			Jane	102
	Louesa	H30			Jane	107
	Martha	H31			Jane	188
FRANCIS,	Ann	167			Jane	H59
	Benjn	165			Jno	101
	Benjn	170			Jno	105
	Dan	168			Jno	139
	Margret	166			Jno	162
	Margret	169			Jno	182
GILES,	Edwd	63			Jno	191
	Maria	62			Jno	198
	Sarah	132			Jno	H75
	Ths	61			Letetia	H76
HUGHES,	Margt	112			Lewis	4
	Morgan	111			Margt	125
HUGHS,	Eliza	225			Marian	193
JAMES,	Eliza	195			Mary	2
	Jno	194			Mary	15
JEREMY,	Ester	160			Mary	106
	Hannah	157			Mary	122
	Jno	155			Mary	181
	Margret	159			Noah	13
	Mary	161			Owen	H57
	Sarah	154			Rees	138
	Sarah	158			Rees	180
	Thms	153			Robert	H74
	Thms	156			Robert	H77
JINKINS,	Mary	57			Sarah	109
	Wm	56			Thomas	184
JNO,	Thomas	231			Thomas	189
JONES,	Ann	104			Williams	192
	Ann	H35			Wm	103
	Benj	187		LEIGH,	Ann	32
	Ceteria	110			Ann	36
	Charlotte	123			Ann	77
	Dan	1			Anna	82
	Dan	121			Daniel	31
	David	108			Daniel	34

LEIGH,	Henry	79	OWENS,	Cadwallader	H50
	Jno	33		Elenor	H44
	Jno	81		Jane	H51
	Mary	35		Margaret	H45
	Samuel	76		Owin Cadwallader	H48
	Sophia	80		Richard	H46
	Wm	78		William	H43
LEWIS,	Ann	72		Wm	H47
	Ann	163	PARRY,	Ann	213
	Calvan	46		Caleb	216
	David	100		Cathrine	217
	Eliza	42		Edward	212
	Eliza	45		Edwd	214
	Jno	44		Jno	67
	Lewis	48		Mary	68
	Mary	71	PETERS,	David	H33
	Sarah	47		Lowry	H34
	Thomas	43		Lowry	H39
	Wm	66		Sarah	H38
	Wm	70	PHILLIP,	Benjn	151
	Wm	73		David	147
MATHIOS,	Ada	135		David	150
	Jonah	137		Elizabeth	152
	Margret	134		Mary	148
	Sila	136		Sarah	149
	Thomas	133	PRICE,	Daniel	25
MORGAN,	Barbara	245		Evan	23
	Cecilia	243		Harriett	24
	Edward	12		Jane	21
	Eliza	244		Mary	22
	Jane	164		Rees	20
	Mary	246		Ruth	26
	Morgan	242	REES,	David	230
	Sarah	247		Eben	54
	Thomas	248		Jane	229
	Wm	10		Jno	226
	Wm	11		Mary	227
NASH,	Eliza	53		William	228
	Isack	49	RICHARDS,	Allice	8
	Mary	75		Ann	9
	Thomas	74		David	7
ORMOND,	Dorothy	H24		David	127
	Eliza	H26		David	H10
	Ellinor	H27		Eliza	28
	Jno	H22		Emma	30
	Jno	H23		Jno	27
	Letetia	H25		Mary	H9
OWENS,	Alexr	186		Thomas	H8
	Alice	H49		Thomas	H11

RICHARDS,	William	29		TREHARN,	Jane	116
ROBERTS,	Owin	H37			Mary	115
ROWLAND,	Ann	177			Sage	118
	Benjaman	19			Sarah	117
	David	178			Wm	113
	Job	16			Wm	119
	Mary	17		WILLIAMS,	Ann	218
	Mary	175			Edwd	58
	Rachal	174			Eleanor	H60
	Rachal	176			Eliza	38
	Thomas	18			Jinkins	185
	Wm	173			Jno	234
STEPHENS,	Rees	249			John	H1
THOMAS,	Ann	141			John	H5
	Ann	144			John Hughes	H3
	Benj	96			Margaret	H6
	Benjn	140			Mary	60
	Daniel	98			Mary	235
	Daniel	142			Mary	236
	Ebenr	69			Mary Ann	H2
	Elisa	146			Mary Ann	H4
	Letitia	97			Naomis	H7
	Margt	219			Rice	37
	Morgan	41			Samuel	39
	Rees	99			Sofiah	59
	Samuel	145			Wm	55
	Sarah	143			Wm	124
TREHARN,	Ann	114			Wm	126

*Listed as David Giles in Appendix B.

Appendix B
Buena Vista Passengers

An "x" in columns 1–8 indicates the following information:

1. A biographical sketch is in Appendix D.
2. A biographical sketch for a family member is in Appendix D.
3. Died between March and June 1949.
4. Died between June 1849 and October 1852.
5. Crossed plains in 1849 in the George A. Smith Company.
6. Known to have stayed in St. Louis or Council Bluffs instead of going to the valley in 1849.
7. Left the Church at St. Louis, northwestern Missouri, or Council Bluffs.
8. A signer of "The Last Greeting," a letter from the emigrants at Liverpool (see Appendix E).

The occupation given on the passenger list is recorded as New Orleans is keyed to the following numbers for column 9: (Those left blank had ditto marks for the one above in the passenger list).

1. Blacksmith	13. Locksmith	25. Schoolmaster
2. Butcher	14. Maid	26. Schoolteacher
3. Carpenter	15. Mason	27. Shoemaker
4. Clerk	16. Miner	28. Servant
5. Collier	17. Milliner	29. Son
6. Deceased	18. Moulder	30. Stepdaughter
7. Dressmaker	19. Nailer	31. Stonecutter
8. Engineer	20. Patternmaker	32. Tailor
9. Farmer	21. Peddler	33. Tinsman
10. Joiner	22. Plasterer	34. Wheelwright
11. Laborer	23. Saddler	35. Whitesmith
12. Lime burner	24. Saints	36. Widow

Names in this list are spelled the same as on the passenger list except when indicated with an asterisk; these are explained at the end of the list.

NAMES	AGE	1	2	3	4	5	6	7	8	9
1. Dan Jones	36	x								24
2. Mary Jones	55									
3. Jacob Jones	6									
4. Lewis Jones	22									
5. Elizabeth Davis	24					x				36

NAMES	AGE	1	2	3	4	5	6	7	8	9
6. William Davis	Inft									29
7. David Richards	50					x				1
8. Allice Richards	22						x			
9. Ann Richards	18						x			
10. Wm Morgan	46	x					x		x	8

No.	Name	Age									Value
11.	Wm Morgan	20						x	x		
12.	Edward Morgan	6					x	x			
13.	Noah Jones	35	x			x	x				16
14.	Esther Jones	30				x	x	x			
15.	Mary Jones	11					x	x			
16.	Job Rowland	35	x				x	x			16
17.	Mary Rowland	58				x	x				
18.	Thomas Rowland	17					x	x			
19.	Benjaman Rowland	15					x	x			
20.	Rees Price	35	x				x	x			5
21.	Jane Price	35			x	x	x				
22.	Mary Price	14				x	x	x			
23.	Evan Price	6				x	x	x			
24.	Harriett Price	4				x	x	x			
25.	Daniel Price	2			x	x	x				
26.	Ruth Price	Inft				x	x	x			
27.	Jno Richards	37							x	x	8
28.	Eliza Richards	34			x	x					
29.	William Richards	13				x					
30.	Emma Richards	5									
31.	Daniel Leigh*	35	x					x	x		10
32.	Ann Leigh	28				x	x				
33.	Jno Leigh	11				x	x				
34.	Daniel Leigh	9			x	x	x				
35.	Mary Leigh	4				x	x				

No.	Name	Age									Value
36.	Ann Leigh	11m	x		x			x			
37.	Rice Williams	45	x					x		x	9
38.	Eliza Williams	77			x						6
39.	Samuel Williams	49	x		x		x				9
40.	Eliza Davis	18	x						x		14
41.	Morgan Thomas	30									9
42.	Eliza Lewis	37	x		x		x				
43.	Thomas Lewis	16			x		x				
44.	Jno Lewis	13			x		x				
45.	Eliza Lewis	11	x		x		x				1
46.	Calvan Lewis	9			x		x				14
47.	Sarah Lewis	6			x		x				14
48.	Lewis Lewis	3			x		x				
49.	Isack Nash	24	x				x				
50.	Charlot Evens	18					x				14
51.	Pheabe Evens	18	x			x	x				14
52.	Margret Davis	18			x		x				14
53.	Eliza Nash	23			x		x				14
54.	Eben Rees	49					x				5
55.	Wm Williams	17				x					28
56.	Wm Jinkins	34					x		x		3
57.	Mary Jinkins	35				x	x				
58.	Edwd Williams	26	x		x		x				5
59.	Sofiah Williams	25			x		x				
60.	Mary Williams	1½			x		x				

NAMES	AGE	1	2	3	4	5	6	7	8	9
61. Ths Giles	64	x			x		x	x	x	5
62. Maria Giles	57		x	x			x			
63. Edwd Giles	15		x	x			x			
64. Henry Jones	31									11
65. Jane Jones	28									
66. Wm Lewis	42	x				x			x	15
67. Jno Parry	55	x				x			x	15
68. Mary Parry*	50		x	x						
69. Ebenr Thomas	40			?						1
70. Wm Lewis	35						x			15
71. Mary Lewis	31			x			x			
72. Ann Lewis	5									
73. Wm Lewis	1						x			
74. Thomas Nash	19		x	x						23
75. Mary Nash	63		x	x						36
76. Samuel Leigh*	33	x		x					x	20
77. Ann Leigh	33		x							
78. Wm Leigh	6		x			x	x			
79. Henry Leigh	5		x				x			
80. Sophia Leigh	3		x				x			
81. Jno Leigh	1½		x				x			
82. Anna Leigh	32									
83. Wm Davis	35									
84. Eliza Lee	33									5

NAMES	AGE	1	2	3	4	5	6	7	8	9
85. Thomas Davis	14									
86. David Davis	5									
87. Henry Davis	2									
88. Eliza Davis	Inft			?						
89. Dan Davis	57	x		x						9
90. Sarah Davis	51	x	x			x				
91. Dan Davis	18		x			x				
92. Ann Davis	19		x			x				
93. Sarah Davis	22		x			x				
94. Mary Davis	12		x			x				
95. Dinna Davis	11		x							
96. Benj Thomas	28	x				x				9
97. Letitia Thomas	24	x				x				
98. Daniel Thomas	1½		x							
99. Rees Thomas	25	x				x				9
100. David Lewis	50					x				11
101. Jno Jones	51									9
102. Jane Jones	47									
103. Wm Jones	25									
104. Ann Jones	18									
105. Jno Jones	15									
106. Mary Jones	13									
107. Jane Jones	11									
108. David Jones	9									

Left table (entries 109–133):

No.	Name	Age	1	2	3	4	5	6	7	Val
109.	Sarah Jones	5								
110.	Ceteria Jones	22								
111.	Morgan Hughes	24	x							8
112.	Margt Hughes	23	x					x		
113.	Wm Treharn	52	x			x		x	x	12
114.	Ann Treharn	55			x					
115.	Mary Treharn	23	x					x		
116.	Jane Treharn	22	x					x		
117.	Sarah Treharn	18	x					x		
118.	Sage Treharn*	15	x					x		
119.	Wm Treharn	11		x						
120.	Evens Jones	92	x		x					9
121.	Dan Jones	45								9
122.	Mary Jones	50								
123.	Charlotte Jones	19								
124.	Wm Williams	49								9
125.	Margt Jones	52			x					36
126.	Wm Williams	22			x					2
127.	David Richards	53								2
128.	Dan Daniels	41	x				x		x	31
129.	Mary Daniels	52	x				x			
130.	Thomas Daniels	17	x				x			
131.	David Daniels	13	x				x			
132.	Sarah Giles	18	x				x			14
133.	Thomas Mathios	40	x					x		11

Right table (entries 134–158):

No.	Name	Age	1	2	3	4	5	6	7	Val
134.	Margret Mathios	37		x			x			
135.	Ada Mathios	12		x			x	x		
136.	Sila Mathios	9		x			x			
137.	Jonah Mathios	5		x			x	x		
138.	Rees Jones	19								34
139.	Jno Jones	24					x			11
140.	Benjn Thomas	33		x		x				11
141.	Ann Thomas	29		x			x			
142.	Daniel Thomas	5			x	x	x			
143.	Sarah Thomas	3			x		x			
144.	Ann Thomas	Inft		x	x		x			
145.	Samuel Thomas	35		x			x			11
146.	Elisa Thomas	19		x			x			
147.	David Phillip	29		x			x	x		9
148.	Mary Phillip	31			x		x			
149.	Sarah Phillip	6			x		x			
150.	David Phillip	4			x	x				
151.	Benjn Phillip	2			x	x				
152.	Elizabeth Phillip	Inft		x	x	x				
153.	Thms Jeremy*	34		x			x			9
154.	Sarah Jeremy	34		x			x			
155.	Jno Jeremy	11			x		x			
156.	Thms Jeremy	9			x		x			
157.	Hannah Jeremy	7			x					
158.	Sarah Jeremy	5		x	x					

NAMES	AGE	1	2	3	4	5	6	7	8	9
159. Margret Jeremy	3		x	x						
160. Ester Jeremy	3		x	x		x				
161. Mary Jeremy	Inft		x	x						
162. Jno Jones	18					x				30
163. Ann Lewis	20									28
164. Jane Morgan	25	x								28
165. Benjn Francis	46	x	x	x					x	1
166. Margret Francis	48	x	x							
167. Ann Francis	16		x				x			
168. Dan Francis	12		x	x			x			
169. Margret Francis	9		x	x						
170. Benjn Francis	7		x	x						
171. Mary Evens	17	x				x				14
172. David Evans*	35						x			26
173. Wm Rowland*	38	x			x		x		x	21
174. Rachal Rowland	18						x			
175. Mary Rowland	11		x				x			
176. Rachal Rowland	9		x		x		x			
177. Ann Rowland	7		x				x			
178. David Rowland	3				x		x			
179. Edw Evens	36						x			22
180. Rees Jones	32						x		x	34
181. Mary Jones	23						x			
182. Jno Jones	75			x						34

NAMES	AGE	1	2	3	4	5	6	7	8	9
183. David Davis	24									34
184. Thomas Jones	22	x		x			⋈			34
185. Jinkins Williams	20			x						8
186. Alexr Owens	34				x		x			5
187. Benj Jones	42	x						x	x	13
188. Jane Jones	42		x					x		
189. Thomas Jones	22		x					x		8
190. Eliza Jones	26		x					x		
191. Jno Jones	Inft		x					x		
192. Williams Jones	19		x					x		8
193. Marian Jones	19		x					x		
194. Jno James	21									8
195. Eliza James	23									
196. Even Jos Jones	14									
197. Ester Jones	5									
198. Jno Jones	1½									
199. Even Evans	45								15	
200. Janet Evans	45									
201. David Evans	22									
202. William Evans	20									
203. Margt Evans	18									
204. Rachel Evans	15									
205. Morgan Evans	13									
206. Edward Evans	11									

No.	Name	Age							Value
207.	Mary Evans	5							
208.	Evan Evans	2		x					
209.	Margt Davis	23	x	x					
210.	David Davis	3		x	x				
211.	Griffith Davis	Inft		x	x				
212.	Edward Parry	48	x	x					27
213.	Ann Parry	25	x		x				
214.	Edwd Parry	3			x				
215.	David Giles*	41				x			18
216.	Caleb Parry	25	x		x				15
217.	Cathrine Parry	22		x	x				
218.	Ann Williams	26		x					14
219.	Margt Thomas	23							14
220.	David Jones	25	x			x			19
221.	Emma Jones	18		x		x			
222.	Hugh Davis	69	x		x				25
223.	Sarah Davis	60	x						6
224.	Mary Oubery Davis	24		x		x			17
225.	Eliza Hughs	76		x					
226.	Jno Rees	32	x			x			35
227.	Mary Rees	28		x		x			
228.	William Rees	8		x		x			

No.	Name	Age							Value
229.	Jane Rees	6							
230.	David Rees	3	x	x			x		
231.	Thomas Jno	35	x		x				16
232.	Wm Davis	43	x	x			x	x	32
233.	Rachal Davis	40							
234.	Jno Williams	43					x	x	16
235.	Mary Williams	40							
236.	Mary Williams	18							
237.	Edward Edwards	37			x		x		5
238.	Eliza Edwards	53							
239.	Edward Edwards	28					x	x	4
240.	Jno Edwards	18							5
241.	Mary Edwards	15			x				
242.	Morgan Morgan	47	x			x			16
243.	Cecilia Morgan	47		x		x			
244.	Eliza Morgan	17		x		x			
245.	Barbara Morgan	15		x		x			
246.	Mary Morgan	13		x		x			
247.	Sarah Morgan	11	x	x		x			
248.	Thomas Morgan	7		x		x			
249.	Rees Stephens	18		x		x			11

*From other sources it is known that the clerk made the following errors:
#31 Listed as Daniel Lee; #68 Listed as Ann; #76 Listed as Samuel Lee; #97 Listed as Solitia; #118 Listed as Ludgel; #153 Listed as Jerremos; #172 Has no last name (Evans?); #173 Listed as Wm Poorland; #215 Listed as David Childs.

Appendix C
Hartley Passengers from Wales

The format used for this list is identical to that used for the *Buena Vista* list with one exception: the number in column 10 represents the numerical order observed on the *Hartley* passenger list.

#	Name	Age									Col 10
1.	John Williams	21						32		x	36
2.	Mary Ann Williams	23									37
3.	John Hughes Williams	30			x			x 16			38
4.	Mary Ann Williams	24		x					x		39
5.	John Williams	33						16			40
6.	Margaret Williams	34				x					41
7.	Naomis Williams	Inf									42
8.	Thomas Richards	36						16			52
9.	Mary Richards	35									53
10.	David Richards	10									54
11.	Thomas Richards	6									55
12.	Morgan Davis	45	x					16			56
13.	Eliza Davis	46	x	x							57
14.	Eliza Davis	18	x								58
15.	Anne Davis	16	x								59

#	Name	Age									Col 10
16.	Hannah Davis	12							x		60
17.	Emma Davis	9							x		61
18.	Rachel Davis*	6							x		62
19.	Mary Bowen*	24		x	x						63
20.	Morgan Bowen	2							x		64
21.	Anne Bowen	Inf		x	x						65
22.	Jno Ormond	52	x					32	x		66
23.	Jno Ormond	16							x		67
24.	Dorothy Ormond	24		x		x			x		68
25.	Letetia Ormond	14		x	x						69
26.	Eliza Ormond	10							x		70
27.	Ellinor Ormond	4		x	x						71
28.	James Eynon	55	x					3	x		72
29.	Elizabeth Eynon	63		x	x						73
30.	Louesa Eynon	25		x					x		74
31.	Martha Eynon	20							x		75

Left section (entries 32–54):

#	Name	Age									Ref
32.	Charlotte Eynon	18			x			x			76
33.	David Peters	38	x							9	77
34.	Lowry Peters	33			x			x			78
35.	Ann Jones	23						x			79
36.	Peter Edwards	12	x					x			80
37.	Owin Roberts	21	x					x			81
38.	Sarah Peters	8			x			x			82
39.	Lowry Peters	6			x			x			83
40.	William Clark	36	x		x			x	33		84
41.	Francis Clark	32			x	x					85
42.	Catherine Davis	21				x					99
43.	William Owens	50	x		x				9		108
44.	Elenor Owens	49			x	x					109
45.	Margaret Owens	19			x		x				110
46.	Richard Owens	16			x	x					111
47.	Wm Owens	13			x	x					112
48.	Owin Cadwallader Owens	12						x			113
49.	Alice Owens	6			x	x					114
50.	Cadwallader Owens	24			x		x		9		115
51.	Jane Owens	6			x	x					116
52.	Nathaniel Eames*	60	x		x				9		117
53.	Sarah Eames	44	x		x						118
54.	Nathaniel Eames	13			x			x			119

Right section (entries 55–77):

#	Name	Age								Ref
55.	John Eames	5	x	x						120
56.	Elenor Eames	2	x	x						121
57.	Owen Jones	30	x			x		16		122
58.	Hugh Jones	28						16		123
59.	Jane Jones	19								124
60.	Eleanor Williams	27								132
61.	Chas Evans	28	x					9		167
62.	Thomas Davis	48		x		x		9		184
63.	Phoebe Davis	43		x	x					185
64.	Mary Jane Davis	21		x		x				186
65.	Thomas Davis	19		x		x				187
66.	Eliza Davis	17		x		x				188
67.	Jane Davis	15		x		x				189
68.	George Davis	12		x		x				190
69.	Margaret Davis	9		x		x				191
70.	Edmund Davis	7		x		x				192
71.	Stephen Davis	4		x	x	x				193
72.	Sophia Davis	Inf	x			x				194
73.	David Bowen*	26	x				x			217
74.	Robert Jones	60						9		224
75.	Jno Jones	28								225
76.	Letetia Jones	22						9		226
77.	Robert Jones	8								227

*From other sources it is known that the clerk made the following errors: #18 Listed as Richard; #19 as Mary Rowan; #52 as Nathaniel Owens; #73 as David Brown.

David D. Bowen
(H73)

Morgan David Bowen
(H20)

William Clark
(H40)

Daniel Daniels
(BV128)

Thomas Daniels
(BV130)

Ann David
(H15)

Elizabeth David
(H14)

Emma David
(H17)

Hannah David
(H16)

Morgan David
(H12)

Rachel David
(H18)

George Davis
(H68)

Thomas Davis, Jr.
(H65)

Thomas Davis, Sr.
(H62)

Mary Evans
(BV171)

Phoebe Evans
(BV51)

Margaret Francis
(BV166)

Sarah Giles
(BV132)

Morgan Hughes
(BV111)

Sarah Jeremy
(BV154)

Thomas Jeremy
(BV153)

Dan Jones
(BV1)

Mary Jones
(BV15)

William Lewis
(BV66)

Thomas Mathias
(BV133)

Edward Morgan
(BV12)

William Morgan
(BV10)

Isaac Nash
(BV49)

Owen Owens
(H48)

Caleb Parry
(BV216)

Catherine Parry
(BV217)

John Parry
(BV67)

David Peters
(H33)

Lowry (Laura) Peters
(H34)

Sarah Peters
(H38)

John Davis Rees
(BV226)

Mary Rees
(BV227)

Owen Roberts
(H37)

Benjamin Rowland
(BV19)

Job Rowland
(BV16)

Eliza Thomas
(BV146)

Rees Thomas
(BV99)

Samuel Thomas
(BV145)

Jane Treharne
(BV116)

Mary Treharne
(BV115)

Sage Treharne
(BV118)

Sarah Treharne
(BV117)

William Treharne
(BV119)

Appendix D
Biographical Sketches

Bowen, David D. (H73), Llanelli, was the cook on board the *Hartley*. After his wife and child died at St. Louis, he married Phoebe Evans (BV51). He left a sizeable journal which contains many interesting details about the crossing, life in St. Louis, and the trek across the plains. He died in 1904 in Nephi, Utah.

Clark, William (H40), Cardiganshire, was widowed while on the Mississippi River. He married Eliza Thomas (BV146) on 14 September 1849 while on the plains. He died in 1890 at Malad, Idaho. Eliza died nine years later, also at Malad.

Daniels, Daniel (BV128), Carmarthen, crossed the plains with his wife, Mary, and their two sons in 1849. He returned to Wales with Dan Jones and Thomas Jeremy in 1852 to serve a mission. He succeeded Dan Jones as mission president in 1856 and became editor of the *Udgorn Seion* for two years. He died in 1893 at Malad, Idaho.

David, Morgan (H12), Llanelli, left Wales with his wife, six daughters and son-in-law, David D. Bowen (H73). Morgan's wife, Eliza, and married daughter, Mary, died at St. Louis. He was eighteen years a Baptist before converting to Mormonism. He died in 1888 at Spanish Fork, Utah. His daughter Elizabeth married William Thomas; she died in 1890. Ann married William Warner; she died in 1900. Hannah married Morgan Hughes (BV111); she died in 1925. Emma married Alfred Rees; she died in 1915. Rachel married George Chambers; she died in 1920.

Davis, Daniel (BV89), Carmarthen, died on 9 May 1849 on the Missouri, leaving his wife, Sarah, the responsibility of one son and four daughters. Traveling with the Davises was their married daughter, Letitia; her husband, Benjamin Thomas; and their one-year-old son, Daniel. Letitia gave birth to a baby girl, Hannah Maria, the only baby to survive that was born during the crossing, on 13 May 1849 just before the *Buena Vista* emigrants arrived at Council Bluffs. Sarah Davis died in 1864 in Box Elder County, Utah.

Davis, Eliza (BV40) was traveling as a maid to someone else of the *Buena Vista* group. Apparently things were not to her liking after arriving at Council Bluffs, for just seven days later Thomas Jeremy made this entry in his journal: "Betsy Davis went back" (24 May 1849).

Davis, Hugh (BV222), Liverpool, was the only "schoolmaster" in the group. His wife, Sarah, was the first person of the original 326 to die. Mary Oubery Davis, the daughter, appears in the 1850 Federal Census for Utah as Mrs. James Switzler and was consequently among the first of the Welsh Mormons to have a "cross-cultural" marriage.

Davis, Margaret (BV209) was the young mother of three-year-old David and baby Griffith. She died 2 May 1849 on the Missouri River just one day out of St. Louis; Griffith died six days later. David was with Isaac and Eliza Nash as they crossed the plains a few weeks after his being orphaned, and he appears in the 1850 census with the Dan Jones family in Manti.

Davis, Sarah (BV223) died on the *Buena Vista* just eight days after departing Liverpool, the first person of the original 326 people to die. Her health, according to Dan Jones, was very poor even as she embarked with her husband, Hugh (BV222), and daughter, Mary (BV224). Jones preached her funeral sermon and described the occasion in considerable detail in his account of the crossing.

Davis, Sarah Thomas (BV90), Carmarthenshire, left two married children in Wales. Her husband, Daniel, died 9 May 1849 on the Missouri River and left her with four daughters and a son. Sarah died in 1864 in Perry, Utah.

Davis, Thomas (H62), Montgomeryshire, became disenchanted with Mormonism after all the difficulties encountered in reaching Council Bluffs and after the death of his wife and four-year-old son, Stephen. Thomas and eight of his nine remaining children settled in northwestern Missouri instead of continuing on. His nineteen-year-old son, Thomas, elected to remain with the main body and went to his grave a faithful Mormon. Thomas Sr. died in 1891 in Kansas; Thomas Jr. died in 1903 in Idaho.

Davis, William (BV232), Rhymni, and his family were the first of William Henshaw's many converts in South Wales. They were baptized 19 February 1843. William and his wife, Rachel, settled in Kanarraville, Utah. He died there in 1865. Rachel died in 1882, also at Kanarraville.

Eames, Nathaniel (H52), Ffestiniog, was traveling with his second wife, Sarah, and their two children. Also with them was Nathaniel, Eames's thirteen-year-old son by his first wife. Other children were left behind in Wales to rejoin them later in Utah. A baby, Jane Hartley Eames, was born to Nathaniel and Sarah while on board the *Hartley*. This entire family, except for Nathaniel Jr., died within a week of each other before reaching Council Bluffs. Young Nathaniel crossed the plains in 1849 with the David Peters family and appears in the 1850 census with his older brother David, who by that time had also reached the Valley.

Eames, Sarah (H53), was the second wife of Nathaniel Eames (H52) and the mother of two of his children. During the crossing of the *Hartley*, Sarah gave birth to another child who was given the name of Jane Hartley Eames. Of the family, only Sarah's stepson, Nathaniel, escaped death on the Missouri River.

Edwards, Peter (H36), Ffestiniog, was the nephew of David Peters and accompanied the Peters family all the way to Utah in 1849.

Evans, Mary (BV171), journeyed from Liverpool to Council Bluffs as a servant to the Benjamin Francis (BV165) family. As four of the six members of the Francis family succumbed to cholera along the Missouri, Mary's services were no longer needed. She traveled with the Benjamin Thomas (BV96) family from Council Bluffs to Salt Lake City. She married Rees Thomas (BV99) in Utah after the trek across the plains. She died in 1907; Thomas in 1893, both at Avon, Montana.

Evans, Phoebe (BV51), Merthyr Tydfil, was a servant girl to Elizabeth Lewis. At Council Bluffs, Phoebe left Sister Lewis because of what she felt were unjust demands made on her and went to live with her sister, Margaret Hughes. As a result, her clothes were confiscated and auctioned off. In 1850 she married David D. Bowen (H73), who had been left a widower by the cholera epidemic.

Eynon, James (H28), Pembrokeshire, and his wife, Elizabeth, were the parents of seven daughters. They were some of the earliest converts in Pembrokeshire, South Wales. Elizabeth died of cholera on the Missouri River. Louisa, one of the three daughters who accompanied their parents on the *Hartley*, became the polygamous second wife to Israel Clark in Utah. When the Manifesto denouncing polygamy appeared in 1890, Louisa went to live with her son Hyrum.

Francis, Benjamin (BV165), Llanybydder, on 30 April 1849 died of cholera, the second victim from among the *Buena Vista* emigrants. Eight days later his widow, Margaret, had only one daughter left after cholera had taken away one other daughter and two sons. The surviving daughter, Ann, married Thomas Howells four years later and eventually had thirteen children. Margaret died at Salt Lake City in 1886.

Francis, Margaret Evans (BV166), Cardiganshire, while on the Missouri River lost her husband, one daughter, and two sons—all victims of cholera. Margaret's only child to survive was a daughter, Ann, who married Thomas Howells four years later and had thirteen children. Margaret survived even this daughter. Margaret died in Salt Lake City in 1886, twelve years after Ann's passing in 1874.

Giles, Thomas (BV61), Monmouthshire, had been a lay Baptist minister before joining the Mormon church in 1845. Several months before Thomas and Maria left Wales, their son Thomas had been left blind by an accident in the coal mine. He later pulled a hand-cart across the plains and gained fame in Utah as the "Blind Harpist." Thomas Sr. died in 1850 at Council Bluffs. Maria died in 1866 at Ogden, Utah. Their daughter Sarah married Lorin Farr in 1851; she was the second wife of six. She bore him nine children. Sarah died in 1892 at Ogden.

Henshaw, William, Cornwall, although not a Welshman nor a passenger on the *Buena Vista* or the *Hartley*, had been instrumental in the conversion of many of the first Welsh Mormon emigrants. He was the first Mormon missionary to proselyte in Merthyr Tydfil, where he experienced considerable success during the three-year period from 1843 to 1846. By the time Dan Jones took Henshaw's place in December 1845, over five hundred converts had been brought into the LDS faith under Henshaw's leadership. In 1851 Henshaw sailed to America on the *Olympus* with his wife and four children. He died at St. Louis in 1870.

Hughes, Margaret Evans (BV112), was the wife of Morgan Hughes (BV111). Her sister Phoebe (BV51), who later married David D. Bowen (H73), was also a passenger on the *Buena Vista*. After reaching Utah in 1852 Margaret divorced her husband and later married Bishop William Pace.

Hughes, Morgan (BV111), Carmarthen, remained in Council Bluffs with his wife, Margaret, in order to save money to continue on their way to Utah. Morgan and Margaret were divorced after reaching Utah. Morgan later married Hannah David (H16), who bore him thirteen children. Morgan died in 1890 at Spanish Fork; Hannah lived to be almost ninety.

Jeremy, Sarah Evans (BV154), Carmarthenshire, left Wales with her husband Thomas, two sons, and five daughters. On the Missouri River three of her daughters died of cholera in a two-day period. Sarah gave birth to three more daughters and a son after reaching Utah. On two occasions she was left with the full responsibility of rearing her family while her husband returned to Wales as a missionary. She died in 1878.

Jeremy, Thomas (BV153), Llanybydder, was baptized in Carmarthen on 3 March 1846, one of the earliest converts from that area. He became one of Dan Jones's most intimate friends. He and his wife, Sarah, lost three little girls to cholera in two nights while on the Missouri River. Thomas returned to Wales on two occasions to do missionary work. He died in Salt Lake City in 1891. Sarah died in 1878. Among their many descendants are Marvin Jeremy Ashton, a member of the Council of the Twelve Apostles of The Church of Jesus Christ of Latter-day Saints, and Wendell Jeremy Ashton, former publisher of the *Deseret News*.

John, Thomas (BV231), according to Dan Jones (letter, March 1851, TD24, 8), was one of the few Welsh who succumbed to "yellow fever." He spent some time mining for gold in California.

By 1854 he was back in Wales, where he wrote a very apologetic letter to Dan Jones for maligning him. The letter appeared in *Udgorn Seion* (29 July 1854, 451) as did Jones's letter of forgiveness (29 July 1854, 451–52).

Jones, Benjamin (BV187), "and his whole family, except his wife, became blemished from unfaithfulness. They went away along the road to destruction at a gallop today" (Dan Jones, letter, 30 April 1849, TD9, 123). Benjamin's son William and his daughter-in-law Marian had been excommunicated two days before the *Buena Vista* reached New Orleans. There is no evidence that Benjamin's wife, Jane, stayed with the main body of the Saints, although from Dan Jones's comment, she appears to have been opposed to the rest of her family in their apostasy.

Jones, Dan (BV1), Flintshire, was a mariner and a steamboat captain many years before joining the Church in 1843. It is curious but not inaccurate that the word *Saints* is entered in his occupation column on the *Buena Vista* passenger list; for nine of the nineteen years between his conversion to Mormonism and his death in Provo, Utah, in 1862, he was a missionary among his compatriots. Dan's wife Jane and daughter Claudia traveled on the *Emblem*, which left Liverpool two weeks after the *Buena Vista*; however, they caught up with him in Council Bluffs. Dan married Elizabeth Lewis (BV42) shortly after they arrived in Utah. And after returning from his second mission to Wales in 1857, he married Mary Matilda LaTrielle. Jane died in Provo in 1861. Dan was survived by six young children (two by each wife) when he died of a chronic lung illness at the age of fifty-one. His daughter Claudia married Hyrum James Dennis in 1866; she died in 1903 at Provo.

Jones, David (BV220), and his wife Emma did not continue with the emigrants past St. Louis. It appears from Dan Jones's letter (30 April 1849, TD9, 123) that they left with Benjamin Jones and his family, and David Giles (BV215).

Jones, Evan (BV120), at age ninety-two, was the oldest of the emigrants. The ministers at Liverpool tried to dissuade him from crossing the sea and predicted that he would not survive the voyage. "But I am determined, through the power of God, to prove them all false prophets'' was his reply, according to Dan Jones. Dan Jones said of him, "He had lost his hair, except for a few strands white as the snow, but by now he has an abundant new crop just like the hair of a child. And he says that he feels younger and younger!'' (letter, 18 April 1849, 15, TD7). Evan Jones did complete the crossing of the Atlantic and the ascension of the Mississippi and the Missouri; however, he died just four days after reaching Council Bluffs.

Jones, Jane Melling, Denbighshire, although the wife of Captain Dan Jones, did not sail with him on the *Buena Vista*. It appears that the plan was for her to remain in Wales until her husband's return after completing his task of leading the group of emigrants to Salt Lake City. The reason behind this arrangement was the birth of their daughter Claudia on 8 February 1849, less than a week from the time the group was to meet in Swansea en route to Liverpool. In those days new mothers were expected to remain "confined" for several weeks. Apparently Jane did not agree with that procedure nor with the plan that she wait in Wales for the return of her husband, for on 12 March 1849, just two weeks following the departure of the *Buena Vista*, she and her baby daughter sailed on board the *Emblem* from Liverpool. They caught up with Dan Jones at Council Bluffs and crossed the plains with him in the George A. Smith Company. Dan and Jane had ten children, only two of whom grew to maturity. Jane died at age forty-two in Provo in 1861.

Jones, Noah (BV13), Merthyr Tydfil, penned "Lament of the Emigrant" (quoted in the text) after the death of his wife, Esther, on board the *Highland Mary*. He cared for his twelve-year-old daughter, Mary, at St. Louis until his death in 1851 of Bright's disease. According to his last wish, some friends took Mary across the plains with them. She married James Dunster in 1854 and bore him ten children. She died at Salt Lake City in 1886.

Jones, Owen (H57), Ffestiniog, lost the sight of one eye when he was a child and the other when he was working in a slate quarry in Wales. Even though he was totally blind, Jones worked for twenty-five years as a mail carrier in Brigham City, Utah, having memorized the layout of the city. He died in 1894.

Jones, Thomas (BV184), was the only member of his family to accept Mormonism. He was just twenty years old and still at home. His parents, having heard the scurrilous stories about the Mormons, forbade him to attend any further meetings. According to his descendants, Thomas "climbed out of his bedroom window and ran away to Utah" (York Jones, 6). Thomas married Sage Treharne (BV118) in 1852 and left her a widow ten years later with six small children. Sage married Samuel Leigh (BV76) in 1868 and died in 1897.

Leigh, Daniel (BV31), Llanelli, was a brother to Samuel Leigh (BV76). Daniel's son Daniel died of cholera on the Missouri. Daniel Sr. crossed the plains in 1849 with his family and settled in Malad, where he died in 1866. His daughter, Mary, married Nephi Campbell; she died in 1932.

Leigh, Samuel (BV76), Llanelli, a brother to Daniel Leigh (BV31), lost his wife and baby to cholera on the Missouri River. The baby was just a week old, having been born on board the *Constitution* two days before the group arrived at St. Louis on 28 April 1849. One year later Samuel married Mary Treharne (BV115) at Council Bluffs. In 1868 he married Sage Treharne Jones (BV118), who by that time was a widow with six small children. In 1876 he returned to Wales as a missionary. He died in Cedar City in 1894. Mary died in 1881; Sage died in 1897.

Lewis, Elizabeth (BV42), Kidwelly, was married to David Lewis when she left Wales with their six children in 1849. Part of David's sizeable inheritance was sold to his brother James just a few weeks before the departure of the *Buena Vista*, and David remained in Wales to tidy up the unfinished business. Much of the money was used to assist a number of the other emigrants to get to Council Bluffs and eventually to Utah. Elizabeth crossed the plains in a "spring wagon" and married Captain Dan Jones two weeks after arriving. The marriage had Brigham Young's approval but was done without the knowledge of Elizabeth's husband, who was still in Wales. She lived in Manti for several years and eventually settled in Salt Lake City, where she died in 1895.

Lewis, William (BV66), Fishguard, was a widower when he emigrated, having left behind a seventeen-year-old daughter and an eleven-year-old son. He later sent money for his children to join him in Utah. William wrote poetry under the pen name "Gwilym Ddu" and had won prizes for some of his verses in Wales. Even while crossing the plains he wrote a poem (see TD21). Shortly after arriving in Salt Lake City he married Charity Arms, by whom he had two children. William died in 1875 at Salt Lake City.

Mathias, Thomas (BV133), Carmarthenshire, and his wife, Margaret, stayed in Council Bluffs with two of their three children. A thirteen-year-old daughter, Ada (BV135), went with the Daniel Daniels family to Utah in 1849, possibly to help a widowed mother of two small children also with the Daniels family. Ada died in childbirth in 1861. Her sister, Zillah (BV136), in 1857 became a plural wife to John D. Rees (BV226) and bore him nine children. She died in 1923 at age 84. Thomas Mathias died in Brigham City in 1887; Margaret died in 1871, also at Brigham City.

Morgan, Jane (BV164), Cardiff, was traveling as a maid to the Thomas Jeremy family. Dan Jones wrote about her during the crossing: "Jane Morgans from Cardiff, who had suffered painful sores on her legs off and on for nine years and had been considered completely incurable by the doctors, is worsening. She has become more and more discouraged about the church ordinances, and her faith has weakened" (18 April 1849, 15, TD7). Jane did not continue to Utah with the Jeremys; apparently she crossed in 1852 with the William Morgan Company. She married John D. Rees (BV226) a few weeks after arriving at Salt Lake City. She died the following year of cancer.

Morgan, Morgan (BV242), Merthyr Tydfil, stayed with his family in Council Bluffs. Eleven-year-old Sarah had died on the Missouri. The family eventually settled in Malad, where Morgan died in 1878. His wife, Cecilia, died in 1887 at Mt. Pleasant, Utah.

Morgan, William (BV10), Glamorganshire, was a widower before the emigration. He was selected to preside over the Welsh branch of the Church at Council Bluffs and led the Welsh in about fifty wagons when they crossed the plains in 1852. All the letters he wrote from Council Bluffs are in Appendix E. His son William died on the Missouri; his son Edward accompanied him into Utah. In 1853 he married Martha Williams Howells, widow of William Howells, the first missionary to France. Morgan died in 1889 at Willard, Utah.

Nash, Isaac (BV49), Kidwelly, in exchange for financial assistance in journeying to Utah, assisted Elizabeth Lewis prior to the emigration in convincing her husband to sign some papers in the sale of his property in Kidwelly, South Wales. Isaac recorded in his journal numerous details concerning the sea and land travels of the *Buena Vista* group. His grandmother and a brother died of cholera on the Missouri. His wife, Eliza, came close to dying but saved her own life by drinking some water while others were asleep. Isaac and Eliza were divorced after reaching Utah. Isaac married two other wives and spent three months in prison in 1885 for polygamy. He died in 1907 at Franklin, Idaho.

Ormond, John (H22), Pembrokeshire, joined the Church in 1845, one of the first to do so in Pembrokeshire. His wife, Elizabeth, did not share his enthusiasm for Mormonism and refused to accompany him when he wished to emigrate. Three of their unmarried children stayed with their mother in Wales and five went with their father to America. How John convinced his wife to part with little three-year-old Ellinor or the other four is not clear. Elizabeth declared herself a widow four years later and remarried. John eventually married three other wives. He died in 1883 at Kanosh, Utah. As for the children who sailed with him on the *Hartley*, Ellinor and Letitia both died of cholera on 8 May 1849; Dorothy died in 1851 at Council Bluffs; John married Jane Jones in 1852 and died in 1913 at Logan; Elizabeth married George Tall in 1856 and died in 1932.

Owens, William (H43), Ffestiniog, left Liverpool with eight members of his family; only three survived to reach Council Bluffs. The parents and four of their children died between 5 May and 18 May on the Mississippi and Missouri rivers. Cadwallader married Elizabeth Jones in 1851 and died in 1898 at Iona, Idaho. Margaret married Robert Wardrop in 1851 and died in 1913. William married Jane Parson in 1857 and died in 1913 at Willard, Utah.

Parry, Ann Jones (BV213), Flintshire, was in the first stages of pregnancy while crossing on the *Buena Vista* and faced a dual challenge of seasickness and morning sickness. When her husband, Edward, died on the Missouri River, Ann was left a widow with a five-year-old son. Five months later during the crossing of the George A. Smith Company to Salt Lake City when they were thirty miles east of Fort Bridger, Ann gave birth to a son, Robert Dan. In 1851 Ann became the plural wife of David Peters (H33) and bore him five children. She died at age forty in Brigham City, Utah, in 1863.

Parry, Caleb (BV216), Newmarket, and Catherine Vaughn Evans (BV217) were married 26 February 1849, the same day that the *Buena Vista* set sail. Caleb's parents were also on board. Eight years after reaching Utah, Caleb became a polygamist. In 1870 he was called to serve a mission in Great Britain. He died a year later in Birmingham, a victim of small pox. Catherine died in 1893 at Marriott, Utah.

Parry, Edward (BV212), Newmarket, a distant relative of Caleb, died on the Missouri. His widow, Ann, bore him a posthumous child five months later on her way to Salt Lake City. She later married David Peters (H33). She died at Brigham City, Utah, in 1863.

Parry, John (BV67), Newmarket, was a preacher with the Baptists and even had his own church, "John Parry's Association," fashioned after Alexander Campbell's views, before converting to Mormonism in 1846. The Parrys were in all likelihood the most distinguished of the Welsh to join the Church up to that time, and it caused great excitement among other Welsh Mormons to count the Parrys as brothers in the gospel. John's wife, Mary, died of cholera the same day that the *Highland Mary* landed at Council Bluffs. John accompanied his son Caleb and daughter-in-law Catherine to Utah in 1849. John was asked by Brigham Young to form a choir with his singing compatriots as the nucleus; the choir evolved into what is known today as the Mormon Tabernacle Choir. In 1854 John married Harriet Parry, who bore him five more children. The last was born when John was seventy-three. John Parry died in 1868 at Salt Lake City.

Peters, David (H33), Ffestiniog, owned a woolen mill in Ffestiniog, North Wales, before he joined with the Mormons. Of the forty members of the Ffestiniog branch, twenty-seven emigrated in 1849, all but three on board the *Hartley*. Eleven died of cholera, mostly members of the William Owens and the Nathaniel Eames families. David sold his factory in order to emigrate, the money from which paid for him and his family plus five others. He married Ann Jones Parry (BV213) in 1851, a plural wife. He died in 1898 at Brigham City; his wife Lowry (Laura) died the following year in the same place.

Phillips, David (BV147), and his wife, Mary, lost three little children in three days to cholera on the Missouri. They crossed the plains to Utah in 1849 with their daughter Sarah.

Price, Rees (BV20), Dowlais, had been a scribe and a trustee of the Rev. W. R. Davies's Baptist congregation in Dowlais before his conversion to Mormonism about one year prior to emigrating. Davies then claimed that Price was not even literate, much less scribe material. In the September 1848 *Prophwyd y Jubili* (131–33) Price published a long letter in which he explained his reasons for leaving the Baptists and joining with the much-maligned Mormons. Price's wife, Jane, and one of their five children died on the Missouri.

Rees, John D. (BV226), Merthyr Tydfil, and his wife, Mary, had a stillborn child when changing steamers from the *Constitution* to the *Highland Mary*. John returned to Wales as a missionary in 1868. He eventually had four wives: Mary Morgan, who accompanied him on the *Buena Vista*; Jane Morgan (BV164), whom he married in Salt Lake City in 1852; Zillah Mathias (BV136), whom he married in 1857; and Cecelia Howe, whom he married in 1869. He was the father of twenty-seven children. He died in 1880 at Malad, Idaho. Mary died in 1907 at Brigham City, Utah. Jane died in 1853. Zillah died in 1923 and Cecelia in 1932.

Roberts, Owen (H37), Ffestiniog, was closely associated with the David Peters family and accompanied them on the 1849 crossing of the plains. He married Sarah Treharne (BV117).

Rowland, Job (BV16), Monmouthshire, had been a Baptist for thirteen years before becoming a Mormon. He was prompted to investigate Mormonism seriously after hearing his minister, the Rev. W. R. Davies of Dowlais, comment that he wished to kill Dan Jones the same way others had killed Joseph Smith. Job married Mary Parry in 1854. His mother (BV17) died at Council Bluffs in 1851. His brother Thomas (BV18) married Isabell Nelson, had eleven children, and died in 1886 at Logan, Utah. His brother Benjamin married Elizabeth Williams, also had eleven children, and died in 1910 at Salt Lake City. Job had five children and died in 1879 at Logan.

Rowland, William (BV173), Hirwaun, was widowed five months before emigrating. He married nineteen-year-old Rachel Evans (BV174), his first wife's niece, just two months before leaving on the *Buena Vista*. The Rowlands had the misfortune of being on board the steamer *Saluda* in April 1852 when the engines exploded. Quite a number of Mormons were killed, including William, two of his children (Rachel and David) by his first wife and the two born to him and Rachel in America (William and Sarah). Rachel, although left permanently crippled, later married James E. Harris and gave birth to eight more children. She died in 1918 at Cedar City. Stepdaughter Mary was badly burned by the accident; she married Thomas James in 1857 and Isaac Riddle in 1861; she died in 1920. Stepdaughter Anne was later adopted by a couple on their way to California.

Thomas, Ann Jones (BV141), Carmarthenshire, lost her husband, Benjamin (BV140), while on the Missouri River and her five-year-old son Daniel while in Council Bluffs. She and her two remaining children crossed the plains with the George A. Smith Company in 1849. Upon reaching the Salt Lake Valley, Ann married her husband's brother Samuel Thomas (BV145) and bore him four children. She died in 1869 at the age of fifty in Salt Lake City.

Thomas, Benjamin (BV96), Carmarthenshire, and his wife, Letitia, were the parents of the only *Buena Vista* child to be born on the Missouri River and survive. This was Hannah Maria Thomas, born 13 May 1849. Letitia's father, Daniel Davis (BV89), had died four days before. Benjamin died in 1887 at Malad, Idaho; Letitia, in 1858.

Thomas, Benjamin (BV140), Carmarthenshire, died of cholera on the Missouri. His brother Samuel (BV145) assumed the responsibility of Benjamin's family and later married the widow, Ann.

Thomas, Eliza Jane (BV146), Glamorganshire, was twenty-one and single when she left Wales on board the *Buena Vista*. In Council Bluffs she became acquainted with William Clark (H40), who had crossed on the *Hartley* and whose wife, Frances, had died while on the Mississippi River in May 1849. Eliza and William were married 14 September 1849 during their trek to Salt Lake City with the George A. Smith Company. They eventually had nine children. William died in 1890 in Malad, Idaho. Eliza died in 1899, also in Malad.

Thomas, Hannah Maria, daughter of Benjamin (BV96) and Letitia Thomas (BV97), was born 13 May 1849 and was the only *Buena Vista* child to be born on the Missouri River and survive. She married William D. Williams in 1870 and settled in Malad, Idaho, where they reared nine children. Hannah Maria died in 1900.

Thomas, Letitia Davis (BV97), Carmarthenshire, was about six months pregnant when she left Wales with her husband, Benjamin Thomas, and their one-year-old son Daniel. They traveled in company with Letitia's parents, her brother and four sisters. Letitia's father, Daniel Davis (BV89), died 9 May 1849; just four days later, while on the Missouri River, Letitia gave birth to a daughter, Hannah Maria. Letitia died in 1858 as the family traveled down to help settle St. George in southern Utah. She was buried by the side of the road.

Thomas, Rees (BV99), married Mary Evans (BV171) after the trek across the plains. Thomas died in 1893; his wife died in 1907, both at Avon, Montana.

Thomas, Samuel (BV145), Carmarthenshire, was traveling with his brother Benjamin's family (BV140), and several months after his brother's death, Samuel married Benjamin's widow, Ann. Samuel died in Salt Lake City in 1893. Ann died in 1869, also at Salt Lake.

Treharne, Jane (BV116), Carmarthenshire, met Edward Ashton while crossing the plains in 1852. Family tradition has it that the meeting took place while each was holding a corner of a canvas as protection for a woman in labor during a rainstorn (Ashton, 89). Jane and Edward were married about a year and a half later, on 6 February 1854, and eventually had seven children. Elder Marvin J. Ashton, member of the Council of Twelve Aspostles, and Wendell J. Ashton, former publisher of the *Deseret News*, are among their descendants. Jane died in 1897. Edward died in 1904.

Treharne, Mary (BV115), Carmarthenshire, married the widowed Samuel Leigh (BV76) in Council Bluffs in 1850 and became mother to four stepchildren. They crossed the plains in 1852 and settled in Cedar City, Utah. Mary died in 1881. Samuel died in 1894.

Treharne, Sage (BV118), Carmarthenshire, met Thomas Jones (BV184) while they were living in Council Bluffs. They agreed to marry as soon as they reached Salt Lake City. Thomas crossed the plains about a year before Sage. When Sage reached the Salt Lake Valley in October of 1852, they were married as planned. They settled in Cedar City, where they had six children. Sage was widowed in 1862 with the death of Thomas. Six years later she became the plural wife of Samuel Leigh, husband of her sister Mary. Samuel died in 1894. Sage died in 1897 at age sixty-five.

Treharne, Sarah (BV117), Carmarthenshire, married Owen Roberts (H37). Information is lacking of any further details of their lives. Sarah died in 1898.

Treharne, William (BV113), Carmarthenshire, left Wales with his wife, four daughters and son; his oldest son, John, was to bring his wife and two children across the following year. William's wife, Ann, died of cholera on the Missouri. The following year John Treharne, his wife, and two children all died of cholera before they reached Council Bluffs. William died shortly thereafter at Council Bluffs. His daughters and young son, William, were left to find a way to get to Utah. William Jr. married Ann Hughes in 1864 and died in 1907.

Williams, Edward (BV58), was one whose way across to the Salt Lake Valley was paid by Elizabeth Lewis. Apparently the money was intended as a loan, as on 23 April 1850 Edward was required to pay $239.17 to Dan Jones "for assistance in helping him from Wales" (Stout, 367). (Dan Jones and Elizabeth Lewis were married by this time; thus, the money could go to Jones.) Williams was also one who cast his vote against Dan Jones's proposal to create a separate Welsh kingdom on the other side of the Jordan River. But in a letter dated 20 March 1853 written from San Bernardino (*Udgorn Seion*, 9 July 1853, 31–34), Williams testified to his parents in Wales that Dan Jones was "a man of God."

Williams, Eliza (BV38), traveled with her two sons, Rice (BV37) and Samuel (BV39). She died on board the *Buena Vista* just six days before the immigrants reached New Orleans. She had been a faithful Methodist for fifty-five years before receiving baptism in to the LDS faith but gave thanks on her deathbed that she was dying a Mormon.

Williams, Rice (BV37) and his brother, Samuel (BV39), although both in their forties, were accompanied only by their mother, Eliza (BV38). Eliza died on board the *Buena Vista*. Rice and Samuel journeyed to Salt Lake City in 1849. Rice had married before the 1850 census.

Appendix E
Translated Documents

Contents

20. William Morgan to William Phillips, 26 May 1850, 204
    Council Bluffs, *Udgorn Seion*, July 1850, pp. 186–88.

21. Gwilym Ddu [William Lewis], "Englynion" (Verses). 206
    In *Cyfarwyddiadau i'r ymfudwyr tua Dinas y Llyn Halen*,
    p. 12.

22. William Morgan to William Phillips and John Davis, 211
    19 July 1850, Kanesville, Iowa. In *Cyfarwyddiadau i'r
    ymfudwyr tua Dinas y Llyn Halen*, pp. 2, 6–10.

23. Dan Jones to William Phillips and John Davis, 212
    10 September 1850, Salt Lake City, *Udgorn Seion*,
    11 January 1851, pp. 17–19.

24. Dan Jones to William Phillips, March 1851, Manti. 214
    In *Llythyr oddiwrth Capt. D. Jones at Wm. Phillips, yn
    cynnwys newyddion o Seion* (A letter from Capt. D.
    Jones to Wm. Phillips, containing news from Zion)
    (Merthyr Tydfil: John Davis, 1851), 8 pages total.

25. Elizabeth Lewis to John Davis, 1851, Manti, *Udgorn* 223
    Seion, 23 August 1851, pp. 272–74.

26. Thomas Jeremy to John Davis, 21 January 1852, Salt 225
    Lake City, *Udgorn Seion*, 8 May 1852, pp. 142–45.

27. Dan Jones to William Phillips, 1 May 1852, Manti. 229
    Private collection. Xerox copy in possession of the author.
    All but the last one-fourth of the letter was published
    in *Udgorn Seion*, 4 September 1852, pp. 287–90.

28. William Morgan to William Phillips and John Davis, 233
    22 June 1852, Pottowatamie, *Udgorn Seion*, 7 August
    1852, pp. 259–60.

29. William Morgan to William Phillips and John Davis, 234
    20 September 1852, Bear River, 80 miles from Salt Lake
    City, *Udgorn Seion*, 8 January 1853, pp. 32–33.

30. William Morgan to William Phillips and John Davis, 236
    25 June 1853, Salt Lake City, *Udgorn Seion*, 27 August
    1853, pp. 143–47.

Hail to California
(TD1)

When pestilence is harvesting the countries—
  Harvesting man like the grass of the field;
When its foul breeze blows
  Laying waste the green earth,
      California,
Yonder across the distant seas, for me.

When the sharp shining sword
  Is bathed in blood;
Yes, blood—the warm blood of men,
  In the worst battles ever fought,
      California—
Yonder to the Rocky Mountains I shall go.

When the seed of the sower descends
  Straight under the soils of the field.
When that sower waits
  To reap—but without ever reaping;
      California—
The country is for me the Eden of the world.

There the crops are abundant,
  There the fruits are sweet;
The end of the winter of Eden's curse;
  The beginning of the Lord's blessed summer:
      California—
There is the chief paradise of the world.

There the tithing is brought together;
  And the great temple is founded;
There it is splendidly sanctified,
  With the Lord when the hour comes:
      California—
Thou shalt be the new Canaan of the world.

You brethren who have stayed behind,
  Hasten to come after us;
Remember, we shall await you
  With a longing look;
                    California—
Sing until you all come there.

Let the dear sailing vessel come,
  Let the brethren come aboard;
Farewell to thee, world of the curse,
  Thou, breeze, blow away:
                    California—
Only California henceforth.

Counsels to the Emigrants to California
(TD2)

In response to the frequent and varied questions which we are asked with respect to the preparations and the expense of emigrating, if the inquirers are not satisfied with the following observations, let them ask again. In the first place, with respect to the preparation for food for the voyage, we say that the state government requires every shipowner to carry on board the ship the various provisions which we mentioned already in our previous observations on this matter in the last issue of the *Prophwyd*; that is, that everything be proportionate with respect to nourishment, for a pound of bread to be apportioned to each emigrant over the age of one each day of the voyage, in addition to 10 pounds of bacon each for the voyage; these supplies will be included in the price of the crossing, that is, the sum which in the last ship was £3 12s 6c for everyone over fourteen years of age. We further observe that the above preparation perhaps may not be sufficient for everyone, and anything else which the emigrants may wish to purchase will be at their discretion, with respect to provisions and abundance. The following list we consider sufficient for each one, in addition to the provisions of the ship; and so each one can determine at his home not only the additional cost he will have to bear for food, but also whether it will be better for those who have such things at home to bring them or to buy them for the following prices in Liverpool:

Provisions

	shillings	pence
10 pounds of Hard Bread for everyone over 14 at 3 pence a pound	2	6
2 pounds of Rice at 3 pence a pound	0	6
4 pounds of Sugar at 3½ pence a pound	1	2
¼ pound of Tea at 2 shillings a pound	0	6
2 pounds of Coffee at 6 pence a pound	1	0
4 pounds of Treacle at 2½ pence a pound	0	10
4 pounds of Raisins, or Currants at 4½ pence a pound	1	6
3 pounds of Butter, at 1 shilling a pound	3	0
3 pounds of Cheese, at 8 pence a pound	2	0
	13	0

Take note that this will be in addition to the price of the crossing. It is seen that the above prices are much lower than such things are sold in the shops; the reason for that is the advantage which is allowed to the emigrants by purchasing large quantities together from the Custom House, without tax on them, because it is intended to use them at sea. To those who can prepare oat bread, good butter of their own, cheese, preserves, pickles, or other things they may desire, it will be very good for them to take such things with them from home. The state government sees to it that all provisions which are prepared by the ship are good and tasty; to the head of each family will be weighed out each week that which he needs for the time being, for him and his family, so they can use it how and when they choose themselves. Those who have children under the age of fourteen will probably not need to provide the additional items above for them, since the provisions of the ship will be sufficient and their cost less by that much. It will be up to each one to provide his own provisions also on the way to Liverpool and then until the ship begins the voyage.

Necessary Clothes

We do not counsel the Saints to buy very much clothing material here, more than will last them for about two or three years in order to be warm and comfortable; for they will earn more than the difference of prices in the interest they will receive from the money they would spend for them; while from the other side such goods would lie in decay and useless in comparison. While we warn against extremes on that side, we urge everyone from the other side to prepare, as much as they can, durable warm and useful clothing; especially let abundant preparations be made for underclothing, dark wool clothes, especially for the children and women; for clear water for washing clothes cannot be obtained on the ocean. Let there be prepared an equal proportion of heavy and light clothing, or summer and winter clothing, such as is prepared for the climate of this country generally. If all the women and their daughters would have a dress of homespun material, or Welsh wool gowns, as are worn in Carmarthenshire, etc., that would be considered valuable for arriving at the end of the journey; if the men could get a suit or two of clothes besides that which they normally have here, that would be sufficient for them to get under way, especially of outer clothes; but as for underclothing, the more you have the better, for one of the main points in the creed of the Saints is cleanliness, comfort and satisfaction. Though we shall experience various climates during the journey, the first part of it will not be too warm to wear winter clothes of this country; and the rest of the clothing, that is, those for the warm weather, we would counsel everyone to get deal chests of the following sizes, if new ones are purchased, that is 3 feet 3 inches long, about 18 or 20 inches wide and deep, and put their clothes dry and neat in them, so that there will be no need to open them for a long time, especially on the sea, for the breeze and water of the sea will greatly damage clothing. Besides that, the chests of the above sizes will be more convenient than to move the belongings back and forth, and after they are filled with spare clothes, they can be put out of way on the ship, and there will be more space for the passengers. Let all do according to this counsel before leaving town; otherwise they will encounter inconvenience on the way, if all their clothes are in confusion and mixed throughout all their chests. Dress the children warmly and healthily, lest they all start crying from colds or other discomforts. Those who have feather beds may take them along; i.e., as many as wish for their use on the voyage. Notice that all must provide their own beds and bedding on the ship, and every other place; and so take care to bring enough blankets and other bedding to be comfortable. The ship provides nothing more than bed boards only, that is, the place on which to put the beds.

Necessary Dishes, Tools, Etc.

The emigrants would be well advised to take with them for the service of their family after arriving home a good proportion of the following things which they will have at hand, that is, plates, knives, forks, spoons, crockery (china, if they wish), and the other things which the women deem desirable for their comfort, for we consider their comfort as much, yes, even more than our own; and we hope to see them at the end of their journey having built homes and living in them—having planted vineyards, and enjoying the fulness of their tasty produce with no one to frighten them or oppress them; and as a result, we counsel them to think for themselves about the dishes, etc., on which they will choose to prepare such feasts after arriving home. They can carry them across the sea, in moderation, at no cost—i.e., for their own service; for if the government officials where we land on the other side think that we intend to sell any of such things, they will put a tax on them, which perhaps will make them more expensive than if they were purchased in St. Louis. But for such things for personal use, they rarely tax them there. Since there will be no need for such dishes for normal use on the voyage, it would be best to put them for safekeeping among the spare clothes to keep them from breaking. We do not counsel anyone to take heavy tools, nor in fact scarcely any household furniture, except what has been mentioned; and we do not counsel the various craftsmen to take very many of their normal tools with them, for they can probably get new ones, better and cheaper, in St. Louis. As for tin dishes for use on the voyage, they can be obtained in Liverpool best as we get under way.

The Way That Will Be Taken, the Distance, and the Estimated Cost

We have already been speaking with the captain of the steamboat *Troubadour* about taking the first company of emigrants from Swansea to Liverpool; and that kind gentleman promised to make every provision for the benefit and comfort of the travelers, and to carry them much cheaper than usual. We shall advertise the time later in greater detail; but perhaps the whole company cannot be prepared before the end of January or the beginning of February. After reaching Liverpool, someone else will board the ship which will be prepared by Pres. O. Pratt and will let us know so that we can be there three or four days before sailing, and that is the time that the wisdom and value of that part of the "Mormon creed" will be seen, i.e., everyone mind his own business, lest the sharpers and the wolves snatch them and their belongings, while smiling to their face; but we sincerely hope that the Welsh flock know the voice of their shepherd too well to mistake the howl of a wolf for it. From Liverpool, the normal time for the voyage to New Orleans is from six to seven weeks; the most part of the journey, after leaving the borders of this kingdom, is temperate, and the breezes are lovely, and more often than not there are too few of them. In New Orleans, large steamboats are available during that season of the year to come close to the ship and take the whole procession and their belongings at once, in about five or six days and for about 10 shillings each, up the great Mississippi River, for over eleven hundred miles to the great city of St. Louis. There another steamboat will be obtained to take them and their belongings up the Missouri River to Council Bluffs, about eight hundred or nine hundred miles, in about a week for about a pound each. All will need to provide their own food along this part of the journey, besides the prices mentioned; and in short, along the way from the ship to the end of their journey, all will take care of their provisions at their own cost. Yet the uncommon unity and love of the Saints will be very advantageous to them to buy everything required in large quantities; and so, everything that is necessary to buy, especially the conveyance along the rivers, will come much less expensive to each one.

After reaching Council Bluffs, you will be outside the western confines of Babylon, among settlements containing thousands of Saints emigrating to Salt Lake City, who make the desert blossom as the rose, and who will prepare themselves there for the rest of the journey; so the Welsh procession will rest in Council Bluffs while preparing wagons and food and buying animals to pull them forward; perhaps this will take several weeks of time before the whole procession is ready to get under way again, besides being more than likely that there will be several thousands of other Saints, besides the Welsh, traveling together from there through the Rocky Mountains. There are in Council Bluffs shops and every kind of necessary skills being carried on by the Saints where wagons and every needed tool can be purchased. In those neighborhoods milk cows cost about 2 pounds each, a yoke of oxen from 5 to 6 pounds; further to the east from here they can be obtained cheaper because the Saints have been buying so many in those areas. We cannot count the cost from Council Bluffs forward to our satisfaction, as well as from there back; but the best estimate we can make is this which follows. If eight persons were to go in together to buy a wagon, one yoke of oxen and four cows, which would carry them and their clothes and their food comfortably, we think that their expense would be not more than £3 10 shillings or £4 each, and the wagon and the animals would belong to them then. Those who have a family of four, five, or six children, will need to get a wagon for themselves; but for families of two or three children, two such families can get together to buy one wagon between them and share the cost. The distance from Council Bluffs to Salt Lake City is considered about one thousand miles, and there is enough game on the journey for sustenance. These few counsels we deem sufficient for this time about the above things, and we wish for all who can see their way open before them to send to us their names, and ages of each one, and the babies also, as soon as possible. We are mindful that these days are the time of gathering and the day of winnowing, that the call is for the children of Zion to come out of Babylon, lest they be made recipients of her plagues; and no doubt each one who neglects the duty to emigrate will sadden the Spirit of God, when God opens his way and provides the circumstances for that. We know of some in this land who began to wither, like the wife of Lot of old, until they became dry trees waiting to be gathered for the fire.

All the latest news from California is very comforting. Apostle W. Woodruff tells us through a recent letter that over nine hundred wagons loaded with Saints have left Council Bluffs toward Salt Lake City during last June and hosts of others are preparing to follow them. Every crop has produced in the valley beyond all expectations; the Saints enjoy generally better health there than in any other place they have been. The medicinal waters which are in the springs there have proven to be a priceless blessing to the sick so far, and what a blessing it would be if we could see all the sick children of God from Wales leaping with joy on the banks of these springs.

The spirit of gathering has taken a strong hold on the Saints in Wales and throughout the world, and we are happy to learn of that. How thoroughly are the words of Isaiah fulfilled when he says, "In that day," not only "shall the deaf hear the words of the book," but he clearly says further,—"The meek also shall increase their joy in the Lord, and the poor among men shall rejoice in the

Holy One of Israel'' (Isa. 29:18–19). What greater "rejoicing" could the poor, meek men of Wales desire in this life than to get a way of emigrating to a country where there is and will be abundance for them, and their race after them to all the generations of the earth. Well, such preparation is already awaiting them in Zion, only to go there to enjoy it. And for the comfort of the poor Saints, we state that we have sufficient faith to believe no matter how great their poverty that "He Who started them in this good work will finish it," through preparing their way and bringing a means to their hands according to their faithfulness, so that the easiest way for all to arrive home is through fulfilling the role which they are in at the present time. But we do not have sufficient faith to believe that God will allow the poverty of one of His faithful Saints to deprive him of this blessed deliverance. And will they not "rejoice in the Lord" at that time, in spite of the extent of their former poverty? We expect to yet see a nation of meek Welshmen who will strengthen a strong host of brave men from the stock of Gomer dwelling happily and peacefully in the centers of the western continent, and all obedient citizens of heavenly laws. We expect to see the poor in their beautiful carriages along the high roads of the earth, enjoying their fill of its abundance. And before long we shall lend a listening ear to hear the mountains and the hills echoing the sweet songs of rejoicing of the children of Zion; and sometime soon we hope to see kings and queens encouraging this great and wondrous work to be fulfilled. Blessed is he who does it with all his might, because that is the work which continues in praise to his name through his generations, while the work of all the foremost people of the world is like grass, stubble, and clay.

Another Thing Which Merits the Attention of All the Saints!

We would like for the Saints to remember, especially those who intend to go toward Zion, that that is a place "where justice dwells''; and consequently, all children of Zion should be workers of justice, as far as they can, even while in captivity in Babylon. The laws of Zion do not allow any of her children to work injustice with any of the Babylonians; and as far as we can know, we do not allow any who are indebted to anyone of the world, justly, to emigrate without either paying them, satisfying them or getting their forgiveness, or in some other way working justice toward them. The Saints were warned of this before, and we remind their pure minds again, so they can strive to free themselves from all they can of this tiresome captivity by the time the happy invitation comes to call them home. It is our desire for the benefit and freedom of the Saints, as well as for the glory of Zion, which prompts us to call the attention of the Saints frequently to this important matter. It is true that the wages are low and the time is bad; yet, there was never a time so bad that the principle of justice could not be shown through doing that which can be done; and then if but a penny of the old debt incurred while one of the Babylonians can be paid, that would show a penny's worth of righteousness and so on as much as possible; and then there would be faith to claim the blessing of the just God on every just effort to work justice, and doubtless it would succeed.

Notice All the First Emigrants!

According to custom all who transport emigrants over the sea, Pres. Pratt expects each one to send one pound of the money for passage in advance, before he will hire a ship, which will secure for each one passage on the ship for his turn to come there in time by the announced time, through paying the rest of the price of his passage according to that which was mentioned above; and consequently, we ourselves expect to save expense, loss and cost, that all will do, or someone for them, to bring the aforementioned pound with them to the NEXT CONFERENCE which is held in Merthyr, which will take place on the LAST SUNDAY OF THIS YEAR; and then, if Pres. Pratt is able to be here on that occasion, as he has promised, he can get them all together; or if he cannot come here, they can be transported to him, and so he can then have a better advantage to hire a ship more cheaply, through getting more time to choose a ship, than if he but takes whatever might be there at the time, and so the crossing will be cheaper for everyone. Notice that a place will not be secured on the ship for anyone except those who follow this arrangement.

The Saints' Farewell
(TD3)

Farewell now to everyone;
We shall sail the great ocean,
In complete longing for God's Zion,
For it is better to go to the land
Given us by our Father;
We have lived captive far too long.
Freedom has come to us in the wake of adversity,
We have been called out of Babel;
At the call, our intention is to go—
To go in spite of the cruel enemy:
Our God, through His great grace,
Will bring us safely to His seemly Zion.

Farewell, British land,
Our home for a long time,
There is a better home before us now;
Hardship, agony and violence
Are perpetually here,
But there is paradise beyond the great open sea.
Who is willing to come to Zion?
It is a place of complete deliverance
From the plagues and troubles
Which come to worry mankind;
It is a safe place to live
When storms cover the earth.

Let us also bid farewell
To the Saints for a short while,
Until we see them all at home:
Our farewell is long
To them who deny the truth,
For they are not of the family of Heaven.
Let us go singing across the sea,
Without fear in our hearts;
God by His kindness shall watch the vessel
When it rides the wave;
And may the Saints throughout this island
Be also in His care.

Invitation to California
(TD4)

Oh, come to California,
   Dear Welshmen, dear Welshmen
Stand here no longer,
   Dear Welshmen;
There are heavens for us there,
We shall have land without rent or taxes,
Prepare to come without delay,
   Dear Welshmen, dear Welshmen,
Do not tarry here except for that,
   Dear Welshmen.

We can get corn without sowing or harrowing,
   Everyone believe, everyone believe,
And bread without baking it,
   Everyone believe,
Houses will grow for us from the earth,
Lovely and attractive palaces,
Oh, this is an alluring place,
   Everyone believe, everyone believe,
A place where pain or sorrow will not come,
   Everyone believe.

There are geese by the thousands,
   Come quickly, come quickly,
Running through the streets,
   Come quickly,
And those after being roasted
Are ready by lunch,
Who would not go there?
   Come quickly, come quickly,
With the feast prepared for him,
   Come quickly.

There are fat oxen there,
   This is heaven, this is heaven,
And thousands of fat pigs,
   This is heaven,

Are waiting by the doors
With the knives in their throats,
Ready, morning and night,
    This is heaven, this is heaven,
There is no one with a sparse table,
    This is heaven.

Soon vehicles will run,
    Listen, listen,
By themselves without horses,
    Listen;
We shall not have to have servants
To serve us, or maids,
There are no problems there,
    Listen, listen,
To trouble the family of Zion,
    Listen.

Clothes come from the clouds,
    Become Saints, become Saints,
Like hail in showers,
    Become Saints;
The cow milks herself,
The milk soon turns to cheese,
The butter comes without effort,
    Become Saints, become Saints,
'Tis a sin for you to doze,
    Become Saints.

Give love to the things of the earth,
    Venture forth, venture forth,
Some are extremely attractive,
    Venture forth;
Joseph Smith is calling,
A very famous man was he,
There is strength in his name,
    Venture forth, venture forth,
Although he had to die,
    Venture forth.

You wealthy farmers,
  Hasten to come, hasten to come,
Provide work for the splendid auctioneers,
  Hasten to come;
Oh, sell your possessions,
Before the heavy judgments come,
And consume you with the plagues,
  Hasten to come, hasten to come,
To gain refuge for your souls,
  Hasten to come.

The man of Glantren is about to get under way,
  A great prophet, a great prophet,
He is zeal from his feet to the crown of his head,
  A great prophet;
He has sold his things,
Already for the journey,
May a fair wind call him to begin,
  Great prophet, great prophet,
Until he reaches the land of the Saints,
  Great prophet.

Near Bogeyman's Hole   A Small Seer

Last Greeting of the Emigrating Saints to California

(TD5)

Dear Brothers and Sisters—With sadness and nostalgia on the one hand, and great joy, love and hopes on the other, we send this last greeting to you who are staying behind in Babylon. We all feel deeply indebted to gratefully recognize the great care and protection of our Heavenly Father over us until now. We, 240 of us besides children on board the ship *Buena Vista*, and 65 other Welsh Saints besides children on board the ship *Hartley*, have organized our whole circumstances as comfortably as can be expected and intend to sail on the great ocean tomorrow. We had unusually good weather on our voyage here; and however many the dangers which surrounded us, and however much was prophesied of adversity for us, and however many Babylonians who tried to discourage us, mislead us and plunder us—we all thank our God today in victory for giving us a leader to guide us safely through it all, without anyone getting hurt or plundered of anything. Much did the enemies of the truth prophesy about our dear President, Capt. Jones, that he would plunder us of our money, and that he would leave us in the midst of strangers and that he would do any number of bad things to us; but justice to his character, justice to the religion which he professes, glory to the God who owns him, our duty is to testify to you that our dear Bro. Jones has been and continues to be more of a blessing to us in the present circumstance than ever before, and we can never repay him enough for his continual care over us and his beneficial directions to us. Through him we got new and comfortable ships to transport us cheaply. The price of our transportation is £3 12s 6c each for each person over 14 years of age, and £3 each for those who are under that age and over one year old, when there are some other ships here now sailing to the same port which are charging £5 each, and without all the necessary provisions, while on the other hand, our ships contain all the provisions we will need. This was for us through his wisdom and fatherly care over us. And not only that, but we know that he, instead of cheating the Saints out of their money, as many falsely accused him, has paid much of his own money to comfort and assist the others, and until now has refused to receive the least pay for that; rather he has paid to the penny the same price as ourselves for his transportation in every regard. In short, his loving and watchful behavior over all has without exception bound the affections of all around him with more and more love, until everyone likes to hear his voice in our midst; and the biggest worry of all of the others was that there would not be a big enough ship to transport everyone in the same place with him.

Dear Saints, all of us are encouraged and praying that the gracious Lord will quickly open the way to you to come after us to Zion. No doubt little Wales is like a boiling pot with the false tales about us, and much will be prophesied about the wrecking of our ship, etc., but pray for us, and we shall go safely under the protection of our God; do not believe them! Also you can defend our character on our departure from Babylon and our righteousness; for you know that our dear President proclaimed and warned beforehand that he would not allow anyone to come away who was in debt to the world or to the Saints; and we are happy to say that there is none of us with a guilty conscience because of that, or who has given cause to disgrace the religion of Jesus Christ; when on the other hand, completely contrary, the Babylonians boast of not paying to us their just debts, as if exerting themselves to the utmost to plunder us of everything they can grab, which unless they repent will testify against them in the judgment. They were so bad, some of them, that they influenced our own families, yes, our dear wives and children! so as to frighten them against coming with us! yes, to cause contention between husband and wife, between parents and dear children. What worse could they have done? They will have much to answer for! Yet, no doubt these themselves [the "Babylonians"] will raise their voices highest to condemn a man for leaving his disobedient, peevish and cruel wife behind when she refuses every offer to come. We assure you that there are no men in our midst who have not tried their utmost to get their wives to come with them, and their children also. Do not the laws of man and God assure to the husband, as the head of his family, the choice of his country? And if they refuse to follow him, his wife or children are the ones who are leaving him, and it is not he who is leaving them!

Many stories were spread before we left that women were going against the wishes of their husbands; but a baseless lie is that; there is none of the kind that we know of in our midst, or anyone who has wronged a man in our midst or who has wronged a man in anything, without reconciling the wrong. The rage of our fellow nation was so great toward us before our departure from Wales that we could not enjoy our civil rights in hardly any place; and it is abundantly true that the life of our dear Brother Capt. Jones was in such danger that his house was attacked almost every night for weeks before his leaving Merthyr, so that his godly life was not safe in sleeping except between guards from among his brethren; and there were scoundrels so inhuman who had been paid to kill him as he left, so that he had to leave secretly the day before. To what end is all this? You know that it was not for any cause given to anyone, rather it is all the rage of the devil against him, because he is an instrument in the hand of God to Zion. The only repayment which Bro. Jones desires is to get an interest in the prayers of the Saints and for them to be kind to his dear wife and child* whom he leaves in your midst until he returns, because his only child was but four days old when he left them—and he practiced every other self-denial for the gospel of Christ and the Saints. No doubt his reward and that of his family for it all will be great in Zion.

Many preachers of the different sects, after slandering us and smearing our characters through the Welsh publications and condemning our dear religion from their pulpits, and doing everything they could to disgrace us and to shatter our feelings, are even here, when we are on board the ship, with practically one foot out of Babylon, and they are trying to frighten the Saints about the sea voyage, about the country and about everything which is good, trying to persuade them to everything except that which they should do. Great are their efforts to put envy between us and Capt. Jones.

---

*We are happy to report that our dear sister has recuperated so quickly that she became sufficiently strong to be able to leave with a ship full of Saints which sailed about the middle of this month; and she intends to join her husband in Council Bluffs before long.

He is the target of all their arrows; but up to now they have failed to influence so much as one. And each one was glad to get back on shore for shame of their own false beliefs. And occasionally one of the more honest of them confessed in surprise that neither we nor our religion were as bad as he had thought. Yesterday they received irrefutable testimony from Capt. Jones and others, and even from their ministers and the Rev. H. Rees as well, until they went back to shore hurriedly and mutely. We hope that it will be beneficial to bring them from darkness to light.

All praise and trust is due to our dear Pres. Pratt for all his goodness to us here. He is worthy of your trust also in all things.

For now, dear Saints, farewell to all of you; hasten to come after us.

We are your brothers in the gospel of Jesus Christ.

Thos. Jeremy, Llanybydder
Benjamin Francis, ditto
David Phillips, Brechfa
Daniel Daniels, ditto
Rice Williams, Swyddffynnon
William Treharn, Pontyets
David James, ditto
Morgan Hughes, ditto
Samuel Leigh, Llanelli
John Richards, ditto
William Rowland, Hirwaun
Rees Jones, ditto
Thomas Giles, Merthyr

William Morgan, Merthyr
Edward Edwards, ditto
Benjamin Jones, Aberdar
Edward Edwards, ditto
William Davies, Rymni
John Williams, ditto
Rees Price, Dowlais
Job Rowland, ditto
John Hughes, Penycae
William Lewis, Blaenafon
John Parry, Birkenhead
William Jenkins, Caerdyf

Liverpool, Feb. 25, 1849

Emigration of the Saints to California
(TD6)

Mr. Editor—I wish to give some of the story of the Saints who emigrated from this country lately, since I accompanied them to Liverpool and consequently am enabled to describe their voyage up to that point.

The emigration was begun in Swansea, where all the Saints of South Wales met on the 13th of last February, and at 9 o'clock the next morning they were to leave on the steamboat *Troubadour*, to go to Liverpool. A preaching meeting was held the previous night in the large and convenient chapel which the Saints have in Swansea, which was overfilled with responsible listeners while Bro. Thomas Pugh and others preached. The emigration had caused a great commotion in the town, and thousands gathered to see the Saints depart. When the emigrants were about to leave the town, through permission of the Captain, they sang "The Saints' Farewell" very beautifully, attracting unusual attention of the observers. Great respect was shown to the occasion by the crowd in general, and many handkerchiefs were being waved in the nearby windows. While the singing continued the ship sailed away, and it arrived at Liverpool about 3:30 the following Thursday. They had a voyage which was especially successful and shorter than usual by four hours. Everyone was healthy and content during the entire voyage, except that a little seasickness troubled some. Upon landing at Liverpool the captain of the ship showed great care for the Saints by landing at a place where there were no "sharpers" of the town waiting, hosts of which had gathered at the usual place to await the steamboat so they could steal from the emigrants. In addition to this kindness the Liverpool Saints had rented a large, six-story house in order to care for their Welsh brothers while in the town. It was sufficiently large for the whole company to take lodging in it. I am pleased to say also that, through listening to their leaders' warning to take care of their possessions, all the Saints kept everything safe so that all the cunning of the predators of the place did them no harm in any way. They spent five days in the before-mentioned house, and during that time no more than 1s 6c each was charged for lodging. The following Tuesday everyone moved to the American ship which intended to sail the next day; but through some obstacles it waited there until the 26th. In the meantime the Saints stayed on the ship, and I also stayed in their midst; and I saw some of the Saints at times taken sick; but no sooner were hands laid on them than they were restored immediately; and I can bear witness that I have never seen more of the power of God than I saw on the ship. While I was in their midst there, I was led by my curiosity to put many of the Saints to the test, especially the weakest ones (and I can name Gwilym Ddu, to satisfy the friends of Pontypridd), in order to see if I could get some of them who were homesick to go back. The answer which I received generally was "However much we love you, we cannot love you so much as to wish to turn back with you. Leave us in peace; it is forward that all of us want to go."

The Saturday before sailing, the Rev. Henry Rees and some of the sectarian preachers of the town came to the Saints on board the ship. They asked me and Capt. Jones if the emigrants were Welsh. We answered, "Yes." Then they asked a second time, "Is it true that there are here widows from the south who have prepared clothes to put on their departed husbands in California and shoes to put on their feet, for we have received letters from respected ministers from South Wales telling us that." "Not a word of that is true," said we; "rather it is a barefaced lie; and those persons knew it was a lie when they wrote to you. Nevertheless, there are on the ship some widows who have kept some things of their husbands out of respect, but not to greet them with in California." "We are very glad indeed," they said, "that the Welsh are as wise as that. We were surprised to hear that the Welsh were so foolish; but now we have witnesses to the contrary." Then we showed our principles to those reverends, telling them that we did not believe anything except that which is in the Bible. With that, they said, "Very well; we wish success to you to arrive at the end of your journey, and may God bless you all." After that they left, bidding farewell to us, and they are probably very disappointed with the Saints.

On Sunday (that is the 25th) a conference was held on the ship, which was begun at 2:00 by the secretary, by singing and praying, and it was carried forward under the presidency of Capt. Jones. Several of the brethren spoke on the occasion and an unusual measure of the Spirit of God was enjoyed there. All the Saints there were embodied in one branch; and then they were divided in eight groups, with a president over each group; and three others were appointed to preside over the whole company. After that, a council was organized to arrange the matters of the Saints, so that everyone could have justice; and then the conference was ended in the customary manner.

After that the time drew near to sail toward home, which would take place the next day at 11:00. On this occasion, the harpists and singers had a place on the captain's cabin, to sing ''The Saints' Farewell'' for the last time, when crowds had congregated to listen to their music and to be eyewitnesses of their departure to California. Many left their tasks to be present, and great was the courtesy which was shown on the occasion. They reached the mouth of the river at about 1 o'clock and

> ''They went singing over the ocean
> Without a single fear in their breast,''

until soon they escaped our sight, and their wish and ours is for them to reach the ''better country.'' Another ship left the morning of the next day full of Welsh, Irish, and Scottish Saints. That the gracious God may bless them and us is my continual prayer. Amen.

W. Phillips.

A Letter from Capt. D. Jones
to the Editor of *Udgorn Seion*
(TD7)

New Orleans, April 18, 1849.

Dear Brother Davis—

According to my frequent promise to the dear Saints whom I left behind in Wales, I shall give an account of our voyage across the ocean up to this point. There are no doubt many tales about us which have been spread throughout Wales, and prophecies about our drowning, etc. Therefore, I beseech you to announce in your *Udgorn* that all these are false up to now—that we are still alive, even though on the other side of the sea from you. I hope that they do not believe that this letter is coming from the *spirit world*. Furthermore, the Captain has not turned the ship to Cuba and sold the Saints into slavery as yet, as was prophesied in *Seren Gomer* and by others that he would do. It is facts like these which prove who the false prophets really are.

But on with the account of our voyage. Since I am writing to many who intend to follow us sooner or later, for whose happiness we are desirous, allow me to itemize the most educational things, so that they may benefit from our experience. According to the account concerning us which you heard from Liverpool, I report that before sailing, that is, the first Sunday after boarding the ship, we established ourselves as an emigrating or floating branch on the depths, yet, in another sense, as an established branch, and the various officers were chosen to fill the different responsibilities appertaining. We held a meeting of the Saints, distributed the sacrament and received open evidence that our worship was accepted by Heaven, through the presence of the Holy Spirit in His lovely influence. And we received open evidence that the enemy, as in the days of Job, had come there also, by his possessing of one sister, until she was driven out of her senses, causing her to scream and utter inhuman things and frightening curses; but her disturbance did not keep up very long, for through the laying on of hands of the elders and the prayer of faith, our Father saw fit to seal the promise of His Son "to them that believe," on land and on sea, that is—"In my name shall they cast out devils"; and Oh, how valuable was the blessing this time.

The ship was divided into eight sections according to the number of the families. Elders were assigned to supervise each section, to see that everyone acted properly and received justice impartially, to foster and nurture love and unity, and especially to see that all kept the places clean and healthful. To that end, it was arranged for two each morning to arise before the others around them and wash the deck clean and dry it. These eight presidents, together with another triad, that is, William Morgans, Merthyr, and Rice Williams and William Davis, Rhymni, his counselors, constituted a council to organize all temporal and spiritual matters. In this manner we prepared ourselves through agreement without exception.

On Monday, the 26th of February, about two o'clock in the afternoon, we set sail from the port, and all the Saints, accompanied by the harp, sang "The Saints' Farewell" as we left the dock. Their sweet voices resounded throughout the city, attracting the attention of and causing amazement to thousands of spectators who followed us along the shore as if charmed. We were followed here by our dear and faithful brethren, William Phillips, Merthyr, Abel Evans, Eliaser Edwards, and some of the other faithful elders, together with David Jeremy from Brechfa. These brethren, having shown every other kindness and assistance they could, like dear kinsmen to loved ones at the graveside, vied with each other in showing yet additional love by buying oranges and throwing them to us in the ship as long as they could reach it. The fall of the oranges out of our reach into the sea proved that we were too far to shake hands with each other any more. It was only this last separation from them that could agitate the fountains of tears in spite of ourselves. By this time, almost unawares, all we could see behind us were their handkerchiefs like flags waving in the breeze, in a language shouting from the aching heart, "Farewell, farewell! to sail across the vast sea to dear Zion"; while all they heard back were the echoes of our warm hearts coming with the breeze from the water, "Farewell, farewell! land of Britain," etc. We thought that not only foreign men but all nature as well had become calm to observe the scene and that the winds of February had turned into summer breezes in our behalf. With indescribable feelings we were dragged by two large steamers out of sight of the city; and before nightfall our ship was rocking just like a hut on the surging waves of the sea. The steamers turned back after escorting us about 30 miles, and inwardly the scene changed on us. Now some would go to light fires, boil water, make tea, etc., while others, made more miserable by seasickness, staggered to their beds. When eight o'clock came and the ship was under full sail—the wind from the west and everything in order as much as possible—a meeting was held for family prayer, and everyone went to lie down, but hardly anyone could sleep; and even though the wind was not stormy and the sea was not rough, still it was sufficiently rough to make almost everyone so sick that I shall not forget that night for a long time. Though hardly anyone could sleep, yet no one slept less than myself and a few of the other elders, as we were back and forth comforting and assisting the sick as much as we could throughout almost the entire night. The sunlight was beautiful the next day, and some of the sick improved; yet they could hardly walk by themselves across the deck without someone guiding them, which service kept me quite busy, but it was no less pleasant than every other guidance in their behalf. This morning I tried hard before succeeding in getting some of the sick out of bed to breathe the healthful air, since seasickness causes such a debilitating feeling. Some were almost angry with me because of my insistence; but I wouldn't be refused, even though I was obliged to carry many a person on the deck. And I was well paid for my trouble through patience, once they realized that the topside and healthful air would improve them gradually and without exception, so that it was easy to see the difference between those who succumbed to their desires to stay in their beds and the others who showed their courage by coming to the healthful air on deck, whose healing, together with the testimonies of these to others, convinced others to follow their example. And I cannot encourage too much those who will yet come to do all they can to come on deck in similar circumstances.

It was not long before those who resisted most strongly to come topside with me were thanking me the most because of almost forcing them to come. This day I got enough men to come to the

"Company Shop" (as was called the storeroom at the back of the ship where the supplies were kept); and the three members of the first presidency and myself became makeshift shopkeepers to weigh the following different foods for each family as they wished; so that each one could prepare it how and when he wished. To all over fourteen years of age the following amounts were distributed with half that to everyone between one and fourteen; that is—ten pounds of hard bread, white and good; four pounds of sugar; three pounds of cheese; three pounds of butter; four pounds of raisins; two pounds of rice; two pounds of coffee; four pounds of molasses; one-fourth pound of tea. This food was of extremely high quality and a gift from Pres. Pratt, something which no one else gave to emigrants; and no matter how sad some of the women's faces were, the sight of such a gift caused them to go cheerfully to the shop; and although they stepped on each other's feet and sometimes fell into each other because of the shaking of the ship, yet I declare that they laughingly called for help "to raise the lowest," and they tried again. There was no respecting of persons in this, rather it was the best on his feet who kept his head up, and everyone agreed that the one leg was too short, or that the other was too long, almost every step.

In the afternoon, since there was a cross wind, the ship stayed along the coast of Ireland, until its steep mountains and jagged rocks threatened to mangle us if we came closer. And we all rejoiced when the sailors turned the other side of the ship to the wind and its point toward the borders of our own beloved country. There were several other large ships in our sight sailing to the west, but it was absolutely incredible how our ship sped by them all one by one so that we could see them no longer. In the middle of the night the winds increased when we were very close to the lights of the Holyhead peninsula. Almost everyone, except for myself and Brother Daniel Daniel, was sick.

[February] 28. We went on deck at the break of day, and the first thing which attracted my attention was Bardsey Island, not far from us. And beyond it the huge mountains of Caernarvonshire lifted up their snowy peaks, vying with each other in height and in the desire to see at the crack of dawn whether the children who had been raised on their breasts were still alive or whether they had

drowned; or if what they heard on the ocean were the lovely voices
of their emigrant sons echoing as before in the forests and glens
of their land. In this eager search, like a nostalgic mother in the
midst of her daughters, dear Snowdon above the rocks of Snowdonia
stretched her neck most and raised her head highest into the
heavens gazing after us and forgot, because of her desire, to take
off her snowy night cap to greet us; yet, there were none of these
sons, except myself, who had strength to echo back her motherly
farewell before she lowered her comely head behind her daughters
one by one in the eastern ocean.

But my vessel did not wait for my affection to embrace for long
its object (that is, the dear land of my fathers) because of her
greyhound-like desire to speed along her way across the seething
white caps, as though frolicking, splendid and fearless, on the tops
of the furious waves. But it was not the green ocean, in spite of
its commotion; the blue sky, in spite of its ferocity; not even the
comfort of my fellow travelers nor how much I wanted this; nor
was it the last farewell to the shores of my country which mainly
filled my thoughts. Rather, I pondered seriously the condition of
her inhabitants. I see myself now with a small handful, a sheaf of
the fluttering of the inhabitants of Wales, looking from afar on the
country which is called the "garden of Christianity"—"the country of the Bibles," which had erected the lofty tops of her numerous
houses of worship to the sky as a monument to her zealous
enthusiasm, yes, behold this and even more. And is it a fact or just
a dream that I have escaped on the water from the midst of my
Welsh brothers with my life by the skin of my teeth? If so, why?
If not, why all the persecution, the slander, and the false accusations I suffered for years from the press and the pulpits? Why did
my residence have to be guarded for weeks? Why was my life safe
only among guards? Why did I have to flee in secret before the
time? Why was I not able to bid farewell to my dear wife and my
baby? It was doubtless not for transgression in the world; for once,
twice, yes, even three times I challenged any man to prove me
guilty of transgression. Oh, it must be admitted, it cannot be
hidden, that religious persecution is what caused it all; there must
be strength in my religion, if nothing else but that could prove it,
for it to have been able to excite the old passion of every false

religion to persecute it. Persecution does not originate from God; neither does the religion which persecutes come from Him.

Oh, yes, 'tis a fact, the sun dawns cheerfully on my head as an exile from the borders of my country; the winds try to beat me back as an exile for his belief; my beloved vessel, my castle, fights to defend me against danger as an exile cast out by his brothers whose benefit he seeks, and she opens her sails to the wind to carry me, as if her kinsman, safely home to Zion, like a victorious soldier to his home. Their thoughts, unawares, drew my affection and my eyes toward the west to ponder on Zion and her glories, until once again, like a flowing stream, it came to my memory that of her dear children thousands are left behind in Wales and that of my gentle fellow nation there, multitudes would love the true faith if they had a chance.

Once again I turned my face to the east and my spirit in prayer to the God Who initiated this good work, and blessed His gospel with success in Wales to make His servants mighty men, and beloved like the sons of the great thunder, to sound the trump more loudly, until the inhabitants of hill and vale are awakened from the sleep of false religion, to embrace the gospel so that His Spirit, like the purifying fire, could refine those who obeyed. But by this time, the blue cover of the sky and the high whitecaps of the waves, between them almost hid under their covers the little green garden, that is, the country which raised me. I vowed that I would not be angry for the evil which I received there. Nor am I exiled forever, rather I shall yet come across the depths to the home of my loved ones to try, if there be a way, to take them to worthy Zion in my embrace in time.

O my country! my love binds itself around your beautiful vales; your rocky shores are all "magnetic stones"; for I want to benefit your peoples. May the gospel of heaven raise its white banners on every brow and hill within your land, and wave in all your breezes. But yet, there is within your land something which surpasses everything I have noted, something far above, more beloved and fair, though so far away now, and closer than anything else to my heart! O my mind, stop, come, return back. Why do I break the strings of my heart? Why do I call? She will not come back. Well, then, just for an instant raise your wings to the wind and feast in

her company. Angels of heaven now surround her bed lulling her
to sleep; her cheeks red and her smile happy as if she sees me; she
reaches out her pure arms; she embraces tightly as if her dear lord
were in her arms. But he is not there, just his image. O little rosebud,
and the only one, hardly as old as a new moon, why did I leave
thee? Even until this morning, my beloved,* for following me across
land and sea, and many countries; for happily sharing the troubles
and comforts of my breast; for many times having caused me to
forget the world and its things, and for so tightly having kept the
keys of my heart for ten years; for everything and everyone who has
ever been even until this morning as my mind shot at the break
of dawn to your bedchamber—I have loved you. Oh, if only my
mind could stay here longer, yes, wait for you to awake. But the
first parting was sorrow enough—why cause a second wound?

Take courage, my spirit; this must be for Christ's religion—it
is not for long, nor is this separation without its everlasting reward.
You, angels pure, I charge you to care for my wife and baby; I go
courageously on. Watch over her until I return; she is precious to
my soul, for she was content for my sake. For this Snowdon will
jump into the sea before I shall ever, ever, forget her. To thy arms,
my Father, I commend everything I have. One look yet—one more
greeting ere I leave. My spirit bows above the place where she lies;
now it takes strength for this adventure! Hush! What is the matter?
Where am I? What, on the high sea? Yes, with a call to hasten to
the sick.

Well, well, I wandered far, but I shall return to my account.
There was hardly anyone able to prepare food today, but Daniel
Daniel and William Jenkins and I agreed on an attracting device
by helping several onto the deck. We made a comfortable place for
a row of the women to sit in the air, and I set about making a gruel
out of oat flour for them, which strengthened them greatly. And
so, pot after pot we apportioned to them in a circle on the condition that they stay up to eat it. It is hard to describe the good this
did them, and I would counsel everyone to take a sufficient quantity

---

*As was noted in the *Udgorn* lately, Mrs. Jones improved so quickly that
she was able to leave after her dear husband, and he has most likely seen
her in Council Bluffs by now—JD.

of good oat flour and oat bread with them, for they shall see that this will taste better to them than anything else for awhile.

In the evening, Ireland was in sight; the wind increased so that it was necessary to lower the top sails to the lowest position and pull all the other sails in. The ship was turned with its stern to the south for awhile, and then back to the other side throughout the night; but whether on one side or the other it was totally impossible for it to remain still or to allow anyone else to lie or stand in his place, rather like a door on its hinge it continually swayed those who were lying down; but as for those standing, it was throwing them along the deck with the boxes and their crockery as recklessly and without warning as the wild horse throws its unskilled rider across the hedge and leaves him there. But without any pity when the rider got up, the ship would throw him somewhere else until he crawled home. It was no use begging her to stop; the grumbling of the one or the groaning of the other together with the voices of the children had the same effect on her, that is to increase her drunkenness. Many agreed with me before morning that it was better to let her have her own way and let her rock until she was tired of it. And so it was. She has hardly ceased yet.

March 1. For a good part of the day we were running a race with the steeple of St. David's, Pembrokeshire. But before night we got ahead of it, thanks to the help of the wind. By this time, many, especially the men, had taken courage, in spite of falling so much like the baby, until they had learned to walk along the sides. A prayer meeting was held in the evening, and soon after that the wind turned to our favor, something which greatly encouraged the sick. Only oat bread tasted good today.

[March] 2. We were out of sight of land and only blue sky and green water around us except for an occasional ship sailing her own way. The majority improving considerably.

[March] 3. Beautiful weather, and the little children playing all along the ship, and the parents laughing upon seeing an occasional pile of them on top of each other on the deck, yet not daring to venture there to interfere. Until today we were escorted by birds of our country, but no longer; rather, having entrusted our care to multitudes of sea birds, they returned.

[March] 4. (Sunday). At two o'clock, we had a splendid, lovely meeting of the Saints, and everyone was perfectly content except for an occasional one of them who refused every counsel to come on deck, who have by now gotten fevers in their beds. All this caused us great concern and trouble, along with sincere prayers before they were restored to health. I would warn others to refrain from doing the same thing. Many beneficial and interesting admonitions were given in the meeting. After the sacrament, several testified of the goodness of God, etc. The sick improving. At night the Saints divided into two prayer meetings, half at each end of the ship. The wind supported us pleasantly.

[March] 5. Beautiful weather throughout the day; constant strolling on the deck; the musicians singing with eleven musical instruments and everyone except a few sick fairly comfortable.

[March] 6. Rather unexpectedly to any of us, our dear sister, wife of Brother Hugh Davies from Liverpool died, over sixty years of age. Her health was very poor when she came on board so that she hardly expected to get across the sea, yet her wish was to come with her family. The captain and the officers of the ship were very kind in view of the circumstances, and everyone throughout the ship felt that our dwelling today is a house of mourning. A prayer meeting was held in the evening, and everyone's health improved. The death had the effect of causing others, who had up until now refused, to rise from their beds, and the result was their improvement.

[March] 7. The climate beautiful and the wind fair, the ship sailing about seven miles per hour. Preparations were made to commit the body of our sister to her watery grave. I preached her funeral sermon at two o'clock on the text "How are the dead raised up and with what body do they come?"—(Paul). I answered the last question briefly, but the answer to the other question was continued along for several Sundays, and it has not been completely answered yet! After the sermon, the coffin was placed on a large plank, the ship was stopped, and after the Saints had sung a hymn the sailors raised the inward end of the plank so that the coffin slipped down the other end to the salty deep, which, because of the weight of the stones which were placed in the coffin to sink it, opened up to swallow its precious treasure and to keep it safe until the day when the command shall be given for the "sea to yield up the dead which are in it." Some have very mistaken ideas and are greatly afraid to think of being buried in the sea. Some think they would float on the surface, a prey to the fish. Even if it were so, it is no worse than rotting in the cold gravel and being food for grave worms; but the fish do not have those who are buried in the sea; the purpose for putting weights with the body is so that it will sink down quickly and lower in the ocean than the fish ever go and lower than they can live. And there it will float in peaceful salt water, which will keep it from decomposing or rotting forever. Yes, until the day of their rising, when the "sea will boil," they will be kept better than the best of the Egyptians were kept through embalming. This understanding does away with the conflict which is in the thought of being buried in the sea and rather makes it preferable. Also I think that this is what the apostle had in mind when he said that the sea gave up the dead, not alive I would think, but the body which was buried in it, and which was preserved in this manner, never to be made alive, for "the body which is sown is not that which shall be," whether it be sown in the sea or land, but an incorruptible body which shall be united with the spirit which possessed the body before. After the sea had closed its jaws on its morsel, and after our little ship had stood for us to be able to behold this majestic sight for a few minutes, her sails were filled with breezes and she galloped across the waves as if nothing had ever happened. The wind continued in our favor, and everything was comfortable, and all the sick had improved with everyone eating his allowance throughout this week. A prayer and counsel meeting was held each night.

[March] 11. (Sunday). The wind, light and against us; the sea, calm, with each having scrubbed himself before the meeting, which began at two o'clock and continued until five o'clock; we were for over two hours trying to answer the previous question, that is, "How are the dead raised up?" It was postponed until the next meeting. Everyone appeared to be happy and rejoicing in the teaching. Before the end of the meeting the wind turned strongly in our favor according to our prayers, and it continued for the most part in our favor throughout the week. Sometimes it blew us over ten miles an hour. We felt the wind and the climate by now gradually getting warmer, since we had sailed still to the southwest.

Several began to complain that their woolen clothing was too heavy and that they could not bear it any longer. Better for everyone to have additional light clothing. We have had hardly any rain, except for a few showers; but it was not raining that time, rather pouring water down from the clouds. At times, we saw several different kinds of fish, some very big, others smaller, jumping from the water. This helped the lazy ones to come on deck, which helped them with every breath they took.

[March] 16. The wind was against us greatly in the afternoon. A prayer meeting was called at seven to pray for fair wind. After the meeting, I said to some who were near me that I felt the desire to go on deck and not return until our Father would give us fair wind. As I was going, having put my foot on the lowest rung of the ladder, those around me were chatting about one thing and another, and one asked what I wanted most. I answered that I would most like to hear the mate on the deck shouting "Haul in the weather braces!"* And before I had moved my foot, I, and the others who had heard my wish, heard the mate above our head shouting loudly, *"Haul in the weather braces!"*—yea, word for word as I had said. And behold a fair wind blowing strongly in our favor which within a few days had driven us about a thousand miles homeward, that is toward Zion. Great was our thanks to our God for that.

[March] 17 (Sunday). Beautiful weather and everyone comfortable. In the afternoon we had an excellent meeting of the Saints with more on "How are the dead raised up?" Meeting in the evening. Fair wind and weather so beautiful throughout the week that it was almost like Wales in June. An occasional squall and cloud breaking to supply us with water for washing. It is beautiful to see the children playing across the deck and entertaining their parents. Some singing here, others talking or reading there; some walking arm-in-arm while others prepare foods of as many kinds almost as could be obtained in any cookshop. The musicians did their best to beautify the atmosphere. Also the harp with its pleasant sounds alone in the evening entertained us as it sang farewell to the king

---

*Order to pull on the ropes which set the sails across the ship and means without exception fair wind.

of the day as he lowered his red head into the western sea. To light the scene in his place, lovely Phebus awakes from her sleep, as if she envied him. No wonder that scenes less wondrous than this excited the heels of David of old to the point that he even took off his garment in the temple—and for what? Hush! shall we reply? What is the use of hiding the fact, did he not do this in order to dance? Yes, yes, and there was hardly anyone in our midst, except for an occasional dry sectarian, who did not prefer to imitate him rather than to find fault. At least it would be hard to deny that it was so here at times, and it did not even cause a storm. "The company store" was open, without books or money, to distribute a sufficiency of either white beans, rice, wheat flour, oat flour, bacon or anything else, and plenty of it for everyone. Some complained of a cold through getting wet in the rain.

[March] 25. (Sunday). Light gusts of wind at times. Again the scene around us was "like a calm sea of glass." And not only the elements, but our ship and all her children as well were observing this holy Sabbath by resting quietly. But the sun gazed too intently on some until it was a relief to retreat to anywhere from its presence. A meeting of the Saints in the afternoon, and a lecture on "How are the dead raised up?" A sermon in English on deck in the evening and nearly all the sailors spoke well of the teaching. The wind rose strongly in our favor in the night. Hardly any scene in particular this week worthy of note, except for an occasional cross breeze, which changed almost consistently in the middle or at the end of our prayer meeting held each night. There was also an occasional appearance of fish to entertain us, and a ship here and there in the distance to gladden the lonely scene. Also the devilish foe, himself, asserted his right with Neptune (the god of the sea) to journey with us, though his company was not so sweet; nevertheless, it was hard work to cast him overboard because of his cleverness. And not infrequently in hard times he would turn himself into an angel of light and as such would occasionally hide in the pocket of an officer. Of everyone who may be left behind in Babylon let this one be the last! He is a poor sailor, a troublemaker, and a worse guide than Ahithophel. Not to the swine, not to the sea, but to some of the Babylonians he escapes at times. And the next time that I cross the sea with a group of the Saints to Zion the other two kinds can stay home! A great benefit is felt by drinking and bathing in the sea water in the morning. Let everyone have his children do so as often as possible. Let everyone take care to refrain from suspending anything which would keep the air from going through the ship. Also let everyone take care that neither they nor their children become constipated—take a laxative. Because of this neglect some have suffered until they were almost incurable. Refrain from eating a lot of heavy food, for this idleness does not allow it to digest. Above any other valuable thing to bring to the sea do not forget to bring a generous supply of *patience*. There will be a great deal of wear on this commodity; let care be taken that it may not fail. Even more valuable than much gold is a little grain of true faith on the sea, for that will buy a fair wind and everything essential. But in spite of everything that has happened, I have not heard anyone repent for having undertaken the journey. It is just that they are desirous of reaching Zion. It has been a great pleasure to hear almost everyone over and over again praising the goodness of God in our behalf—the fair weather, the beautiful breezes, the excellent food, and the general success which we have had better than expected before getting underway. And truly it was not a small pleasure to see the cooks by the fire making their puddings, their pancakes and their fries piling up and inviting the one and the other to drink tea with each other. And in the evening "they arose" happily as did those earlier "to dance." In this manner frequently many pleasant days came and went on the ocean. Who can blame them?

April 1 (Sunday). This Sabbath again all nature agreed with us to pause and gaze on the excellence of the creation of our God. Two other ships did the same in the distance. A very lovely meeting of the Saints; a lecture for two hours on "How are the dead raised up?" Several took off all their woolen clothing, like myself, and caught cold. Take care against this. Although summer clothing is lovely now, it is better to check yourself (so say my sufferings). For in this climate the clouds suddenly rend under the weight of their watery burden. And especially do not wear wet clothing. At noon today our time here was four hours later than London time. When it was twelve o'clock or noon here, it was four o'clock in the afternoon in London, which proves that we are 60 degrees to the west of London, with 30 degrees and 9 minutes to the west to run yet before reaching New Orleans. I observed the sun today again through the sextant, and I determined our latitude to be 23 degrees and 54 minutes north, or within 14 miles of the tropics where in the middle of summer the sun would be above our heads. But since it is in the south now and lovely breezes temper the weather, we did not feel uncomfortable heat. Our distance from New Orleans today is about 2,000 miles. Our distance from the land we expect to see on our journey, that is "Hole in the Wall," one of the islands of the Bahamas, is between 900 and 1,000 miles. Our southerly distance from Liverpool is 1,806 miles.

[April] 2. We had some storms and rain and rough winds from several directions which threatened to swallow our little shell into the depth of the salty cauldron; in spite of all this, through the protection of our God and the skill of our captain and his sailors, our ship climbed upwards from wave to wave, as the swallow would fly through the slight breeze. The sea shook our little vessel and all the passengers as does the whirlwind with the crow's nest in the oak tree without being able to disturb even one of the small chicks therein. Upon perceiving, however, that its awful and fierce waves did not deter us, the sea desisted in its effort and smiled pleasantly. The sun, which had earlier worn sackcloth, with a stern and ugly gaze, now took off his clothing a cloak at a time and laughed at the battle, promising fairly as he lowered his head amidst the red sky that we would have a fine night for sleeping. For this everyone offered thanks and made the most of it. Perhaps the next statement will be incredible to the ignorant, but it is absolutely true, nonetheless, that we saw almost every day after that fish flying! Sometimes we saw scores of them together. They flew at times a good mile or more, and then they would wet their wings in the top of a wave and off they would go a second time. They are chased by other fish who jump several feet out of the water after them. It is a good thing for the defenseless that the Creator in this case had provided them with wings for their protection. These fish do not fly very high—but higher when the wind is strong than when it is peaceful. And other times, in these areas I saw them fly against the sails of the ship and fall on the deck. And inasmuch as they can rise only from water we caught them. They are not as big as a common mackerel. Their wings are not feathers, rather a kind of bright and very thin skin. In the water they close and serve the same purpose as wings. Their length is from six to ten inches. They cannot fly unless they keep their wings wet, and they are seen only in warm weather.

Now Mrs. Williams, originally from Ynysybont, who has been sick with a fever for several days, is gradually improving. Jane Morgans from Cardiff, who had suffered painful sores on her legs off and on for nine years and had been considered completely incurable by the doctors, is worsening. She has become more and more discouraged about the Church ordinances, and her faith has weakened. Ever since we reached warm weather we have arranged for each section on its day to have a turn to spread out its beds and bedding on the deck in the sun, something which has been very healthful for all. Let everyone do so as often as possible. Our captain has graciously given us some kind of liquid to sprinkle along our sleeping places. It purifies the air wonderfully and we use it frequently. We have several elderly people on the ship, and they are all improving as they come to the deck every lovely day. One old gentleman, close to 100 years old, says cheerfully that he is happier than he has ever been. He says also that many of the sectarians in Wales and even in Liverpool, the Rev. H. Rees and other reverends, tried to dissuade him from coming, prophesying that he would not arrive across the sea and many other things. "But I am," says he, "determined, through the power of God, to prove them all false prophets." He had lost his hair, except for a few strands white as snow, but by now he has an abundant new crop just like the hair of a child. And he says that he feels younger and younger!

Fair and lovely wind. On Saturday the 7th I had been up all through the night looking for land until four o'clock in the morning, and I had hardly slept before the loud shout and its exciting effect on everyone else, that is, "Land ahead," had awakened me. Great was the joy this caused to all the emigrants; there was nothing else mentioned or noticed for a time except land. By sunrise we were sailing nicely along to the south along the coast of Abaco Island, one of the Bahamas. This is quite a deserted island, populated mostly by fishermen, and people who cut firewood and carry it to other parts to sell it. Earthquakes chase everyone away from here from time to time and cause much damage. Not a very pleasant sight. Nine o'clock in the morning we turned the ship to the west to round the southern edge of the island within three miles or less of land. At this southern tip there is a lighthouse on a rock and a dwelling nearby in which the lighthouse keeper lives. There were three other ships sailing along with us past the lighthouse, but keeping more to the south toward Cuba. By midday the island had disappeared out of sight behind us, and there appeared several other islands and rocks to the south of us less than ten miles away. For the understanding of those who will come this way, since they will come close to the aforementioned lighthouse, I should have commented that its name is "Hole in the Wall"; thus, those who see it will remember it through the eyes of someone who has looked on it before them. I call their attention to the meaning of the words, or their origin. You can see a large hole through the high rocks on the rocky mound where the lighthouse is located. It looks like a bridge or a large "arch" of man-made work, but either nature or the struggle of the elements is what has made it. There was earlier another more remarkable bridge reaching from the top of one rock to the other round rock which is now by itself about 300 yards out to sea from it.

This area is considered the most dangerous place to navigate in the whole world. For several hundred miles we are surrounded by islands, sandbanks and rocks, some above the surface and others below. We see some small ships fishing and some other small ships called "wreckers," that is, ships which know the seas and sail around continually, depending for their livelihood on the misfortune of other ships. Whenever ships have lost their way, these lead them back to the right way and save many lives. If this were all they do their work would be good, but they are accused of using false signals to mislead ships from their path in order to get thousands of dollars for guiding them back out of danger. Many ships must lose their way to support the numerous wreckers surrounding us now. But there is no need for their assistance, and I hope that such will continue to be the case.

At sunset the bottom of the sea was no further than twenty fathoms down. We navigated slowly and carefully through the night, and our leader brought us safely to see the light of Sunday

again. It was Easter Sunday, and although hardly anyone had many
new clothes to wear that day, we saw many new and wondrous
things around us. We saw a lighthouse on another island and several
Frenchmen who lived on the shore, having built their houses, or
rather their simple mud huts, along the shore. We sail now to the
south along side the Grand Bahama Bank.

There is a lovely wind from the southeast, and the ship is
traveling six miles per hour through the water. Also the water is running with us from three to four miles per hour. This southern current
is less than a mile wide from which the Gulf Stream to the north
runs totally contrary. Here the bottom of the sea is in green water
ranging from five to twenty fathoms, and the water is cold. A few
yards away to the south, however, the color of the water is black;
it is much warmer and runs directly opposite. We saw on the rocky
shores the remains of shipwrecks. Several wreckers sail along with
us. Everyone is contentedly observing the land. We are especially
delighted to leave it so quickly behind us and pull toward the end
of our voyage. The island of Cuba is to the south not far from us,
and the ridiculous and loathsome prophecy of *Seren Gomer** that
the Saints would be sold as slaves here is the subject of scorn
between almost every two people along the deck. That correspondent
has immortalized his foolishness with poor taste and has brought
Cuba more notoriety than anything else. This now serves to bring
to the recollection of the emigrants the lies and false accusations
which were said and published about them and their dear religion
by their fellow nation until it loosened their love, knot after knot,
even from the country of their birth. And instead of thinking of
turning back, it prompted them to turn their faces not toward the
east but into the sunset for freedom to worship God, and for those
rights of which they were deprived by "zealous Christians" of their
own country! Yes, the constant prayer of everyone throughout the
ship is "Blow, east wind, blow us fiercely to the western ocean."

Oh, it is beautiful to contemplate this scene! Hope is what fills
everyone's breast as the ship sails along, propelled by the lovely

---

*Is it erroneous if asserted that the Rev. H. W. Jones, publisher of the
Seren, is the above false prophet who was writing under the name of
"Anti-Humbug," in *Seren Gomer*, October, 1848?—J. D.

breeze. All on the seas give many thanks to their Savior. In Zion, however, is the lodestone from which they derive all their comfort. But we shall not continue to put forth our own thoughts, lest this letter be too long for the *Udgorn Seion*. I shall concentrate more on the account, and each one can think for himself. Perhaps that is what I should have done from the beginning.

I forgot to mention that we had a meeting of the Saints Thursday night last, as we did several times before, but this time was the first in which we put the gifts into practice. And great was the commotion this caused up and down the ship amongst the Babylonians! They clustered along with the officers of the ship at the entrance of our place and listened in amazement. We wondered greatly what had caused this; then we perceived that ''Achan'' was in our midst—that two or three of the Saints who had transgressed were there with them, translating for them and causing them to believe evil things about us, so that the officers of the ship and the captain also were more bitter toward us then than ever before, and I had a hard time calming him down. To our dismay their interference obliged us to cease practicing the gifts in the middle of the meeting, but not before we had received great comfort through them and learned some things about you, yourself, there in Wales, etc. We were informed that the party of those who failed in their designs on me as I was about to leave Wales is plotting revenge on my dear fellow officers who were left behind me; but they will not succeed. O Lord in Heaven, watch over them. Also, we learned that many of the Babylonians are praying for our failure and the Saints for our success.

Afternoon, wind fair. We had an excellent meeting of the Saints. We had retired to the back of the ship where neither the Babylonians nor the traitors in our midst could prevent us from enjoying the gifts of the Spirit, which gave us great comfort. Daniel Daniel and Benjamin Francis were ordained elders. Many counsels were given concerning health and clothing and the necessity for each one to care for the condition of his stomach. The latter counsel cause nearly everyone to come asking for medicine, inasmuch as the oil was depleted. This is necessary to forestall diarrhea. Let everyone take care in this matter.

[April] 9. Our God brought us safely through the dangers of this night also and smiled on us by continuing the wind in our favor. At 8:00 a steamboat came by us on its way from Havana to New York, and we also saw three British warships. Afternoon, we saw the borders of Florida, American continent. The land was low and sandy, a few trees here and there; and only judging from the smoke rising in columns to the clouds from one place and another, there are also some kind of inhabitants living here. We sailed along the coast until nightfall. We saw two lighthouses: one there and the other on a cluster of small, rocky islands which are named Fortugas [Tortugas]. After rounding these at the break of the next day we changed our course to the northwest; and here we left the Gulf Stream behind us with scarcely 500 miles to reach New Orleans. The "N.E. trade winds," which have carried us steadily and quickly for almost the last fortnight, are fair here still. More water was apportioned out for washing, as we have plenty on board to last for another month. And I cannot liken this bustling scene with the sisters all around the deck doing their washing any better than to the scenes I remember seeing by the hot waters of the iron furnaces in Merthyr on washday! The lowest deck was washed, and under the beds, with chloride of lime, in order to purify the air. Mrs. Williams is more ill. All are busy preparing their chests, etc., and to be ready to leave the ship before long. More food was offered from the "company store," but everyone had such an abundance that they did not come to get it. They said that all their sacks and vessels were full so that they had no room to hold any more. And many said that they had never before had such a variety or abundance of foods in their lives. And I maintain that anyone who is not happy with this food should be shut in the oven for a while, like the lap dog of the gentle lady.

Tuesday afternoon. Wind light, the sea calm and the weather uncomfortably warm. We saw some ships which appeared to be coming out of New Orleans. Mrs. Williams, of Ynysybont near Tregaron, is worsening fast, and signs are that she will not live long. She told her sons and me that she had little choice whether she died now or whether she would be granted to live longer. "My greatest desire," she said, "is to reach Zion; and I fear that my dying on the sea will discourage others in their old age from venturing across the ocean after me. I am content to die rather than be an obstacle to the cause of God; on the other hand," she said, "I wish to go to rest now in the bosom of Jesus, if that is pleasing in His sight." She said that the greatest honor she had ever received was to be able to become a member of the true church of the Son of God, that there was no fear in her breast concerning the other life and that her religion now proved its strength more than ever before. She was asked if she was sorry that she had left the Methodists, with whom she had been a respected member for 55 years. She replied that she preferred now more than the whole world to have been able to live to hear the preaching of the gospel by the Saints. And she solemnly counseled her sons to continue faithful until death so that they would obtain with her a better resurrection. She depended through her feebleness on the ordinances of the Church, and no complaint was heard from her lips. She continued lucid through the night, and at a quarter past four the next morning her spirit departed in peace, leaving a smile on her lips. She received every care, assistance and kindness from everyone, and especially from her faithful sons who revered her as they did their own souls. They did not weary in serving her almost day and night, comforting her and attending her. She had reached far more than 80 years of age.

Thursday, April 12. Every funeral preparation possible having been made, Sister Williams's funeral sermon was preached. Afterwards she was committed to her watery bed in the presence of hundreds of emigrants who looked simply and orderly on this sobering sight while a choir sang. And after that our oscillating dwelling made her way forward away from the mournful scene. Alone on the huge sea, she proceeded slowly with the black darkness as her garment of mourning. The sun also, despite its great strength and courage, was already trimmed in its cloudy cloak of mourning in the distant west when it perceived that one of the mothers of Israel had fallen on her way to Zion. All, all with a look of sadness. That night passed and only the shark, that cruel fish with its long, forked teeth, as if a faithful dog by the grave of its master, stayed as a marker of the resting place of the departed. Though she is among the fish in the severe ocean until the resurrection, peace be to her remains and praise to her name. The next morning at the break of dawn, welcome pleasant east wind. It zealously took pity on our condition and blew away the garment of mourning. Our sorrow was bestirred from her sullenness—like Phoenix from the ashes, her appearance was changed from head to foot. In short, like David of old after his son died, our ship in full sail, like a stallion to battle, hastened over the untamed waves. She strove to cheer up her mourners with the hope of seeing their port tomorrow. In spite of that, before morning came she had turned treacherously against us, and other winds blew us toward the eastern world. The sun by this time, despite its mourning and sympathy the night before, became a tormentor. From its hot cage it issued forth strong punishment with its scorching rays.

Friday. Several other ships were seen. Also seen was the greatest wonder which some had ever seen in their lives. In spite of seeing a burial yesterday in the somberest of scenes, today we saw a strange and majestic marriage between the "waters which are beneath the firmament and the waters above the firmament," intermingling through powerful and mighty *water spouts*. The elements in their boasting tried by resounding together to eliminate all else in our firmament and mix everything together in a water world. In this endeavor they roar frightfully; they stir an acre or more of the briny foam as if in a cauldron. In the depths of the cauldron the fish, in spite of themselves, are seen flying helterskelter from their element to the sky. In its self-activated womb the enormous and heedless vat gives birth to a powerful whirlwind which with the wall of its element blows its opponent like chaff across the surface of the waters. Despite their thickness the clouds part, and from the pieces is woven a long, thick, and spinning neck. Quickly downward the neck goes and the lowest part frolics to join with it! Now a union occurs. They combine—a beautiful marriage between the great salty liquid and its element above! Such an embrace is a surprise! Yes, mixing and kissing until all the sea perspires with the effort. Truly, this is the element which turned in marriage previously. Now, through sweetening that which was salty, the elements imitate the miracle of their Lawgiver! For a moment one thought that the water would prevail and swallow everything into its turmoil. But in time, just as when our earth was flooded, mercy from heaven smiles. A rainbow, the covenant-sign of Noah, was given, a phenomenon which revived the faith of the onlookers. Then God released wind "from His hand" to help the feeble whirlwind below. They join in a terrible attack and before them they sweep the wondrous water-spouts into fragments back to their places. And although they try time after time to lift their heads from their watery grave, they are unable to rise any higher than the top of their waves.

Not only the elements around us today are stirred up, but also the emotions of the sojourners. At the bidding of the prince of the air there are some which are boiling. Those in his treacherous army become tailors, and their work is to make a mask of the darkness to enshroud the heads of their magicians. 'Tis painful to say that they succeeded in so doing. Their caps fit so comfortably that I fear that they will be worn by some to their very destruction. The mighty king of Babylon has not only land armies, but I understand by now that also his navies wave their flags on all the seas. May his kingdom be shattered speedily. May his subjects on land and on sea turn traitor on him. Would that his majesty be swallowed by a whale on his way to the depths of the ocean with a lock on his mouth—with myself keeping the key!

Saturday, the 14th. Wind contrary. The land birds flying to the ship are tired, and the children catch them and tame them. We are diligently looking out for land.

Sunday, the 15th. Wind rather contrary and blowing hard. Many are half sick between homesickness and seasickness. It was passed in the council to excommunicate William, the son of B. Jones, Aberdar, and his wife. Others of the family are not much better. They cause much worry to the Saints through their false accusations to the captain, disgracing our dear religion, etc. There is every hope that Ebenr. Thomas will repent. Much trouble has resulted through too much association with the people of the ship back and forth. One of them, in spite of our best efforts, succeeded in bemusing and confusing the maid of one who had been so kind as to pay her cost from Babylon. I shall take more care next time that generous people will not be deceived by lasses who come to make love instead of to serve. Prayer meeting was held at 2:00 and at 6:00. The sea thrashed violently through the night.

Monday, the 16th. At 8:00 in the morning I went to the fore of the ship and saw a column of smoke in the distance rising to the air. We soon perceived that it was a steamboat from New Orleans coming to meet us; another steamboat from the other side came running toward us as fast as it could. And within two hours the two were by our sides. We gave a large rope to one of the two which pulled us to the mouth of the Mississippi by noon. Great was everyone's joy and gratitude for arriving here. We have 100 miles yet to the city. We arrived Tuesday, the 17th, all healthy. Soon we shall leave from here to go up the river to St. Louis.

Now hastily, I shall say farewell this time, since other matters are calling me. Dear Saints, be faithful to the heavenly calling which you have received and hasten to prepare to follow us. Listen to the voice of your presidents. That the Lord will bless you is the constant prayer and heartfelt wish of

Your brother in the gospel of Christ,
D. Jones.

Letter from Thomas Jeremy
to the Editor of *Udgorn Seion*
(TD8)

New Orleans, April 18, 1849.

Dear Brother Davis,

Be so kind as to give me the loan of your "Trumpet" to blow in for the first time from a distant country. What I especially wish to make known in it is the story of our voyage from Liverpool to here. Monday, the 26th of February, about two o'clock in the afternoon, we began our journey. And as we left from the Waterloo Dock, we sang "Farewell of the Saints." At that time there were in me some very strange feelings; yes, so strange that it is too difficult a task for me to describe them on paper and ink. I remember the cheerful faces of my faithful brethren—William Phillips of Merthyr, Abel Evans, Eleaser Edwards, John Davies, David my brother, and

Daniel Evans, Felinfach, Ystrad, Cardigan—who came from Wales to escort us as far as they could. Oh, how lovely was the association I had with some of these brethren on numerous occasions in Wales. Sometimes the day was too short for us to talk about the things pertaining to the kingdom of God, and we would frequently take the night as an extention to it. And sleep would stand in the distance from us while others would be abundantly comfortable in its grasp. At that time it came to my mind, "When will I see them again?" I imagined hearing something in answer that it would not be long before seeing them over in Zion. And at that I took courage.

As we were going out of the port I saw my dear brethren following after us along the bank of the river as far, I think, as they could. I imagine that I hear their voices carried along by the gentle breeze saying, "Oh, Father, watch over them," while we ourselves echoed back:

> God of Israel, keep them
>   In the midst of the host of enemies
>   Like the sons of thunder on the field,
>   Until they conquer the black enemy.

After we had gone out to the sea about 30 miles, the steamboats who had escorted us turned back, leaving us alone on the huge ocean. The wind was rather contrary to us the first day, but the weather was very lovely.

Tuesday we came in sight of Ireland. The land seemed barren and the mountains very high; nevertheless, dwellings could be seen very frequently at the foot of the mountains. The following Wednesday and Thursday most of us were in rather bad spirits because of seasickness, although some made it without one sick day. In these days our revered president, Capt. D. Jones, was very attentive to the sick. He showed his love for us greatly, walking back and forth along our large ship administering to the sick. He and Bro. Daniel Daniel from Brechfa, together with William Jenkins from Cardiff and a few other faithfuls, painstakingly made gruel for us. This was the most tasty food of any other during that time. It was better to stay in our stomachs than anything else. I did not request salt or butter in the soup then, nor was I able to eat bread with it. It was the same with my dear wife and the children. Mary, our youngest daughter, was not sick during the entire journey, although some had predicted before we left Wales that she would surely die on the sea, because she had not yet been weaned. But thanks be to God for keeping us all alive. We were sick but a few days, and I see now that the sickness was beneficial to us through cleansing our stomachs. I advise everyone who comes yet to Zion to bring oat flour and oat bread with them. They will find that this is the best food when they are sick. The best way for those who yet come after us to Zion to stay healthy is to try to stay often up on the deck. This will be advantageous counsel to them from our sad experience. Bro. Jones was very diligent to get some to the deck. Some tried to linger in their beds and tried to hide from him when he went past; I was not far from doing so myself. Jokingly, he at times would threaten to pull the pulley down from the deck and put a rope around us to pull us to the top even if we did not want to go. But everyone went to the deck on his own without Bro. Jones's having to carry out his threat.

Love for us is what compelled Bro. Jones to continually do everything in our behalf. I saw all his worth in our midst from the time we started our journey to this place. And there is no doubt in my mind also that Bro. Jones will do his best yet to do everything in our behalf until we reach the Valley of the Mountains. And I also believe that his chief effort there will be to make us happy and able to enjoy temporal and spiritual blessings.

Dear brother, you can publish in your melodious ''Trumpet'' that all are false prophets who prophesied from the press and the pulpits that Bro. Jones would sell us as slaves, take our money, etc. It is very obvious to me and all the Saints to perceive which spirit it is that leads them to imagine such things about him.

But to return to the acccount of our journey. Hardly anyone of us continued sick after the first few days. I do not intend to give the account of our journey day by day in this letter, as I had first thought, since Bro. Jones gave such a detailed account of our journey in his letter. Let it suffice for me to testify that he has given the account properly. I have a daybook in which I put down the most wondrous things we saw each day, together with what kind of weather we had. At times we saw rather large fish swarming to follow our ship and jumping up a little higher than the water; their length was between four and five feet and some larger. They are called sea-sows. Also we saw the dolphin which was lifted up on deck alive by one of the sailors. This is considered the most beautiful of all the fish in the sea and is about the size of the common salmon of the Teifi. We saw the flying fish, dozens of them. They were flying above the water from one place to another. On the 19th of March we saw a fish about twelve feet long which some called a shark and others a young whale.

We left many ships and islands behind and each day our vessel hastened toward the sunset. We had lovely weather and fair wind frequently each day. In fact, it was much more pleasant for us than I had thought it would be. The middle of March was like the middle of June. While in one part of the ship the musicians were playing, edifying books were being read somewhere else. Others were chatting about our dear compatriots, about the success of the gospel in their midst and about how many of their relatives had been obedient to the truth. My prayer for all my relatives and everyone thoughout Wales, especially those who heard my preaching in the counties of Carmarthen and Cardigan, is that they will grasp the true light. May the seed which I sowed grow luxuriantly. I do not doubt that it had good soil in different places and that it will give fruit. May my brethren who are still there care for the weak shoots so that nothing will destroy them, and may they sow all their seed in fertile soil so that it will give much fruit.

We held prayer meetings almost every night instead of family prayer. Our Father poured out His spirit greatly on us from the heavens. He answered our prayers and even caused the wind to obey our request. Every Sunday we held meetings of the Saints in remembrance of our blessed Lord. At times in these meetings we received knowledge through the Spirit about you there in Wales. Yes, great things were revealed to us. And, oh, how sweet was the teaching which Bro. Jones shared with us about the resurrection of the dead, that is, "How are the dead raised up and with what body do they come?" There is more mystery in this than many think.

I see that my letter is getting long. I must close despite how enjoyable it is for me to give the account of our lovely journey. But before closing I wish to inform my dear brothers and sisters who intend to follow us yet to Zion to take care to obey their leaders in every counsel which they receive from them from time to time. In this way they can have great joy in the Holy Spirit. On the other hand, if they forget this counsel and disregard the holy priesthood, it is better for such to stay behind until they come to have enough of the Spirit of God to be humble, meek, gentle, and tractable.

Dear brothers and sisters, hasten to come after us, remembering to keep the above counsel in your minds. And remember the saying of Jesus Christ that "blessed are the meek, for they shall inherit the earth."

Now dear Bro. Davis, having been so lengthy, I close by telling you that we have arrived here in health. My wife joins me in remembering you kindly, and wishing you every goodness.

Your dear brother in Christ,
Thomas Jeremy.

Letter from Capt. Jones to Pres. William Phillips
(TD9)

St. Louis, April 30, 1849.

My Dear Brother Phillips—

Following the detailed account of our sea voyage which I sent to Bro. J. Davis from New Orleans, I shall add hurriedly that we all arrived here Saturday, the 28th.

In New Orleans we caught up with the emigrants of the ship *Ashland*, which started from Liverpool with about 200 Saints several weeks before us. I hired a steamboat, and I took them and the Welsh Saints with me in it; the price for carrying us 1100 miles up the river is (for us) $2.25, or about 10 shillings! And in addition we can take 100 pounds of freight. The steamboat came alongside our ship to take our goods aboard, which spared much expense and loss. The cholera is very bad in New Orleans, and many are dying on the steamboats along the rivers, especially the immigrants. On one ship which went before us there were forty-two who died from cholera; on their other journey, nineteen, etc. But they were not Saints. Through being careful to observe the rules of cleanliness, to refrain from drinking the water of the river without letting it settle, putting alum or oat flour in it—through being faithful and godly—through refraining from eating fruits, meats, etc., in short, through striving as if for life in every sense, and through the blessing of God on His ordinances, thanks be to Him, the Welsh Saints have come alive and been healthy up to this point, except one dear brother by the name of Jenkin Williams from Aberdare, who was a good and faithful lad the whole voyage, except that he went contrary to the counsels which were given, and he hid the cholera as long as he could by taking his own way to treat it through brandy; and the sad result was that he died here within a few hours after arriving, and he was buried with due respect. A few minutes before he died he left a remarkably good testimony after him and said that he was completely happy as he faced death.

Also a young child of R. Price of Dowlais died of consumption. These are all the Welshmen who have died until now. But of the English Saints two women and one child died of the deadly cholera. The officers of the boat were surprised how few deaths there were in our midst, and they asked in surprise each morning, ''Are there none of you dead yet?'' A baby was born to the wife of Samuel Lee, Llanelli, and also to the wife of John Rees of Cardiff, a stillborn. The mothers are improving greatly.

Yesterday I hired a steamboat here to carry us to Council Bluffs for 16 shillings per person, with 100 pounds free and 2 shillings for each additional 100 pounds of freight. From among the Saints who are here we completely filled the cabins and everywhere else. The other boat will come alongside us to take us and our goods in; thus, from Liverpool to Council Bluffs it did not cost any of the Welsh a penny for moving their goods!

Everyone is healthy today and heartened and rejoicing in their privilege and desirous to move forward. Better news from the West still. There are here between 3,000 and 4,000 Saints. Mormonism is winning in popularity now so fast that the treacherous tricks of its malicious false accusers are being revealed. ''The fact is too obvious to be concealed any longer, that they are a powerful, intelligent, diligent and courteous people and good citizens," say the publications now about the Saints and everyone courts their favor. This is good; they have been disregarded long enough. Here we purchased iron to make wagons in Council Bluffs, and flour and meat, groceries and everything necessary for the journey to California and to settle there. We have every opportunity to hold public meetings every day and every night, in every boat; when I was here before, it was worth the life of a man to say that he was a Mormon.

May the 1st—We hired a steamboat and moved to it yesterday to carry us to Council Bluffs, 900 miles up the River Missouri, for 16s 8c each, half price for children between four and fourteen; and younger than that no charge; we can have 100 pounds of luggage without paying, and we pay 2 shillings per hundred for the rest. We shall start from here tomorrow. We purchased our food here to get us to the Valley. Also our stoves, iron to make wagons, clothes, arms, goods, etc., etc. To this point, our journey has not been as expensive as I noted in the *Prophwyd*. And as far as I can tell, the costs will be hardly any different from what I noted there. The deadly cholera is killing hosts here now. One dear and faithful elder died this morning, namely Benjamin Francis, leaving great sorrow behind him. It would be difficult to find any more faithful than he in his life, and he died happy. His wife and children will come along with us.

Benj. Jones and his whole family except his wife became blemished from unfaithfulness. They went away along the road to destruction at a gallop today. David Giles and David Jones and his wife went with them, completely unknown to me. I shall take greater care next time to refrain from bringing any but the faithful Saints with me.

I heard that my dear wife is on the sea following after me; if so, may the gracious Lord keep her is my constant prayer.

Dear brother, be faithful and fearless through all persecution to lead properly the dear flock which I left under your care. You officers, remember my counsels to you, nurture the Spirit of light, love the Saints, and feed them with truth; and may the God of Israel bless you abundantly. Amen. Remember me to everyone at once, to my brother and his family, and your own family, etc.

Your brother in the gospel,

D. Jones.

Letter from Capt. Jones to President William Phillips
(TD10)

Country of Indians, Omaha, July 13, 1849.

Dear Brother Phillips—

Hastily, and almost before a dog opens his mouth in the camp, I take this early morning opportunity to send you a few lines. There is not time to portray the sight around me nor to preamble, for the mosquitoes are biting, the sun is almost up, and I am awaiting the call to get under way with fifty wagons to the Far West, beyond the furthest borders of every civilized country to the midst of the red-skinned people of the forest.

Wm. Morgans and William Davies from Rhymni have followed us this far at my request, so they can tell you our course in more detail, which time and my duties do not permit me to do now. And at this time I say to you only, do as they direct you by letter; for I had the opportunity to speak with them much that I cannot write about now. In Council Bluffs I established a part of the Welsh company which came here, and a Welsh branch of the Church, with Wm. Morgans as president. The prime objective of this is so they will be ready in this center point to receive, welcome, and direct such of our dear nation as may come after us. For they can give details of the advantages of the country, and of the Welsh who have stayed in that part of it. I shall only say, allow those of the Saints who wish and who you think best qualified to come here as soon as they can; and those who cannot go as far as the Valley of the Mountains can come to this beautiful country and earn enough soon to help them the rest of the journey.

There are of us Welsh twenty-four covered wagons loaded going forward now, and we have come about eighteen miles on our journey successfully. You shall receive the names from Wm. Morgans.

All news from Zion is good. You shall receive the newspaper which is also published here from William Morgans.

To the dear Saints in Wales I say, "Be faithful in the calling to which you have been called from darkness to the light of the

Jubilee; hurry after us to build Zion; come one, come all, according to the directions of your presidents, out of Babylon, from the midst of pestilence and disease, wars and battles of a transitory world to the freedom of the children of Zion—to the safe place of the redeemed." It is possible to come here for the cost which I noted in the *Prophwyd*, that is between 6 and 7 pounds apiece for those fourteen and older; and it is possible to soon earn assistance to proceed, which cannot be earned in Wales in a long time.

Everyone from this company here is very content, and very eager to see their relatives, etc., following them soon. My dear wife and baby arrived here safely a few days ago and in time to go along with us. The cholera imposed heavy losses on our small army along the rivers, especially on the accursed waters of the Missouri; yet, the effect was small in comparison to that on other people throughout the neighboring boats and towns. Wm. Morgans will go into detail as to who was prey to it; I hope that a greater proportion of the Saints there are not in its clutches. You shall have great comfort in reading the interesting letter which I received lately from Parley P. Pratt from the Valley, which I shall send to Bro. Davis to publish.

Those who wish to write to their friends who are going to California should address the letter like this: "_____ _____, care of Capt. Jones, Great Salt Lake City." Put the letter in an envelope and address it to "Mr. Orson Pratt, 15, Wilton Street, Liverpool," and he will forward it at no cost except for the postage.

Give my warm regards to Bro. John Davis and Abel Evans. Be one; put your shoulders unitedly under the ark—to all the conference presidents and all the officers; dear brethren, feelings of nostalgia are beating in my breast for your company, for your voices in the council and the congregations, and my hope is to behold your happy faces before long, and your hosts with you in worthy Zion. May God, our Father, hasten that blessed day is my sincere prayer continually.

Give my warm regards to all the dear Saints. Your benefit, your success, and your temporal and eternal joy are the heartfelt wish of
Your humble servant in the gospel of Christ,
D. Jones.

NB. I was hoping greatly to hear whether my dear brother Wm. Howells had ventured forth on his mission again. May the God of Israel bless him with success. My health is improving gradually, although my voice still continues hoarse; so hard to be still with so much to say.   D.J.

A Letter of Capt. D. Jones to J. Davis.

The following is an excerpt from a private letter which Capt. Jones sent to us:

"Do your best to sell my books which I left and send the rest of the money with some faithful brother who will lead the next company to come here. Doubtless, they will be very useful by then to support my family, so that I can devote my time to serve the Saints, and perhaps to look for the Welsh Indians. I desire an interest in the prayers of all the dear Saints for success in this, and so that I will be able to be of more and more benefit to my nation, regardless of which country I am in.

"Farewell now, dear brother; may the Lord God of Israel bless you and clothe you with the spirit of your calling, so that you can enlighten your compatriots and sound your "Trumpet" so that the huge rocks of Wales will echo the calling to her inhabitants to hasten to Zion.

Your brother, etc.
D. Jones."

A Letter from [William Morgan at] Council Bluffs to President W. Phillips
(TD11)

Pottowatamie County, Iowa, 2 Sept. 1849.

Dear Brother Phillips—

It has been a good five months since I saw you in Liverpool, and I think that neither you nor I will ever forget the day we took the last look at each other for a time. There are close to 8,000 miles between me and the country of my birth at the present time; but in spite of that, my mind can fly across the great deep like lightning, frequently to gaze on the faces of my dear brothers and sisters who stayed back there; but I am confident that before long I shall see many of them following to this desirable country, so that I may speak to them face to face and rejoice together in the Lord, in the same country, and under the same roof, as in earlier days. But I dare not, at present, give vent to my feelings. I must be about the work which links all the dear Saints in general. We, the Welsh, here have divided into two groups; one group has gone ahead toward the plains of the Salt Lake, that is twenty-two wagons, under the presidency of Bro. Jones; the other group is staying here for the purpose of putting a Welsh settlement in the place. This will be to the advantage of the monoglot Welsh who follow; for there will be people of the same language and from the same country, and most likely many who will know them and have been associated with each other many times, to welcome them to this new country; for there are only English here for several hundreds of miles— and we, a small handful of Welsh in their midst, brothers and sisters, enjoying our freedom like the birds, with no one to say a word against us, but all of them very friendly. I live in the house where Apostle George A. Smith lived, and William Rowland, of Hirwaun, in the house of Apostle Ezra T. Benson. Counting adults and children we number 113 in all—there are more Welsh in this branch than there were in the Merthyr branch when I was baptized; and I hope that it will stay at 113 until more come from Wales, for I have no more room to accommodate any more, for the Saints are covering the land; yet perhaps some will come from the worlds above. The Welsh Saints here love each other, and some have married also. I shall not name them now; you will yet hear. We, the Welsh, have almost all our land adjoining; and Brother Jones has purchased a land claim which is 150 or more acres, near our lands, and has entrusted it to my care for a gift to the Welsh. We intend to build a meetinghouse on it, as soon as we can; and I think that will not be long, for the hard part of our work is over; our wheat harvest is past, all of it under cover. I wish for you to remember me to the Saints in general. All the Welsh Saints here greet you, and they would be delighted to see a shipload coming across next spring. If they can get as much as £7 each, they can come over here; and if they cannot go further, they will have in three years, or two perhaps, enough oxen and cattle to go ahead. I am sure of this, for some in this company who had not a penny when they landed here have cattle and sheep now; in fact, I know of no family in this country who has not a cow or two. I am in a hurry, and I end by wishing for the gracious Lord to bless you and your family, and all the Saints who are under your care.

Yours,
William Morgan.

P.S. Bro. Jones wishes for you to send Abel Evans with the next company, if you can spare him. You shall hear from me again soon. I would be glad to receive an answer to this letter and some information about my sister Anne. Bro. Jones is improving in his health, and Sister Jones and the child are quite well. Seven pounds I said would be enough for one to come over; think of those who can spend £14, yes, £28 if they choose, with taking many steps on the streets of Liverpool. And if one or more will overspend their money, I hope that no one will blame me for saying that £7 is enough. You shall yet hear in greater detail concerning the prices of things on the journey and the prices of the provisions which will be necessary. You can expect that within a month, or earlier perhaps.

[From George A. Smith, Ezra T. Benson, and Dan Jones]

(TD12)

Camp of Israel,
on the hills of the Sweet Valleys,
near to the Independence Rock,
649 Miles from Winter Quarters,
September 21, 1849.

Brothers W. Morgan and W. Davies, Presidents
of the Welsh Saints in Pottowatamie, Iowa, G.A.

Dear Brethren—

Our most sincere wish always is to give counsel, assistance, or suggestions which may be of benefit and ease to our brethren. Although we are so distant from you, we consider it a suitable thing to offer for your observation some things which we have learned through experience, which will benefit you if you adopt them, and not only you, but everyone else who may immigrate across the deserted and interminable plains to the Great Salt Lake Valley. We wish for you to understand that we are not taking upon ourselves any leadership or taking upon us your presidency, for that belongs to others. But we think after we have reached the end of our journey, it will be too late in the winter for the presidency in the Valley to give information to you this winter, and Bro. Hyde will ask us to put this to the attention of those who are under his direct presidency. In the first place, we wish to impress on your minds the great importance of your situation with respect to the offices which you hold; you can set a good example for the Saints, that is, give unity, pious secrecy in all your counsels and in your daily transactions; be patient, long-suffering, meek, temperate, virtuous, just, loving and in every thing worthy of emulation. In the choice of your animals for the immigration, we would counsel you to insist on those which are used to the yoke and easy to handle, not older than ten or younger than five years old. Be sure that your wagons are built from good materials, strong and light, and the wheels six inches higher than they usually are. They are good for crossing rivers by keeping the water from your supplies. The wheels should be 1¾ inches in width, with 2,000 lbs. on one wagon, and three yoke of good oxen to pull it; but the most convenient load is 410 lbs. on a light and strong wagon with two yoke of good oxen; such loads will go across damp places without sinking and getting stuck on the spot as some of the heavier ones usually do. Never should you put over 2,000 lbs. on one strong wagon with three yoke of good animals; and be sure to have other animals besides those in the yoke, so that you will have ready assistance if one of those in the yoke happens to be injured or die. Take care lest your animals get whipped to excess or any other mistreatment. We believe that the gold seekers have lost more of their animals because of the whip and other mistreatments than because of their load, their journey, or alkali poisoning. The bones of their animals are scattered along the way of the trail, and it is astonishing to think of the loss as one looks at them. Let that be the freedom of those who are fond of flogging dumb creatures. When the hoops of the wheels come loose because of dryness or something else, instead of breaking the wheel as usual and then joining it as a shorter one, make a wooden hoop corresponding to the length and width; set it tightly between the hoop and the wheel and nail it so that it is secure; it serves the same purpose and does not require a lot of time to make.

About the manner of your journey, we would counsel the one adopted by Pres. Young; no fewer than fifty wagons in each band; no fewer than twelve good horses for the purpose of rounding up the animals and of looking for a place to camp, and they will be useful when the animals get out of control and run, goring each other; in short, without the horses you cannot follow the animals, overtake them and bring them back, etc. To keep the animals in order, we would advise you to tie them up each night until the grazing gets scarce, when each will prefer to look for his morsel or to rest than to threaten with his horn and shift himself. Be careful and watchful in all things; put from eight to ten faithful watchmen around your camp and your animals every night. Do not permit anyone's fine tale about your safety, such as ''There is no need to guard them—you are safe here—no harm will come to you, etc.,'' keep you from organizing faithful watchmen as we have mentioned.

Let each group have iron bolts, that is the biggest ones, together with the next size to them, pertaining to wagons, in case some break when the blacksmith's shop is far away, also linchpins, etc. Take care in the choice of men as officials for the immigrations that they be meek, patient, long-suffering and slow to be excited to bad tempers, slow, determined and understanding. Do not be in a hurry to travel; if you go forward sixty miles each week, be content; driving animals hard in hot weather causes the black disease to spread and causes them to die soon. Allow your animals to go slowly when the grazing is good, so that they will be in good condition and strong when you go to a more sparse place. Through that plan, they will be enabled to go across the deserted and fruitless plains when necessary to travel several days through the day without food or water. Be careful that your animals do not drink the waters of the poisoned alkali, which this part of the earth is full of from the highest crossing of the Platte to Independence Rock. In short, be sensible and cautious in all things, especially with respect to your animals in the crossing, for it is on them to a large extent that your temporal salvation depends. Another thing we consider of great importance and which we would desire to impress on your mind, is the use that is made of strong liquor. Our brothers come from a distant country where liquor is scarce and hard for anyone to get except for the wealthy, and so liquor is seldom used by the poor. But when they come to America where liquor is so cheap, and they not being accustomed to the drunkening effect, they are very likely to make too much use of it, to their own harm and great loss. For that reason, we counsel everyone under your care to abstain completely, and refrain from making use of it, only except when necessary in the case of illness. If you cannot get wagons as we have suggested, insist on some as similar to them as you can. Tell the Welsh to buy good "Russian duck" in Liverpool to cover their wagons. That is the only material which will keep the rain from getting your beds and your supplies wet on your journey. Insist that your wagons be made like boxes on the sides and the bottom, so that no water can get through the sides or the bottom. Purchase those things which will be necessary in New Orleans or St. Louis, such as stoves, crocks, irons, tea kettles, etc., and which will be needed on your journey. Last spring we gave an order to the merchants of Kanesville to buy those things which we needed for the immigration; they promised to do it, but they failed to fulfill their promise. That is why we urge you to buy in other places, as you are able, those things you will need, lest others are disappointed as were we. Insist on a few good Americans who know how to drive and who are gentle with animals to be drivers in every group, and an expert guide to lead every group of immigrants. Do not depend on cows to be of any use in the yoke for the purpose of helping the oxen, but take along as many as you can, for they will be very useful in the Valley. Every group should have axletrees of hickory wood, lest some of them break, and some oak wood for spokes. Let everyone weigh his load, and refrain from taking anything he can do without. Buy some good grass ropes to tie up your animals; and have ten feet of rope for each ox. A herd of animals has stampeded before, and it is frightening and dreadful to behold them. Terror, running, the earth trembling, chains rattling, yokes snapping, wagons falling apart, watchmen trampled, some perhaps killed, others wounded, are the effects which go along with a herd of animals in a stampede. Tell our friends in Wales to come to the plains of the Great Salt Lake as soon as they can; and those who cannot prepare to come to the plains, let them stay in Pottowatamie County, Iowa, where they will meet with friends and many of their brethren. The Welsh company is with us; they are going forward well with Capt. Dan Jones in their midst; they are happy and content and make the camp resound with their evening song. They are enjoying health and a good spirit, and undeniably have been blessed; and we say, "May the Lord continue to bless them." We offer the foregoing suggestions for your benefit and for that of everyone else who immigrates to Great Salt Lake City. May the Lord bless you, and give you wisdom to be prudent and faithful stewards and shepherds over the inheritance of God which you have been placed to preside over, is our prayer.

A Letter from Capt. D. Jones to President W. Phillips

(TD13)

Bank of the Green River, October 12, 1849.

Dear Brother Phillips—

From between what seems like showers, with the frequency and importance of tasks, I snatch the opportunity at midnight to greet you, yes, from the extremes of this distant wilderness. And even though our local distance increases continually, yet that, nor anything else which befalls me on this lengthy and strange journey, will alienate my thoughts, my feelings of love or my prayers from you, from my other dear brothers in the priesthood—the kind Saints—children of my begetting in Jesus Christ, nor cause me to forget the vineyard of my Lord, the garden of my planting and my flock in Wales.

My conscience is peaceful ever since I left you with respect to every teaching which I preached, every discipline which I ordained, and every organization which I established before leaving you, and daily I pray the God who owns the vineyard to watch over it in all things. I entrusted the Saints seriously to the care of their various presidents, and I taught and proclaimed their duties to them, so they did not have to be ignorantly led about in error; and great the privilege, awesome the responsibility, grave the consideration— you and your counselors were selected as watchmen over everyone there. O, remember my counsels, follow my example as I followed the sound doctrine of our Lord Jesus Christ. Be an example to the Saints in humility, tenderness, patience, love and all the fruits of godliness; so that when you are as close to the chief earthly fold as I am, you will enjoy looking back on your work, and joyfully think about giving an accounting. O, how lovely it is for me now to think of my efforts day and night while there, even though in my body every day I felt torture and pain which they caused me.

I do not feel so fearful about the cause there after leaving you as at first I thought I would feel; the reason for that is that I know that God is with you still, and His Spirit is guiding you according to your request from Him; and frequently we receive here a short and exceedingly sweet message with the speed of the mind, by means of a mail coach of which the world knows nothing; for our Father, at our petition, tells us about you!

Perhaps you are thinking that we are at the end of our journey by now; but the main causes which have kept us longer than some who went before us are that there were so many rainstorms on the first 300 miles of our journey that it was difficult to travel because the wheels of the covered wagons would often sink very deep in the mire, and also that after we came to the highland, the grazing was and still is very scarce for the animals. And this is not strange when you consider that from 6,000 to 7,000 covered wagons, each pulled by three to six yoke of oxen, besides several thousand cattle, sheep, mules, and horses have passed along this road during this summer toward the paradise of the Saints and the country of gold; these consume much of the grass, but if you add to these all the thousands of buffaloes, antelope, elk, etc., who own, by poor grazing, this wilderness and desolate, parched land—this together with other considerations caused us to slow down and be content if we could travel but ten to twelve miles each day, and it was proved to our satisfaction before that this is the only way we can complete our journey. There is hardly a day that we do not come across skeletons of the oxen of those who went before us on the roadside, a monument to their foolishness in traveling too fast at the beginning of a journey as long as this one.

Not so with us or the other Saints, thanks to the God who preserved us. Whereas others leave their animals, their covered wagons, and thousands of dollars' worth of their provisions along the road, we are enabled, through the blessing of God, to wend our way steadily and comfortably along, although slowly; and while we find the graves of others often alongside the road, we rejoice and give thanks, as will you, that no one has died in our camp since we left Council Bluffs, nor has there been hardly any sickness. We have been on this journey now for over three months and have traveled 863½ miles, have ascended to the height of over 7,000 feet above sea level; and almost unawares we have been surrounded on nearly every side by snowy tops of the Rocky Mountains, which perpetually dwell in the white clouds. O, majestic sights!! They are beyond description.

There are between us and the Salt Lake Valley still 164 miles; yet I am confident that this journey will be finished within fifteen days, with the blessing of our God. O, hail, blessed day! All the Welsh who are here with me are living as befits the Saints, acknowledging God in all their ways and praising Him morning and night for keeping them until now from the captivity of persecuting Babylon, until their sweet voices resound in unison in the massive rocks around us, and we almost believe that they with their melodious voices charm the wolves who play outside our camp at dusk and so far have rendered them as harmless to us as our flock of sheep.

Since about a week ago nature has put on her white wedding gown as if to receive some new inhabitants in the fissures of these everlasting mountains; it spread a white carpet before the door of everyone one night, and spread a snowy white blanket lightly on some who had not taken care to close the cover of their wagon before night! The snow piled up between the wagons so that we did not see some of our neighbors until the evening; but we did not die in the snow this time according to the prophecies of our enemies. The sun shone pleasantly the second morning! The earth soon changed her garment, and soon between 200 and 300 wagons could be seen in a majestic row climbing the steep slopes while all were singing the songs of Zion; and we made camp in the evening under the crimson smile of the sun of the Western world. The Saints from the Valley sent more than eighty yoke of oxen over 300 miles to meet us, and great is the help they are to us. This is brotherly love worthy of emulating, and we anticipate more each day. All the news we have from the Valley brings joy to our hearts. May thousands of the race of Gomer soon come after us to the freedom of this country.

The Saints have formed a state in California by the name of the state of "Deseret" (search the Book of Mormon for the meaning of the word!) and have sent a petition to the American government for a dispensation to that effect, which, if granted now, will fulfill many a prophecy, such as "Your officials will be from yourselves," etc., "I shall restore your judges as before, and your councils as in the beginning." At this time the state officials will be inspired, and without this arrangement it is impossible for the "kingdom of God" to be fully established and for its laws to be administered on earth. Everything works to the good of the Saints in the end, and the whole earth will know that before much longer.

The Welsh are holding up under the difficulties of this journey, and are learning to drive oxen better than my expectations, and are winning praise from all the other camps of the Saints for their organization, their virtue and their skill, and especially for their singing.

I need not enlarge further here on advice concerning things and preparations for the journey to those who shall come after us, because Apostles G. A. Smith and E. T. Benson and myself have written all those things in great detail to Bro. William Morgans, who is the president of the Welsh settlement in Council Bluffs, and have asked him to send it to be published in the *Udgorn Seion*. How far will Brother Davis sound his "Trumpet" now? My heart longs to hear its voice; I haven't seen one since I saw you. Send me at least fifty of every number, as you are able, through the hand of Bro. Pratt. I hope that Bro. Davis is receiving regularly the newspaper which O. Hyde publishes in Council Bluffs, according to the agreement which I made there. If the above-mentioned directions reach you, publish them in the *Udgorn* so that the other Saints who follow us can have, for free, the information which we had to purchase. May they study them carefully for their benefit.

I know not when I shall get to see you and the dear Saints there; but I know this, that it is the true wish of my heart to see all of you here with me in Zion. I long more and more continually for your friendship, your church meetings and the marvelous conferences which we had.

Some of the Saints are worried because the Cholera Morbus snatched away so many of our dear brothers and sisters on our journey from St. Louis to Council Bluffs, lest that counteract the cause of God in Wales and keep their dear relatives and friends from following them; but I say, as Job of old with an easy conscience, "The Lord giveth and the Lord taketh away; blessed be the name of the Lord"—in spite of how painful it was to my feelings under the circumstances for death to cruelly tear my dear ones from my bosom. And I fear that the persecutors of the Saints in Wales have a more necessary task nearer to home than to set anything foolish against the religion of Christ because of the death of His Saints.

With respect to the emigration from Wales here, I will say again as I wrote before, Come one—Oh, that all could come rapidly. Open the gates, proclaim all the bondsmen of Babylon free to come to Zion, yet in an orderly way; not through flight for a while yet. In spite of that, everyone who can get hold of 7 to 8 pounds in his pocket to get underway, counsel him to come to Council Bluffs, where he can meet with loving Welsh brothers and sisters with their arms wide open to receive him, and direct him if he cannot come along the way without stopping. By saying this I do not intend for you to harm the vineyard of God by driving away too many of the workers at once, but do this also in an organized way. May a shipful come at once, and select seven brave and faithful elders to be in council in their midst, which will be of one heart and one mind, to keep them all out of the clutches of the devil, for they will be without doubt tried worse and a thousand times more than in Wales. There is but the Day of Judgment which will prove the work, the worry, and the fatigue which I went through to keep them all from the wolves until now.

With respect to the wealthy who pay the cost of the poor to come over, let them prepare their hearts to forgive them everything if, in spite of everything, they repay them with unkindness; yet, let them not weary in well doing, for their reward will be greater from God. The elders will have their arms full to guide all of them here who profess every faithfulness before beginning, yet they strive more and more. O, how valuable is the Spirit of God on this journey for nuturing unity and love and warding off conflict; without this, not even an angel could lead a company across, I suppose. Pray daily for more of it.

My health is not yet as good as I would wish by far, nor as good in the last weeks as it was; and if it be possible under the weight of this heavy burden for any man to get better, I request an interest in the prayers of my kind brothers and the dear Saints, for strength each day to serve them continually.

Remember me and my wife and all the Saints here to your dear wife and your family and your counselors. Be one in heart.

Remember me lovingly to the council and Saints of Merthyr, Dowlais, Aberdar, Hirwaun, Monmouthshire, etc. But what am I doing by starting to name names; like children of my bowels I love all without exception. May the gracious God bless them and keep them to eternal life.

Remember me to the faithful presidents of the conferences, and the branches. Let them remember my counsels to them in the last conference and always, and that which I proclaimed.

Remember me lovingly to all the Saints, which is all I can say to them now so far from them, by earnestly pleading with them, as God would plead with them through me for them, for the sake of their own souls, to behave according to godliness in all things, so that the very glorious name which they took on themselves will not be scorned; bid them to listen to the advice of the priesthood, to pray to God, and live lovingly, honestly, chastely and righteously; for thus they shall have an abundant entrance into the eternal resting place of their God.

Now, dear Saints, farewell to you all for a while, although I have more things to declare than I am able now from here. May the gracious Lord bless you all with His spirit abundantly, and keep you in the midst of persecution and strengthen you in trials and save you all in His kingdom is the sincere prayer of

Your brother, etc.

D. Jones.

A Letter of Capt. Jones to W. Phillips
(TD14)

Salt Lake City, November 20, 1849.

Dear Brother Phillips—

By chance I had the opportunity of sending this letter from these remote parts in this season of cold across the Rocky Mountains. Some of the American soldiers, I heard now, are going to the States and will be ready to start before I finish this letter. We arrived here healthy and happy on the 26th of last month, and we were very pleased about everything here on the whole, temporally and spiritually, so much better than we were told, as was the wisdom of Solomon beyond the comprehension of the Queen of Sheba. This is nearly all I have time to say about the place; you shall have a more complete account next spring. All the Welsh are content and are joining together to enclose about 600 or 700 acres of land on the banks of the West Jordan River about four miles from the city, which country is called New Wales, as fruitful and beautiful a land as any under the sun in the Western world. It does not cost anything, but is cheap to everyone, and as much as everyone can cultivate.

It is surprising what great work has been done in a year in this splendid valley! Yesterday I had the pleasure of baptizing close to forty of the Welsh here in order for them to renew their covenants and seal their faithfulness to the Lord God of Israel; and great was the joy and the rejoicing in their midst through the day! Our only worry was that there were not thousands more of our dear fellow nation here; yes, all the honest in heart with us. We established a Welsh branch of the Church to God to hold their worship meetings in the language into which they were born, with Thomas Jeremy as president and Daniel Daniels and Rice Williams as counselors.

I have put all the Welsh into comfortable situations to get plenty of work of gold, money or supplies, etc. The wages of the workers are 6s 6c per day, the craftsmen from 10s to 12s per day, and if all the Welsh craftsmen were here, there would be people running after them with gold in their hands to pay them. This Valley is so healthful that I haven't heard of old age or sickness or disease since I have been here. I heard our dear President Brigham Young say publicly that he could not remember when anyone was buried here, and I haven't heard any mention of such a thing since I have been here.

I am building a house in the city, on the inheritance which was prepared for me before I arrived; I received a lot, or an acre and one quarter, for each of the Welsh in the city who chose to build on it also. Mrs. Lewis got a paradise-like lot near the temple and she has a house on it almost finished already in addition to a farm in the place which I mentioned; and she, together with all of the company, are rejoicing greatly that they have come to this place. Others are building houses in the city, that is, of the Welsh, and all are happy in their countenances. In short and in great haste, understand me when I say that all is well with everyone here, and an abundance of food and as good shops as are seen in Wales.

As for me, although the world says that I am getting all this ease at the expense of the Saints, I shall say that all the Welsh except myself are getting to rest here in ease to serve themselves and to make themselves happy; whereas, I had not been here a week before I was counseled to prepare to go from 800 to 1,000 miles further to the southwest on a mission for God, and that at my own expense, across the tops of the snowy mountains through tribes of savage Indians along a road on which white man has never before set foot. Tomorrow morning is the hour to get underway; I know not when I shall return. My mission is to search out that branch of the race of Gomer which are called the Madocians; their story is well known, and I go with the intent of bringing them into the fold of the Good Shepherd. Oh, Saints, pray for my success and that my life will be protected among bloodthirsty savages. You shall hear more when I return.

I and all the Welsh received a hearty welcome to the Valley; the presidents came miles to meet us and to welcome us, and great was the joy. Everything is well.

My fatigue is vexing my health still so that I am hardly better than when I started from Wales; yet, God will strengthen me miraculously day by day. Oh, dear Saints, pray for me now; for my work is still increasing. Oh, that I had the opportunity to tell you of the hopes which are shortly before us to be fulfilled for you, but I cannot. Be patient a while yet. My wife and family are well and, together with all the Saints, send their regards to you and the dear Saints there. Farewell now, dear brother and all, in great haste.

Your brother,
D. Jones.

A Letter from Council Bluffs to Pres. W. Phillips
(TD15)

Council Bluffs, December 25, 1849.

Dear Brother Phillips,

I think it would be beneficial to give a few of my thoughts with respect to the necessary things for the distant journey which many of my brothers and sisters will be facing before long. The first thing to have is a good supply of patience; for grumbling does no one any good; and if they are to have a trouble-free and successful journey, let everyone resolve to keep the counsels of the president. If they do not do that, they are likely to lose the Spirit of God from their midst; the evil one will enter, and then it is not easy to get him out. Even though many of our company fell victim to the cholera, I know of but one or two of them who did not find fault with the president's way of doing things; thus, the voluntary obedience was not from the heart—some were not content with those whom Bro. Jones selected to oversee some matters because so and so was older in the Church, etc. I repeat, take care and beware of that spirit; remember the counsel of the Lord Jesus Christ—i.e., listen to the voice of your shepherd. If so done, the journey will be a successful one.

Now I shall mention some other things. All kinds of garden seed would be good to bring over. We counsel the craftsmen to bring their tools with them. Writing paper would be of great service, such as a quire or two. Those who can, bring tin dishes for treating milk, also crockery, glasses, iron and steel. The spades for coal and ore mining here are not worth much, but shovels are expensive, i.e., from 4 shillings to 5 shillings each. You can get shovels in Liverpool for about 10 shillings for half a dozen. I would be grateful if some of the brethren could bring half a dozen shovels from Liverpool for me; it will not be much trouble for them to do so. Also half a dozen pitchforks. I would be glad to get them; a shilling each is their price here. It is worth bringing all sorts of iron-ware here except axes; those are better here than in Britain. The price of common iron here is twopence and a halfpenny per pound;

small iron is threepence and higher. Calico is twice the price; earthenware vessels the same; glasses also are expensive here.

We advise everyone who will be emigrating to take care that their boxes are strong, made of dry wood; some have suffered losses because their boxes were not dry, and so their clothes become mouldy. Potatoes on the ocean would be very desirable, and herrings, oat flour, bacon, dried beef, pepper, mustard, salt, pickles, onions and oranges. The oranges, in my opinion, are not of much use; apples are better, the ones which can be baked or put in cakes. Brandy is beneficial to warm the stomach when it is cold and the sea is rough. For seasickness, it would be good to take some things about a fortnight before starting in order to cleanse the stomach so that it will be as free from bile as possible. Small children are better sailors than adults; they stand on their feet while their parents have one leg too short or the other too long to walk without difficulty. I have written to you before; I hope that you have received my letter and that there will be an answer before this one reaches the end of its journey. I sent two copies of the *Frontier Guardian* to John Davis. I would be glad to get a copy of *Udgorn Seion*. Is it possible for the ''Trumpet'' to sound across the sea? Many Welsh Saints would be glad to hear it if its voice can reach America. I would like to know the terms; perhaps we could put together a plan so that there could be communication every month or more frequently. I shall be grateful to Bro. Davis for his opinion on the matter. I should like to have a letter telling when the Welsh intend to set sail, who will be the president, etc., so that I can write a letter to St. Louis or New Orleans to meet them. No doubt that between now and the time they set out I can give direction as to some things they can buy there and sell here for a rather good price. It is expected that the gold diggers will come here in the spring in hoards. If they come, there will be a chance to make some money quite easily; some make about $400 each in a few months by buying things for the gold miners. The Welsh can do the same thing easily with no obstacles on their journey. I had a chance myself the first day I set foot on land in the Bluffs to earn $49 by selling to them. By now you see the good I can do for the Saints by sending a letter to meet them if I don't come in person.

We as a Welsh branch are happy, and I have performed four marriages: John Williams, of Monachlog, and Mary Jones, from the neighborhood of Mynydd Aberdare; Edward Evans, Hirwaun, and Alice, the daughter of David Richards, the blacksmith. Alexander Owens, Twynyrodyn, has died from yellow fever; please inform his wife. Let no one fear the sea; it is lovely to sail on in fair weather; from Liverpool to the Sounding is the roughest part. Our tabernacle will be finished by the time you bring the emigrants here; it is in the square now. I have heard but once from Bro. Jones after his departure to the Valley; he was 500 miles from the Bluffs at the time—he, his wife and child, and the whole company were healthy and going along successfully. I expect a mail pouch yet from the Valley in the near future. We have heard about the cholera in your midst; there is no more cholera in St. Louis now, and there has not been any of this devastating illness in the Bluffs so far.

Remember me to the officials and all the Saints, and may the gracious Lord bless you and bring you safe to beautiful Zion is the wish of my heart.

I am your brother in the new covenant,
William Morgan.

P.S. Let it be known that Wm. Jenkins, from Cardiff, is staying in the Bluffs. We heard through the gifts that some of the brethren are suffering because of fire and that the destroyer is there in your midst. I received letters from Morgan Morgans, E. Thomas and Morgan Hughes. John Ormond and his son and two daughters are here.

A Letter of Mrs. Lewis to J. Davis
(TD16)

Salt Lake Valley, April 10, 1850.

Beloved Brother in Christ—

At last I date my letter from the blessed place which I longed so much to see, and for which I broke through many obstacles to reach; and though it is not perfect heaven, nor is everyone in it perfect, yet I am not sorry for having come here, and the evils which were prophesied to me back there about this place and its inhabitants have not been fulfilled; and I believe that it is my duty to my Good Lord and His cause to send my witness back, for the sake of those who have not had this experience as I have had, and so they can take heart also to come here.

Do not expect me to give you a detailed account of a place which is so full of wonders as this one; you shall have more from others; but I shall say, like the Queen of Sheba earlier, that I was not told half the good things about this place and its inhabitants. The city is being built with miraculous speed, and the country around it is being worked incredibly well. There is a convenient worship house already finished in which we meet with several thousands of dear Saints each Sunday from every country, and we hear the voices of the best people on earth, and our dear President Brigham Young and his counselors, the Apostles and others teaching us in the law of heaven with pleasure and great sweetness to me and showing the great power, wisdom and love of God in the plan of salvation; and not only people who love the heavenly teaching are taught here, but more than anything is that everyone else is following suit, and peace, prosperity, and love reign; and God is praised more and more for this salvation. I have not seen a drunken person in this place or anyone quarrelling with another; I have only heard of someone threatening to take another to court, except that he was too ashamed to be the first one in the place to do that. I have yet to hear an oath or swearing on the street; not one murder or theft that I know of in the place, nor have I seen any immorality. And as for the highest officials here, they are surprisingly humble, meek, and godly—like a father to his children is all their behavior, from what I have seen. I fear greatly that sickness, pestilence, poverty, and oppression are causing much suffering to my dear brothers and sisters in the gospel in Wales, which causes me to desire and to pray a great deal to be able to see them by the thousands in this blessed place. May all the best Welsh soon come here, and what a time we'll have then. There is no one here begging or any poor here. The men who came here the same time as I did are such freeholders that it is difficult for me to get anyone to work my small farm. A busy time for sowing is now here. The wages of workers here are two or three dollars per day, and work buys what cannot be had for gold. All the Welsh who came here are doing well and are very respected by everyone. We farm with each other ''on the banks of the Jordan,'' and the place is called ''New Wales.'' Capt. Jones has just returned from searching for the Welsh Indians. I write in haste because the mail is about to leave. I write to you because I hope that my relatives are on their way here.

If my dear husband, father and my sister have not started from there, tell them to come soon; I would be glad to see them here together with my brothers and all my relatives. If you have a chance, remember me to them lovingly; and my heartfelt wish is for them all to obey the gospel speedily. If you choose to send this, my testimony, to them, I hope that it will have the blessing of God for them. Tell them and everyone who mentions Capt. Jones that he has not been the evil man that they prophesied about him, rather until now his behavior has been the direct opposite. We all found him kind and benevolent, and his entire behavior is like a father toward his children, and great is our duty to thank him and the God who sent him to be a good leader to us. He has not received nor has he tried to get any of my money, and I have not heard that anyone of the company has been the loser of one penny because of him; and the prayer of all of us is that God will bless him with health which he has lost serving us and recompense him in the world to come.

Dear brother, exhort all the Saints for me to continue faithful in this Church, for I am certain that this is the religion of Jesus Christ.

Remember me lovingly to you and all the Saints,

Your sister in the new covenant,

Elizabeth Lewis.

Letter of Capt. Jones to J. Davis
(TD17)

Salt Lake City, April 12, 1850.

Dear Brother Davis—

I have so many things to write to you by now that I hardly know what to start with, but this Epistle will tell you many of my thoughts; and besides this, briefly, I shall say to you and all the dear Saints there, Oh, brethren, be faithful and diligent in the heavenly calling to which you have been called, since you know that your labor is not in vain in the Lord. Make good use of your time in the vineyard of God there, before you are called here, for there are difficult days ahead. Everything is fine here, and all the Welsh are healthy and happy here.

I returned here from the south in February, after traveling about 1,000 miles, and being within less than 100 miles from the abode of the Madocians as I was told afterwards by Indians who had been in their midst. I could not have gone further, as our horses and our supplies were depleted and the rainy weather was flooding the country. We nearly lost our lives traveling across the snowy mountains for hundreds of miles through snow between three and eight feet deep, and sleeping in it at night with nothing more than a blanket to cover us. We left behind some days a half dozen of our horses and mules to die or as prey for the wolves. We were for several days without food before arriving at the Utah settlement on returning. You shall have some account of our discoveries in the Epistle, but it is not the time to tell everything to the world there. We intend to fulfill the purpose of this adventure yet, perhaps this year; at least, we shall not give up until I get hold of the Madocians, and get the main road opened to the Saints to come from Wales across the railway of Panama to the California channel, up the Colorado River and there overland to the settlements of the Saints, which will be near the port at which the steamboats will land from there to here in every valley before long. The good intentions of God toward the old race of Gomer are becoming manifest strangely and rapidly to our dear President and to us. Dear Saints, remember and keep

the counsels which I have given to you there. Respect the priesthood
and pray for me and for yourselves.

> I am, your brother in the new covenant.
>
> D. Jones.

NB. When will the "Trumpet" sound? Send it here every chance
you get. For goodness sake, do your best for me with my books,
and send the money; I was on the above journey at my own cost
and I shall go likewise again before long.

A Letter of Capt. Jones to W. Phillips
(TD18)

> Great Salt Lake City, April 12, 1850.

Dear Brother Phillips—

A few lines only can I write to you now; you shall see the letter
from Brother Davis which says much about myself; yet, I hope, yes,
and I pray daily for God to keep you from the evil which surrounds
you, and give you influence on all the Saints, as a good shepherd
has on his flock, that you may keep them in unity, love, growth
and continual success; and I hope, I say, that hosts of those who
persecuted me as the worst man in the country, before this have
obeyed the gospel of my Lord, come to know me better and to love
you; and that will cause me to love the most hateful of them, yes
and embrace them if I could see them here. I fear that the government hardly gives you any protection; but, if not, do not become
disheartened; the King of Kings is watching over you; He will pre-
serve you if you are humble and pious before Him. Do not forget
to pray to Him and serve Him. You cannot fulfill your important
office there without His assistance. Oh, I would be so happy to see
your face here and for us to get to tell each other our troubles and
our hopes, but probably we shall do that first over there. Doubtless
the poverty, pestilences, and deaths of every kind, together with

hatred of the world, are causing much worry to you and the Saints; but rejoice in this, there is salvation here from every evil but death, and very seldom does the King of Terrors visit this place. Yet, we are not here without our trials and temptations to the extreme, though different from there; and some, I am sad to say, even among the Welsh, are giving themselves to false influences, especially that which is called "yellow fever," that is, the desire to go from here to the country of gold to get rich. I imagine that many beloved Welsh are on their way here for some weeks, and may the gracious God keep them from the evils which surround them, and especially from the Cholera Morbus on the Missouri River. Oh, William, that was the strangest time I ever saw in my life to see the power of God and the power of the devil. *****

My wife and little Claudia are well, and all the Saints, and they send their greeting to you and to your dear family, and all the Saints there. Farewell now, from

Your brother,
D. Jones.

NB. The American soldiers did not take the other letter until now because of the weather, and so I send it now. I hope that the other letters I sent have reached you promptly. I have heartfelt longing for your conferences and your association, but I must be content now.

A Letter from Great Salt Lake City [Thomas Jeremy]
(TD19)

Great Salt Lake City, April 14, 1850.
Dear Brother Davis—

Would you be so kind as to lend space in your melodious "Trumpet" for this letter, so that those who wanted me to write to them can have an answer through it; for it would be too much work

for me to write to all I would like to personally. I hope that my
old faithful brothers and sisters around Llanybydder and Brechfa
and other places will do their best to spread the *Udgorn* through
the country so that those who wish will get to read our account.

By the goodness of my Heavenly Father toward me and my
family, we arrived here, that is, to the neighborhood of the Valley,
all healthy on the 29th of October. In the meantime our revered
President, Brigham Young, and his two counselors with him have
come to visit us, that is all the Welsh; and great was the comfort
we all received by listening to his welcome to the Valley to us, and
his excellent counsels pertaining to this settlement. He counseled
us to go to the west side of the city, to stop about three miles from
the city so that our animals could get better grazing. We camped
on the bank of the Jordan River, which runs directly from Utah Lake
to Salt Lake; the width of the river is about 100 feet, in proportion
to its depth of about five feet. In this river there is an abundance
of large fish; and also hosts of wild geese and ducks descend to it
and to the small lakes which are along its banks. This is an excellent
place for those who derive pleasure from shooting game, with no
reason for fearing anyone. There is free agency to everyone to kill
the number they desire. As a family we lived in our wagons for a
month's time here before getting a house; we were very comfortable in that way, because we had a good top on our wagons, and
a stove in one of them for the preparation of food, etc. Then we
lived for about four months in a room which we obtained in the
city; but now we are in our own house, on our city lot, which we
call "privilege city." The size of the lots is an acre and a quarter,
which everyone owns without money and without value, only to
pay for measuring it and recording it, that is, $1.50. The Welsh
chose to get their city lots on the west side of the city on a beautiful
plain; the biggest part of three blocks is in the possession of the
race of Gomer. The blocks are generally 10 acres, which makes eight
lots in each block. I believe that we have obtained the most fertile
land in the city, although it is all extremely good. My reason for
thinking that it is so good is because it is flatter and lower than
other places of the city. Our land is rich, black soil; I'm not sure
how deep it goes, but I do know that in some places it is six feet.
I observed this by seeing the marks left by some who had dug down

to get water conveniently by their houses; the appearance of the soil in that depth is black and rich. The biggest part of the Welsh intend to build on their lots this year. There is plenty of room for thousands of Welsh to come yet nearby us. It hardly costs anything to keep animals. Because of the size and the richness of the Valley, horses, oxen, and cattle are kept outside through the winter; but some keep their cattle by their houses, and give hay to them, so they will be more convenient to milk. All the Saints here get as much land to work as they wish without paying anything to anyone except to measure it and record it. We, the few Welsh who came here, have chosen our own land for planting (i.e., land for farming rather than for building) on the west side of the Jordan River about five miles from the place where I live. Unusually abundant crops are raised here of wheat, barley, Indian corn and oats, potatoes, squashes, watermelons, cabbage and every kind of garden vegetable as big as you wish.

I shall give a bit of history of the fruitfulness of this large valley. Mr. Halliday planted one bushel of wheat, called "touse wheat," and got from it about 183 bushels; another planted one bushel of potatoes and got 330 bushels. It is said that you can get from barley obtained from California about 100 bushels from planting one. Perhaps this account is too good for some Welsh to believe, but yet, that will not make it any less true. What good would it do me to send false testimonies there? Those who come here can know for themselves. I think that the reason that the tillage gives such a good yield is that you need to sow only very lightly. I heard some say here that half a bushel of wheat is enough to sow an acre, the same amount of barley. Because of the fertility of the earth, the tillage spreads unusually well here by growing; and the goodness and love of our Heavenly Father which blesses us temporally as well as spiritually is acknowledged here. The holy prophets foresaw this valley and spoke of it. See Isaiah 32 from the 15th verse to the end of the chapter. The last two verses in the chapter and some others also are easily understood; for we see frequently the "hailstones descending on the trees" when there is nothing coming down on us in this low city. It is good to sow near all the streams here because there is not as much rain here in the summer as there is in some other countries. It is necessary to water the land here at times; I,

myself, am very thankful to my Heavenly Father that my land is
on the bank of the Jordan River, and I can drive the feet of the
oxen there whenever I want. Perhaps the above verses will not be
believed literally by everyone in Wales, but it is very likely that they
will inspire them to think something else, if they have not
abandoned the old custom. Oh, how lovely it is to be surrounded
here by high mountains, whose tops can be seen at times above the
clouds, and which are covered with snow year round. There is a look
on them as if they were testifying that not one enemy can come
here to do harm to the Saints. You have heard about the excellent
springs there are here, which are especially medicinal. It is so nice
to bathe in the hot spring; there is another one here so hot that
you can hardly keep your finger in it any longer than while you are
counting from 10 to 15. There is sufficient water in it to turn a
large mill or more.

There are excellent prices here for men for their work. A
stonemason here earns $2.50 per day; a carpenter, $2.00 per day;
from $6 to $10 is paid a tailor for making a coat; laborers, $1.50
per day; and remember that one need not work as hard here as in
Wales. Some of the Welsh brothers here earn from $3 to $4 per
day by digging by the job. The Americans are not used to digging.
So, you see how easy it is to live here. The price of the wheat here
now is $4 per bushel; Indian corn, $2; a yoke of oxen here costs
from $70 to $100; a cow costs about $30; a good horse from $150
to $200; a dollar here is 4s 2c of your money there. I am not send-
ing for my dear brother, David, and my dear sisters, this time,
because Bro. Jones sent back from along the way that David would
get to come here this year with the faithful brother Abel Evans,
and Bro. Howell Williams, and others. I hope they come; there
would be great joy here to see them. I hope that my dear father
comes also on the journey here. I wish greatly to hear how my sister
Sarah is, if she is not on her journey here, together with the
Cefncrwth family, of Meidrim. I hope they are now members of
the Church of Jesus Christ and that they will be in Zion before
long.

My dear brothers and sisters, this is a lovely place; this is where
he who holds the keys of the kingdom of God on the earth is; the
Twelve Apostles are heard here preaching excellently on the

mysteries of the kingdom of God; but there is not so much need to exhort the Saints to come here, for if they keep the Holy Ghost within them, He will show them the necessity for this salvation. I know not when I shall come to Wales. None of the Welsh at the last conference was sent on a mission to any place; but some were sent to England and to various islands of the sea. The conference was held on the 6th and 7th of this month, in the Tabernacle, which is very, very big; but nonetheless too small to hold all who went there. The Welsh were exhorted by our revered President, Brigham Young, to sing the song of "Joseph and Hyrum." The English here love very much to hear the Welsh sing. Oh, how lovely it is to escape from the wearisome captivity to the midst of the best people on earth, where justice and holiness abide, where we can worship God with no one to disturb us or to frighten us, about 1,000 miles from everyone except the Lamanites, who are here and there in the mountains, that is, the seed of Joseph who was sold into Egypt.

Before I finish, I wish to say a little to those who have not obeyed the gospel of Jesus Christ; and this is it—Remember to listen to the servants of God there, that is, the preachers of the Saints, for there is no one there who can teach you the way of salvation except only them; for that reason listen to them, and obey their teaching so that you can be saved. If I reasoned with you at length, I could not give you better counsel.

I hope Mr. Davies, Clynglase, parish of Llanwrda, sees this letter. I sincerely hope that he and his dear family are in the Church now.

I do not have time to write more; the mail leaves here tomorrow morning.

Dear Saints, farewell "for a small moment, until we see each other all at home." My family joins with me in remembering all the Saints in Wales, especially in Llanbydder and Brechfa and Cardiganshire. I hope that the dear Saints whom I love so much continue faithful; and may the gracious God who called them from darkness to light bless them with the spirit of love, unity and peace and save them in the end in His heavenly kingdom, which is the constant prayer of

Your dear brother in Jesus Christ,
Thomas Jeremy.

NB. I would very much like to have several letters from my brothers and my friends in Wales. Let them send them to: "Thomas Jeremy, Great Salt Lake City, California, North America." I sincerely hope that you, dear Bro. Davis, will correct every mistake which you see in my writing.

A Letter from William Morgan
(TD20)

Council Bluffs, May 26, 1850.

Dear Brother Phillips,

Bro. Abel Evans brought his company of Saints here on the 23rd of this month; and on his testimony and your licenses, they were received as regular members of the Welsh branch in Cambria's Camp.

Dear Brother, there are some things taking place among the young people, things which are natural according to the custom of the old country but which would be good for them to turn from. One thing is making promises of marriage. My opinion is that it is best to refrain, and that it would be wiser to get married before getting underway, for those who wish to do so. Bro. Abel Evans and myself also failed to see that earlier; but he had opened his eyes before coming to the Bluffs and married a lovely girl from near Carmarthen, Mary Jones from Wern Branch. Usually families live better here than widowers; and so, then, those who wish to get married, let them get married, and those who wish to refrain, let them refrain; but let all boys and girls and all widowed men and women leave the old country without making promises to get married. Thus, there will be no danger of breaking promises; and they will come free to a free country and leave those who remain behind free also. That was the opinion of Bro. Jones also, as I recall, i.e., to covenant until the emigration. I have performed marriages for eight in this country and expect six or eight again soon.

Our town is like a boiling pot these days, and as full as Merthyr market on Saturday, so that one cannot drive a wagon without stopping along the streets. They are gold people, and they leave some of their gold behind, or you might think so, for flour is $6.00 for a hundred pounds, Indian corn is $1.50 a bushel, and some have sold for $3.00. I was told by Dr. Bennett, a doctor of one company, that there are 4,000 acres of wheat in Illinois with no one to cut it and likely to be trampled by the animals. The Mormons preached the gospel—yes, the Prophet Joseph was the first to proclaim it there, but they did not believe his witness, rather they shouted, "Away with him," just like his Master. It was Mormons who discovered gold in California, and strange how truthful is the witness and how accepted it is by people in general; but there is not a grain more of truth than the testimony of the Mormons in Merthyr with respect to the gospel; but the spirit of the world is running after its toy, that is, the root of all evil, and as a result it cannot receive the Spirit of Christ, which is truth and love, glory to God in the heavens, and on the earth good will. Well, good luck to them and their gold. Let whoever wishes become merchants. We, however, shall build Zion, the city of our God in the Valley of the Mountains; and when the time comes for her to raise her head, her King will come and her glory will envelop her; and at that time the false men will be afraid.

I received ten packages of *Udgorn Seion* from one of the English brothers who came here with the first shipload, addressed to Capt. Dan Jones. They will be on their way to him before you receive this letter, but not all of them; for after they came to our territory, we judged that we are entitled to a tithe, and we kept two of each package. You see that we have not tithed as heavily as the old country, according to the law of tithing. We have paid for six months of the *Frontier Guardian*, and it is to come across there regularly as it comes off the press. I have seen but one letter from you, nor have I received the *Udgorn* monthly as you said; and I do not know whether the *Frontier Guardian* which I sent has been received or not; it is being sent to Merthyr and Dowlais. I received a letter for Elizabeth Thomas, from the county of Glamorgan, and I sent it over last April to the Valley. Let no one be disheartened who has sent letters to the Valley to relatives and to Bro. Jones, for answers will be forthcoming as soon as possible. I expect to hear from the Valley, from Capt. Jones and the Welsh Saints, between now and the end of June. Bro. Prythero from Abersychan and his family are staying in my house at the present time, and they have taken some land in another part of the country and will be going there soon.

Remember me to all the Saints, together with the officials; and may the blessing of God be with you.

Yours in the eternal covenant,
William Morgan.

Letter from William Morgan, Kanesville, Iowa, To W. Phillips and J. Davis
(TD21)

Kanesville, Iowa, July 19, 1850.

Dear Brother Phillips and Davis,—

I received the following letter in the mail which came from the Valley this month, that is July 1850, with a request from Bro. Jones for me to translate it and send it to the *Udgorn*. Here it is at the editor's service, but not without mistakes, which I am confident the editor will correct; but the sweetness of English writing as wrought by its famous authors is out of the translator's reach.

[The letter which Morgan received from George A. Smith, Ezra T. Benson, and Dan Jones, dated 21 September 1849, is then presented. The English translation of Morgan's Welsh translation from the original English is Translated Document 7 (TD7) in this appendix. Toward the end of the letter, reference is made to the Welsh Company: "They are happy and content and make the camp resound with their evening song." Morgan adds his own comments in a footnote as follows:]

*I am an eye and ear witness of that. I think, as do the Apostles, that the spirit of music has descended on them from out of the evening before their departure from the territory of the Honuhous. About six o'clock Friday afternoon, Bro. Jones ordered me to call the camp together for the purpose of reading the rules of the journey; and in a short time each was by his post. I had the honor of beginning the first meeting for 1850 years, at least, on that land, for the purpose of organizing the Welsh journey. Bro. Jones followed; and after that, the word was given out to sing to close the meeting. As we sang the first part of the verse, that is, ''When the Saints shall come, etc.,'' we saw the English and the Norwegians and everyone I would think, with their heads out of their wagons. With the second part, the wagons were empty in an instant and their inhabitants running toward us as if they were charmed. I heard good singing in Wales, but nothing like the strength and sweetness of the last song I heard by my brothers and sisters, co-travelers, on the land of Honuhous. Some asked me where they had learned and who was their teacher? I said that the hills of Wales were the schoolhouse, and the Spirit of God was the teacher. Their response was, ''Well, indeed, it is wonderful; we never heard such good singing before.''   —Wm. Morgan.

To that which Brothers Smith, Benson, and Jones have written about the journey, and the preparations for it, I shall give the prices of several things which I suppose might be useful for the small-holders or the farmers. The price of an iron plough is 25 cents per pound, or a shilling and a halfpenny in the money of the old country. Understand that iron ploughs here are in one piece, the point and iron the same kind as the casting which is sold there by the ironmongers; the whole thing weighs about 30 pounds. The iron harrow, that is, the teeth, 8s 4c. Files for sharpening saws, 7½c each; for a large saw, or a whip saw, 1s 6½c. A scythe handle, 4s 2c; scythe of a larger size, 6s 6c. A spike for the hay, 2s 1c. Wheel rim iron, 2½c per pound. Four iron wagon wheels cost, that is, the four rims as some call them in the old country, £1 14s, before the blacksmith puts his hammer to them. In my opinion it is better for everyone to buy his milk pitcher, that is, the tin kind, in Wales. The pitchers for keeping milk for making cream cost 1s 8c

each here; their size is between 12 and 13 inches in diameter in
the widest spot, that is, the top; 8¾ inches at the bottom, and
3¾ inches deep. Pottery is close to three times as expensive here
as it is there; the worst cup and saucer which are for sale in Wales
cost 5c here; and other dishes are proportionately higher. Bed ropes,
1s 5½c each; half-inch ropes, 1s ½c per pound. The ropes of the
old country are better than the ropes of this country in general; the
hemp goes black here before getting any use from it. I saw much
of it in St. Louis half-rotten, and I saw one steamboat full of it
catch on fire, until it burned to the water level; but I don't think
that that was a big loss to the public. I have not seen any sickles
here, but they would be very useful; and I suppose that it would
be well for the farmers when they come here for them to have
brought their sickles from the old country with them, and not to
sell them and leave them behind as did those who came first from
Wales. Closed billhooks are useful in this country. The axes in this
country are better and as cheap. Tongs, fire shovels, and bellows
for blowing the fire in the morning would be very useful here; also
knives and forks, brass candlesticks, soup spoons, and teaspoons.
It would be best for the women who go, to buy parasols; women
are not seen walking very often without them here; and truly a veil
is something quite good—women are not seen very often without
them, even some of the Welsh. The blue cotton which is sold for
4c in Merthyr costs 8c here. I would counsel those who go to bring
moleskins for everyday wear; they last longer than the other materials
here. I shall make an end now on this end; in a previous letter I
gave my thoughts about a few things which I considered beneficial
for the emigrants to come across the sea; and as far as I can
remember concerning that which I wrote, I have not changed my
mind about the directions which I gave, and I do not think that
I will have to blush in the presence of the emigrants who make use
of them; at least, my conscience is clear that everything originated
from an intent to be of benefit to my Welsh-speaking brothers and
sisters and others also.

I received three numbers of the *Udgorn*, together with a note
from Bro. Phillips, and a letter from you to Capt. Jones, which I sent
ahead on the fourth of this month. We received letters from some
of the brethren who are in the Valley, that is, Daniel Leigh from

Llanelli, D. Peters, and Capt. Jones. They are in agreement about
the fruitfulness of the country; D. Leigh says that the Valley of the
Mountains is the best under the sun to raise crops. He says that one
bushel of wheat planted in the ground gives the marvelous yield
of 166 bushels, and one bushel of potatoes gives 133 bushels.
"What is all the fruitfulness of the land," he adds, "in comparison
to the teachings which are received from the Apostles? They are
worth more than anything I have ever seen." Evan Rees and Edward
Williams are digging for coal, and Mrs. Lewis is living in the town.
Elizabeth Thomas from Waunfro near Cardiff married William
Clark; perhaps Bro. W. Thomas will be glad to hear that he is
increasing in family so far away from him.

There are some things in the old country which I would be
glad to see here, that is, all the honest in heart wishing to do the
will of God continually, and that which is owed to me in the old
country. One is as just as the other; if not, I do not expect anything
from this which I may consider owed to me. I wish for Bro. Phillips
to try to collect my notes, and I shall be thankful to him, and to
those who pay.

Bro. Capt. Jones has sent only a little piece by his own hand,
but he sent in print an account of the conference in the Valley.
That which you want will be in the *Guardian*, if it comes to hand.
The substance of the letter of Bro. Jones was that I was being
tested; "and it happens, dear William," says he, "that you are not
tried by your best friends until you are at the end of your journey.
Keep at it, great will be your honor, in spite of everything." He
ended by saying: "I know not where I shall be when you come to
the Valley, nor do I ask to know anything but that which is com-
manded me. All the Welsh are well. Remember me and Jane to
all the Saints.   —D. Jones."

I was in a hurry when I wrote the last time (as if there were a
time when I was not in a hurry), and perhaps some will make use
of that which I sent in a way I have not considered, although really
it is not my official duty upon arriving at this side of the sea, and
I do not consider there to be more strength in that which I write
than there is in that which some other brother or sister writes from
this place. Yet, perhaps there are those who have not forgotten that
which Bro. Jones wrote from the Indian territory; listen to his

counsel. Well, then, my opinion is that it is better for all who are engaged to be married to free themselves before starting from Wales, if one comes before the other; and those who are coming at the same time, and are engaged, it would be well for them to do the same or get married before starting. But perhaps better than marrying would be to undo the engagement. The sea is free and the country they come to is free; and between freedom of the sea and the freedom of the land, covenants are broken even by those who are traveling together. Well, then, it is better not to be under promise, in my opinion, in every meaning; for not much time is needed to get married here. They can see each other for the first time ever at nine o'clock in the morning, and if they wish they can become husband and wife according to the law of the land and the Church also, before twelve o'clock the same morning.

Your letter says that there are many Saints who are coming across next autumn. Bro. Pratt will be there before that; but let them come whenever they wish, for I have nothing to do with the emigration; therefore, I shall keep my mouth shut on the subject of the time of the year. But I shall be thankful to you for sending a letter here a month or two before they come, mentioning their number of each skill, and the sum total, men, women, and children, and the day of the month they will be leaving Liverpool. If they come here, perhaps that will be of benefit to them. My paper is full, and I am tired, and there is not time to do any complaining this time. I shall close now by wishing for the gracious God to give to you and all connected with you and under your care, wisdom, so that you will be wise as serpents and harmless as doves, in these latter days, in broadening the kingdom of God on the earth. Amen.

I am, your brother in the new covenant,

Wm. Morgan.

P.S. All the Welsh Saints greet you.

Verses
(TD22)

Composed on the journey, by Gwilym Ddu,
formerly of Pont-y-ty-pridd, Glamorganshire.

Some of the sectarians insist,—that to sell us
    In shame, like animals,
    Across the sea, our leaders would do:
    Such was the group's cry.

"The Captain," they say, "enticed,—in the area
    Of Merthyr a huge number of Wales's children,
    That they might be sold,—
    Yes, a shipful from among the host."

Oh! blind men, poor souls,—if they continue
    In their course of an angry disposition,
    When the judgment and the plague come upon them,
    Their false tales will be as the wind.

Our Moses and mighty chief—he is Jones,
    Our supreme and heavenly teacher;
    Full of the energy of holy wisdom
    To lead us into the land of praise.

[Taken from page 12 of *Cyfarwyddiadau i'r ymfudwyr tua Dinas y Llyn Halen* (Direction to the emigrants to Salt Lake City), a twelve-page pamphlet published in 1850 by John Davis in Merthyr Tydfil. "Gwilym Ddu" is the poetic pseudonym used by William Lewis, a member of the first group of Welsh immigrants to enter the Salt Lake Valley in 1849. He composed the above "Verses" during the crossing of the plains with the George A. Smith Company in that year.]

A Letter of Capt. D. Jones
to Elders W. Phillips and J. Davis
(TD23)

Salt Lake City, September 10, 1850.
Dear Brothers W. Phillips and J. Davis—

Until now for the life of me I have not had a chance to greet
you, in spite of my desire, since I wrote before; and now, short words
are my song, for I am about to leave again from here further away
to settle, that is, to the valley of San Pete, and that according to the
counsel of Pres. Young to me, and as many other Welsh brethren
as can come. I know not yet who will come. This place is splendid
country to settle in with an abundance of water and wood close by.
It lies about 130 miles from here. We went through it last year as
we searched for the Madocians, and I shall be as much as that on
my way to fulfill that venture yet, which thing, if God wills, I shall
do before I rest. I do not have time to say hardly anything about this
place or its happenings, but I shall send to you the *Deseret News*,
which is published here, to do its part of that for me.

I had received only one small letter from you since I left Wales,
nothing from anyone else, until the mail came in very recently; and
yesterday I received the *Udgorn* for last year. I cannot describe my
feelings as I took hold of a book which came from the hands of my
dear brothers in the dear country which I left; a host of things which
have gone by came to my recollection! But when I cut its pages and
my eyes rushed across its pages, I saw the names of a number of the
brethren whom I love so greatly shining through it like diamonds
amid the rocks along the seashore—proving they were yet diligent
in the field, faithful in the vineyard of their Lord, which vineyard
is of my own planting. The bonds of my heart are nearly bursting
with *hiraeth* to see them, to shake their hands once again; yes, for
their company eternally. I cannot be completely happy without all of
them, those whom I loved so much; and yet, instead of returning to
feast in their company and to battle together shoulder to shoulder with
you in the army of Jesus there, He sees best now to send me even
further! Well, I am content. His will be done, says my soul. So be it.

Yet, oh, dear brethren in the priesthood, what shall I say to you
one and all to comfort you? This you know, that you are servants,

as am I, of great Jesus, and that He is expecting all of us to fill the circle into which we have been placed; and He shall call us together sometime to give our account. Well, dear brethren and children in Christ, be sure to appear there happy. Remember that which I told you when I was there and do it; and thus God our Father will bless you forever and ever. I was about to say kiss my dear co-workers there; what else shall I say to them to show my love for them? Yet, that would be nothing. I have not time nor space to even name them, as they are too numerous. Go forward, dear Saints; the crowns are ahead of you and eternal life to clothe you. I dreamed lately that I was in the middle of a room full of you in council, and embracing my dear brethren W. Phillips and J. Davis endlessly, and it was exquisitely sweet! Oh, such heaven it was to me, but it was but a dream! Oh, teach the dear Saints tenderly in love the way to keep the counsel of God. Thanks to my Father for answering my prayers in your regard. Remember me to dear Howells and his family lovingly; that the Lord be with him and his family is my constant prayer. Remember me to all of the Saints. My wife and little Claudia are well, together with the rest of the Welsh. Remember me and my family kindly to my brothers, John and Edward, and my relatives. Oh, that they were here; I shall pray for them all to be faithful Saints anyway. I heard that A. Evans is not coming here this year, but that he is staying in Council Bluffs. * * *

The roads here are still white from the wagonfuls of immigrants. They are like doves coming to their windows from the four corners of the world. The sickness which gathered on my lungs through hard work there has not gotten much better yet. Dear Saints, remember your poor servant and pray for him, he who served you almost to the death; and for him be faithful and diligent in the work of God. We had an excellent conference here last week, and everything here is successful and wonderfully organized, for there is an able leader at the helm and an abundance of assistants. I cannot get a chance now to write an account of my journey to the south last winter; you shall have that as soon as I can write it. You shall have an account of the Council Bluffs Welsh from Bro. W. Morgans. They are welcome to dwell on the land I bought there for them. At last, I must close. Brethren, here are for the three of you my love and my heart forever and ever. Amen.

D. Jones.

A Letter from Capt. D. Jones to Wm. Phillips Containing News from Zion

(TD24)

Manti City, March, 1851.

My Dear Bro. Phillips—

With pleasure I commune with you by means of a letter for lack of any other means, even though a letter is but a poor means to transmit my frequent thoughts with respect to, and my nostalgic feelings for you and my dear brethren in the priesthood together with all the dear Saints there. Believe me that you are never out of my thoughts for even a day, and the best wishes of my heart are offered up at the family altar daily in your behalf to Him who is able to keep you safe and gather you together to the place of deliverance where you can hear the sound of the lovely songs of victorious Zion instead of having your ears stunned by the transitory moans and groans of friends, relatives, and loved ones; where you meet a brother and friend with a cheery smile on his face, an index of a happy and guileless heart, instead of like it is there, being pained by an angry look and gnashing of teeth at you along the streets by those whom you wish to benefit, as I received while there. The wish which fills my mind, in spite of everything which happened, is to see hosts of the Welsh enjoying the teaching, the quietness and the peace which are here; and the deliverance from sickness, plagues, and the oppression which, according to all accounts and prophecies, continue to sweep the wretched inhabitants of the world there to the spirit world, ready or not, and trampling the rest under their iron hooves into the dust without hope of salvation.

May the day soon come when you all shall find yourselves here, and I shall have the pleasure of your company in the valleys of these peaceful and healthful mountains, and you shall have your fill of fruitful land to work without paying rent or hardly any tax to anyone for it and plenty of wages to satisfy you for every trade. Yes, when you shall have, as does everyone else here, the full enjoyment of all the elements, possession and endowment of our Father to His children. And you shall have also the perfect law of freedom to defend you in all your rights and to urge you to do every good thing, and also to punish you for your smallest transgression which you do knowingly.

Our church and state officials here are from among ourselves at last, as Isaiah prophesied they would be for the Saints in the last days. The news came here lately that the United States has permitted us to be a territory and choose our respected Pres. B. Young as president. And they have granted generous privileges to the new territory, considering who they are. Our borders reach to the south to a latitude of 37 degrees north. Our King rightly said: "Be wise as serpents and harmless as doves," and it would be good for all His subjects to remember that continually.

The situation of the Saints here is extremely successful, spiritually and temporally. These valleys produce wheat, barley, oats, potatoes and every kind of crop and vegetable that can be grown in Britain, but much more abundantly with less trouble, except to irrigate, which is a task which must be done carefully and diligently, for there are insufficient rains in the summer without that. The way that corn is irrigated is by opening furrows with the plough after sowing the seed a few feet from each other in such a way that the water runs slowly along the furrows. The water is obtained from the nearby streams through ditches which are dug for this purpose. And these lands are of such a nature that the water penetrates through all these furrows in a few hours; and then the water is turned away for perhaps a week, more or less. In this manner, 40 bushels of wheat per acre are generally produced, and frequently more; and I know of some who have gotten the incredible sum of over 200 bushels after the sowing of one bushel, something uncommon, although true of the above-mentioned California wheat, which is what is sown here most and which produces much grass from each seed, sometimes scores, for I counted them myself. And the ears of corn fork into several of considerable size because of that which is called the seven-headed variety. The price of wheat now is $2.50 to $3.00 per bushel. Its price some time ago was much higher, and last summer, to the immigrants, it was as high as 25 cents per pound of flour, oats and barley being a little cheaper; potatoes about $1.00 per bushel, butter 50 cents, cheese the same price or less. The wages of craftsmen are from $2 to $4, workers from $1 to $2 per day. By the month from $12 to $20 per month for the year; and I am now paying one of the Welsh boys in salary $200 per year plus his food and washing, and to one other lad about fifteen years old, $100. Also to a maid $1.50 per week, and $1 to the other, that is, Welsh ones. The common wage for maids is $1 per week, and there was great demand for Welsh women until they became too greedy for wages. I am writing like this about these valleys in general, and not about any place in particular, lest you misunderstand me.

At the last conference, Pres. Young wished for me by naming me in public to emigrate to this place, that is San Pete, and so I came in the autumn. This is a spendid valley, advantageous to settle in, although not as large as the Great Salt Lake Valley, yet more advantageous in some respects, such as there is here a greater abundance of land, easier to work and irrigate in proportion to the inhabitants, than there is now there; for you would be surprised how they have settled there already! Much easier to get trees, shelter, firewood, etc., here. In the account of my journey to the south last year, you have the history of the settlement of this place; and it has increased already until there are several hundred comfortable houses, and families who are the most loving, devout, and peaceful that I have ever seen. Not a cross word, no profanity, no oppression or injustice have I seen since I have been here. We have a worship house which is large and comfortable, which is overflowing every Sunday with cheery and happy people; school is held in it every day and it is too small so that we had to build another schoolhouse lately. Some meetings are held in them every night through the week. Also built here since I came are a corn-grinding mill and a sawmill for laths and shingles. There is a shop here in which you can get nearly all the common supplies you want, and the prices are not so different from those of the States as you might think, except for some things.

Several thousand acres of land are worked in one enclosure, and it is pleasant to see with what unity and brotherhood everyone works together for the benefit of all in everything. And, in fact, it can be said of this people that "whatever they put their hands on to do, they do it willingly and with all their might." It was thought that the desire of each one is to build the kingdom, and by doing only that each builds himself.

The next news will cheer your hearts every one, I know for myself. Sing, you, the scattered of Zion through the world! Yea, rejoice in the British Isles of the sea, for the Lord God is shortening His great work for you, and will do it shortly in justice! A temple to Him is to be built in Zion in which your own thirsty soul can drink deeply from inexhaustible fountains of knowledge about God and the proper way to worship Him, about Heaven, its laws, its enjoyment and its glory, and where you through preparations and godly ordinances can become fit to associate with its inhabitants and be taught also in the perfect ethics which are used in its eternal dwelling place. Yea, in your time and according to your faithfulness you can possess the fulness and strength of the priesthood which reigns there and in every other place. And after completing your work and giving to God and to His servants sufficient proof of your faithfulness and worthiness, you can gain a goodly entrance in through the gates of the Temple first, and there from gate to gate unto the most holy! Blessed are those happy souls. Is not the expectation of such bliss—of the strength of faith, of getting that faith which was once given to the Saints—worth every effort and suffering? Here is mention of something similar to the substance of religion and godly wisdom. This only will satisfy the desirous souls who have tasted the firstfruits of the Holy Ghost. Well, dear Saints, for your comfort and your devotion I assure you that the blessed time is at the door; yes, the appointed time for which your souls have longed. The thing which I taught you frequently when I was there, and with heavenly sweetness, was that it was close. Oh no, my dear friends, Mormonism is not false in anything which I taught to you, although there are some who deceive themselves through it. To them will be the unspeakable loss, but to all the faithful will come more than tongue can tell of blessings and glory and eternal lives to enjoy. What else shall I say from this distance? You know your duties; obey the priesthood which is in your midst, and if you support the leaders through your faith and your prayers and your obedience, they will lead you all safely in time to the enjoyment of all which your hearts desire; yes, and more than your hearts can imagine. But remember that it is necessary to have a test of your faith in all things always. God says that He will try His people in all things, and so it does not mean in some things only. Expect that then, and watch and live properly today while there is a today, and thus you will endure to the end.

Further on this topic I shall say that I understand through recent communication from Pres. Young that when he begins the foundation of the Temple they intend to begin to give to those first who are going on overseas missions their endowments in the Council House, which is a spacious and beautiful building, newly finished. Before its foundation, they will build a wall of rocks around the Temple Block, which contains 10 square acres. This wall will be 4 feet thick and 8 feet high; on top of this will be a wall of bricks 8 feet high, and 6 feet of pickets on top of that. There will be in this wall several gates which will be guarded by watchmen. And the firm decision is that through these gates no unclean thing will enter in any way or under any circumstance. For on these conditions only, if you notice, the Lord gave a promise of His presence in the other temples which were built. Yet some who were unclean and evil crawled into those because the circumstances of the Saints were such that they could not withstand them as can be done here. An iron railway is being made to carry the rocks from the mountain to the wall. And that is not all that is going on here, but much else which I cannot express to you through a letter. In short, this new world is already clothed in the cheerful countenance of antiquity, and her diligent inhabitants are fulfilling the character of the little, diligent creatures whose name was given to the place, that is, "Deseret," which translated is "honeybee."

There are here four cities already established, dedicated, inhabited and being built surprisingly fast: Great Salt Lake City, Ogden City (40 miles to the north), Provo City (46 miles to the south), and Manti City (130½ miles to the south of Salt Lake City), i.e., the place which was first called San Pete. Coaches have been prepared and established to run each week from here to Ogden. This service will begin as soon as spring arrives. Bridges have been made across the rivers, and the road has been made the whole distance. Several settlements have been established here and there across Utah Valley and in the north corner of this valley, and mills have been made this winter. In short, the valleys of the mountains for hundreds of miles are already alive with inhabitants!

Surprising, the gathering that we have here from the eastern world. One would think that nearly all its inhabitants have left home, between the Saints who have come here and all the thousands who have come through here to the country of gold. There is some unrivalled commotion going on at least! Besides this, a company containing many families, I know not exactly how many, but far more than 100, under the presidency of G. A. Smith, emigrated from the Great Salt Lake Valley to the Little Salt Lake Valley last January, together with all the preparations and tools advantageous for establishing a settlement in the valley, which I mentioned on my journey, in the place where we kept our wagons, etc. They took supplies for a year and seeds of every kind of corn, etc. The intent is to raise supplies mainly to satisfy the thousands of miners of iron, coal, etc., that it is intended to send there next summer to make iron, etc. The government here now is making plans to begin an iron railway from the Great Salt Lake Valley to the Little Salt Lake Valley. And as soon as they can, it is intended to drive it through to the port of San Diego on the Pacific Ocean. Amasa Lyman and Charles C. Rich (two Apostles) are now in the city preparing a numerous company and are by now about to leave to settle in William's Ranch, near Los Angeles, and within 40 miles of the port which was mentioned. A rich, healthful country and a temperate climate which is said to never have frost or snow; but all the fruits of the tropics are produced abundantly.

You can see from all these movements that the prophecies or the imaginings which I wrote to you before are being quickly fulfilled, that is, that the purpose of all this is to open the way for the Saints to come here from the south, instead of coming along the accursed waters of the Missouri and the long and painful journey across the land and the Rocky Mountains. I believe that it will not be half the distance, the cost, or the time to come here when the railway is finished which is being hurried along across the Isthmus of Panama, and from there in a ship to San Diego, and from there along the railway to the place which you choose. This is good news, isn't it, to the oppressed children of Zion, especially when we remember their longing for their freedom and their homecoming— when they have no hope, thousands of them, that they could earn enough there in their lifetime to pay their cost to come here.

In spite of that, I have better news still for the faithful and the patient, which proves the great care of God and His servants for all His children. I think that many in view of the foregoing promises will sing and weep, rejoice and grieve alternately. For, they say, what good is the temple or its ordinances to us who are too poor to be able to go to the place where it is? And they worry day and night because of their inability to come to Zion to enjoy the privileges of the Saints. But take heart, poor people of Wales; you will not be lost because of your poverty. And the arm of your God was not shortened so that He could not gather all the poor from the corners of the earth. Although there will be a curse of thousands on the heads of those poor persons whose cost was paid to Zion because of their dishonesty and their unkindness; yet, they do not close the ways of God nor can they prevent His work from prospering. Instead of that way of gathering the poor, a society has been established here sponsored by the government, with B. Young presiding over it, through gifts which are already tens of thousands of dollars. Its purpose is to gather the poor here, where they will work on the public works until they pay back that which they received. Bishop Hunter and others were deputized and sent to the States, and they returned in the fall with hundreds of the remnants of those poor who were in Nauvoo, etc. All the income from their work is returned to the treasury, and so it increases all the time, besides the continuous contributions until, I hope, its beneficial effects will be felt even in Britain and Wales also before long. Behold to you, poor people, proof of that which I promised through God to you when I was there, that is, that you would not be left behind because of your poverty. Rejoice, then, in this; be faithful and patient until you are sent for.

Another bit of news that I have to tell you is that we, ourselves, in this place have begun to build a temple—that all are agreed in the matter, and I have no doubt but what it will be finished before the end of next summer. There is an abundance already promised for that. And after that our joy will be even fuller.

Other news is with respect to the Madocians. Besides that which I wrote in the account of my journey, I heard in the fall in the City, from a gentleman who lived in Mexico and was on his way home from the States through here, that he a few years ago had found on his journey a nation of white people. And he described them very similarly to the way Mr. Ward and others described them and as settling in the same place. He says with respect to their houses that they are either hewn in the rock or built of rock in a nook between high rocks and impossible to get to except through a narrow descent—that they climb ladders to the tops of their houses from the outside and go down into them from the ceiling to the bottom. Others say things different from that. He and his friends were welcomed to their midst by about 300 young women coming dressed in their petticoats and white pettigowns with their heads adorned with flowers, etc., that each had a little pouch and some Indian corn flour in it which they scattered along the path before them. This custom shows their abundance together with their generosity and their kindness. They filled their needs cheaply when they went away.

Besides that, Col. Doniphan from Missouri announced that part of his army in the Mexican War, after proclaiming peace, offered their service to restore peace among some of the neighboring Indians. They lost their way for a time, and at last they came across some white people who received them with a welcome, and they wintered there. In the spring they escorted the soldiers to Santa Fe. For that kindness the Col. sent a regiment to accompany them home safely. After that he published their story in the newspapers of the States, but I have not had the privilege of seeing them. One said to me that he had read the account together with two treatises which were published by other travelers who were in their midst. And the former assures me, I know not how, that it was Welsh that they spoke there. These accounts agree remarkably in the peculiarities about them.

Even more explicitly, I understood through the Indians who visit us here that some of their elders used to go almost every summer to the south about a ten-day journey to trade with some white people, who, they say, make and wear clothes similar to the Mormons; and that their women are much fairer than they. That they work the earth and plough with one large fat horse with an iron plough—that their implements for horses are kind of a strong web of their own making. They showed me wool blankets which they bought there which are similar to the home spun of Wales. They make some of several colors, and black rows or blue in white in others. These Indians say that they are rather superstitious—that they believe in diviners, wizards, etc., and that one man rides home from the forest on a huge piece of wood without anything visible pulling it along! Poor things, if they are more superstitious than these Indians. I expect more of their history when some of the persons who were in their midst return, and you shall have an ampler account yet. Bro. Davis complained that the pieces were long last year, but I fear that you will be of the same mind as he now if I do not end at last. But it is either feast or famine between us still, and it cannot be otherwise now. But I must end at last feasting on the accounts I have about you in the *Udgorn*, etc., until next fall, it seems, when I shall expect a feast through receiving your stories for the year through the *Udgorn* and comprehensive letters which I shall expect from many of you.

All the families who came here are alive and healthy as far as I have heard, and they cannot help but do well in this country, all who try. Several Welshmen came through here to the country of gold, and with them no one of the Welsh went but Thomas John. I am so pleased to see if only the names of my old zealous brethren and co-workers, such as Thomas Pugh, Howell Williams, T. Giles, David John, Thomas Rees, John Thomas, Eli. Edwards, Robert Evans, Jos. Davies, D. Williams, Wm. Williams and his family, etc., etc. But there is not space to name them all or the half who are close to my heart always, but no one more than yourself and my dear brethren, John Davis and Wm. Howells. I translated his letter and it was published in the *Deseret News* at the request of Pres. B. Young. I intend to write to him soon and let him hear this letter. Pray for him as do I every day. My warmest love to the above brethren and their families together with all my acquaintances and all the dear Saints there. And my chief wish is that you be zealous, meek and godly, and pray continually for each other, for the success of Zion and for your unworthy brother in the Lord.

Dan Jones.

A Letter from Elizabeth Lewis to John Davis
(TD25)

[Manti, 1851.]

Dear Brother in the Gospel—

My excuse for writing to you is that I am not sure where my parents or my relatives are living now. And if they are alive you can tell them about me. Also, I promised to many of my dear friends, Saints and others, that I would write from here about the happenings and nature of the country, its inhabitants and the religion professed. Many promised to believe my testimony from here if I testified that Mormonism still seemed true. Although their delay to believe until then was not wise, yet, I consider it my duty to fulfill my promises to them. Thus with your permission to give space to this in the columns of the *Udgorn* I can still hope, though from afar, to help them break the debate that was in their minds.

With respect to the country in general, briefly, for the space does not allow me to go into detail: this is a mountainous country broken into valleys, great and small, rich and lovely, with rows of high, rocky, wooded, snowy and cold-looking mountains, which are in contrast to the rich meadows and the summer-like weather which is around their feet, which without exception form a majestic sight.

Its present inhabitants, besides the remnants of several tribes of Indians that live almost inhumanly and unnoticed along its lowlands and its hills, are the Saints, who, like myself, immigrated here from different parts of the world. They, without assistance in the world almost, except the freedom of the elements in their natural condition and hope to stimulate them, can here enjoy the freedom to worship their God, something which was forbidden them in almost every other part of the world. They took hold of something without shape, and already, not only are they a people independent of the world, possessing a fulness for their maintenance from the fruit of their own labors, but also they have peace and freedom which are priceless.

Our officials, temporal and spiritual, are from amongst ourselves, and the laws like the subjects receive justice. Needless to say, these inhabitants are religious, for nothing else is fashionable, much less tolerable here. There are here four cities speedily being built and inhabited, some containing already thousands and some tens of thousands of inhabitants; and the country surrounding with respect to agriculture looks similar to Wales, except that the fields are richer, flatter and a bit larger, some fields containing thousands of acres! Every craft is thriving, and schools in every settlement. Worship houses are numerous and full of Sabbath worshipers. Normal health is enjoyed throughout the settlements and peace reigns through the regions altogether. But I cannot say half of what I feel or what I see of the rights and enjoyment, not to mention the religious privileges of these saved inhabitants.

When I see the temporal advantages of these valleys, my thoughts escape back frequently to compare the conditions of my fellow-nation in Wales, and their poor ground, their rents and their hard taxes, and all which makes a hard world there, with the ease, the fulness and the freedom they can enjoy here, with moderate diligence. But when I understand about the plagues, the choleras, the disease and the deaths, the thefts, the murders which are ravaging mankind there, and embittering the sweetest pleasures, I cannot help but worry that they are not here by the thousands; and I know of nothing which would make my happiness more complete than to enjoy Welsh company here.

With respect to the religion, the truthfulness of which I testified so much about when there, I testify more firmly today than ever that this is the true gospel of Jesus Christ in its strength. I get additional testimony of this continually, and such that I could not get there, which has set its truthfulness beyond doubt in my mind a long time ago. And if my friends there could hear my testimony now, it would be stronger than any; and my exhortations would be more intense by far for them to get baptized by the servants of God for the remission of their sins and to be saved in the kingdom of God. Oh, you, my dear relatives, believe this my testimony. Be wise for your own benefit. You, my acquaintances whom I implored so much for your obedience to the plan of God to save mankind— from this distance, may this last inducement strengthen you to break the argument at last, that it is better for you to obey the ordinances of heaven than to take pains to try to conduct yourselves

zealously according to the human traditions of the age, which in
contrast are but mere shadows of the substance. Choose the good
part and be saved is my constant prayer.

Remember me lovingly to my dear parents, my brothers, and
my gentle sisters if you see them, and to the faithful Saints, hoping to see them here soon, "like doves coming to their windows."

The Welsh who came here the same time as I did are alive and
all healthy and successful as far as I know. All my own family and
I, thanks to the Grantor of all blessings, are enjoying excellent
health, with cheerful prospects ahead. The health of our dear Pres.
Capt. Jones is better than it was, but his diligence in every way
keeps him feeble. Likely he will write to you himself, and several
others, from whom you shall have a more detailed account than
I can give to you. Capt. Jones was elected Mayor and Chief Justice
for Manti City lately. I am your sister in the gospel of Christ.

Elizabeth Lewis.

A Letter from Great Salt Lake City
to the Editor of the *Udgorn*
(TD26)

Great Salt Lake City, January 31, 1852.

Dear Brother Davis—

With delight and pleasure I write to you again from the Far West,
hoping that this little paper will reach you safely, and that you are
enjoying health and temporal and spiritual success, which is the wish
of your old friend. The earlier time in Llanybydder comes to mind
often when we were small babies newly born in the fold of the Good
Shepherd. Great was the joy we felt at that time when there were
but four of us holding our meetings in my old home (Glantrenfawr),
and asking for great things from our kind Father; and greater was

our joy when we would get an answer to that which we had requested, and that we also knew at the time that our closest neighbors, and our relatives whom we loved so dearly, were bereft of those truths about which we had already come to know.

We had not been there long before some others enlisted under the same banner as we, ourselves. Some of our neighbors complained at that time that old Captain Jones (as they said) had deceived us, that we had promised all we had to him, etc., which neither they nor anyone else could prove one word of truth in it to this day. In that time several faithful brethren came to us, i.e., Brother Abel Evans and Thomas Harries, and others, who were of great benefit to us through their valuable counsels, and the greater experience which they had had in the Church of Jesus Christ. When in that condition, and increasing gradually, the father of lies and his children raged greatly against us, until we came to be the target and the scorn of some nearby reverends; but all worked out to our good. You will remember that letter which I received from Capt. D. S. Davies, Dolau, threatening me so greatly because of the religion I professed, calling the Saints, poor things, ''The damned night deepers that leadeth the people away down to hell''; but the Lord saw fit to bless us in proportion to the persecution which we suffered. It would be too lengthy for me now to mention old Daniel the Blind, and other cruel persecutors, for I know that they all shall receive justice in the forthcoming day, when the secrets of all hearts will be examined.

Forgive me, dear brother, for writing that which you knew already; it is a pleasure for me to write and remember former times.

Now, I venture to give some of our story here to you. Several of the nation of the Welshmen came here last fall, and all of them are enjoying excellent health. Shortly after they came here, I had the honor of baptizing about eighteen of them the same day; they were confirmed in my own house; after I baptized them, the Lord poured out His Spirit on them abundantly, and on us also as we administered in an extraordinary manner. No wonder we feel good, for love and joy dwell in every heart. The ordinance of baptism is necessary for all of the Saints to obey after coming here. Our revered Pres. Brigham Young and his counselors, and the Twelve, gave obedience to the above ordinance when they came here, renewing their covenants to the Lord to live faithfully, etc. Everything is going along well here; the storehouse of the Lord is being filled quickly; we anticipate more and more blessings continually, because the promise is on our side. The Lord said through the prophet, "Will I not open you the windows of heaven, and pour you out a blessing, that there shall not be room enough to receive it?" Hosts of the Saints last year received their endowments, and endowments continue to be given again this year. Several of the Welsh had the extremely high honor of receiving them also. I say to you, Bro. Davis, blessed are those humble and faithful (and I fully believe that you are one of such), for there are many blessings for them which they have not hitherto had. I do not possess the words or expression to describe the excellence, glory, and wisdom of the holy order which my Master, my goodly Father, has set out to bring His children to receive an inheritance of eternal life. Several large houses were built here last year by the Church, and preparations are now being made to make large walls around the Temple Block; soon no doubt an excellent temple will be seen here, the kind of which has not been seen in this dispensation, if the Saints continue as faithful as they are at present. Their diligence and faithfulness and their success are a matter of wonder for the world, and they know not what to say or to think about us; but they admit that there is something wondrous about us. Oh, that they were wise, that they understood that the invisible hand of the Lord is protecting and keeping His children daily, although He suffers the enemies of the Saints to persecute them from place to place, from city to city, until finally they persecuted them to the wilderness, about 1,000 miles from all settlements of white people. This is good that we are so far from them; we may have calm here to worship our God, "with no one to hurt us or to make us afraid," for the mobs of Missouri and Illinois are too far. We do not hear in this quiet city here the cruel blasphemies, i.e., deceivers, satanists, and false prophets, etc., etc. Oh, how lovely is the dwelling of brothers together far from the Pharisees and hypocrites of this age; but no matter how far we are, several of the Gentiles come by us, who are sick from yellow fever. They are desirous of gathering before their golden god in Lower California; they stay here but a short time. Why? Because the Spirit of the living God reigns here; for fear, terror, and horror are on sinners in Zion. Yet, we baptize an occasional one of those who are honest in heart of the blood of Ephraim who comes here in their midst. Such are happy and rejoice with us in the salvation of our God. When will I see you here, dear brother? Doubtless you would like to be in the great source of light and knowledge, which with its crystalline waters goes quickly to the four corners of the earth; but yet, perhaps duty calls you to stay there for a while; if so, you lose nothing, but it is a loss to those who refuse to come here when the way is open to them to come.

How sweet it is to listen to the counsels of our President Brigham and his counselors, together with the Twelve in their turn: they show so clearly our duties in this church, and the great reward which comes from carrying them out. What is the wisdom of the Colleges of the world compared to God the Father, and His Son Jesus Christ, and the strong deeds of the Holy Ghost? I answer, nothing; for their wisdom is natural, earthly, for they do not think about the things from above; they oppose godly wisdom and the power of God in our age, just as they did in every age when the priesthood was on the earth.

I must finish; and if you see this letter as worthy of appearing in your *Udgorn*, you are welcome to use it; and if it appears in the *Udgorn*, I say again to those of the Saints who read it, "Flee, flee to Zion according to the counsel of the servants of God, the presidency in Wales." I wish very much to hear from my relatives, my father, and David my brother, and my sister Sarah, if they have not started toward here. I wish for the family of Cefncrwth, Meidrim, to send a letter to me; I would very much love to see them here, and I hope that what I have said to them will stay in their minds. I wish for my mother-in-law to send a letter to me frequently. My wife joins with me, together with Bro. Benjamin Jones, Sadler and Richard Jones, in sending fond regards to you and Bro. Thomas Harries.

Farewell for a while, dear brother.

Your humble servant,
Thomas Jeremy.

Letters from Capt. D. Jones

(TD27)

Manti City, May 1, 1852.

Esteemed Brother Phillips—

After an extended delay I again write to remind you and the beloved Saints in Wales that I am still alive here and continuing in the enjoyment of many privileges and blessings, temporal and spiritual. The cause of the delay was Pres. Young's counsel to me last October to prepare for a mission to Wales. And so I expected to carry my own letter; however, he together with scores of other brethren came through here yesterday to visit the southern settlements and instructed me to prepare to search further for the "Madocians" next fall. He said that lately he had heard quite a number of interesting stories about them which would be too long to report in this letter. I shall follow his instructions.

Dear Brother, you and your important mission occupy my thoughts and my prayers frequently, and it causes no small comfort to me to hear through letters, etc., that the Lord is keeping you and strengthening you through His Spirit, to lead the Church there with success—to hear, I say, that unity and charity are prospering to the point of attracting sinners to obey the gospel of Christ. And no doubt if the Welsh understood what is being enjoyed here, together with the things which await them also there, they would readily obey as a nation. But God arranged that "through the foolishness of preaching is the saving of those who believe." So, they must believe your witness before they can see through the veil which is between them and their future destiny, one way or the other.

No doubt you await some stories from me this time. The best of these is that the inhabitants of all these valleys are enjoying general health and peace. The countenance of their Father smiles on them and their possessions, and their labor, temporally speaking, and we enjoy more privileges, blessings, enlightenment and knowledge from God, our Father, and the great plan of salvation continually. And in this church there has never before been seen such unanimous devotion and unwavering and general determination to build the kingdom of Jesus as there is through these valleys now. This enthusiastic unity and zeal brought down from heaven in the last conference more blessings and knowledge than ever before. The natives who live around the settlements are peaceful now. The kingdom has come in our midst here, which coming our ancestors desired so much to enjoy a part in. Agriculture is so fruitful that all the storehouses of the country have overflowed with labor, and an abundance of wheat can be obtained for between 2 and 4 shillings per 60-pound bushel. Cheese from 6 pence to 10 pence; butter from 10 pence to 1 shilling; horses cheaper than ever here; horned stock continue in the previous prices; clothes about double the American prices. But there is a shortage of money here presently, which causes the merchants for the most part to transport their goods to the gold mines from here.

There are brave efforts in favor of independence from the whole world and its markets, through an increase of home skills. And there is already a large part of the inhabitants making their own clothes and necessities, insofar as the climate allows the materials to grow. And there are settlements continually spreading to the south where everything can be produced which can be produced in any climate. While the peace and protection continue at home, which cover these valleys at present, neither you nor we need to be uneasy about the jealousy and the fury which are appearing against us in the States or in any part of our Father's footstool.

With respect to the immigration here this year, there is no room to doubt any longer but that it will be far beyond any past year through the States. Preparations are being made here to send scores, if not several hundred wagons to meet the immigrants traveling on foot, who will be along the way by the thousands. Food, etc., will be taken to them about halfway from the States.

With respect to the emigration from Wales, you no doubt are getting all pertinent counsel from the Presidency in Liverpool, yet I shall add this for the consideration of the emigrating Saints from there—Let them strive to keep the Spirit of God with them so they will not lose the spirit of gathering, or forget their inciting purposes there, nor the final selection after arriving here. This gathering is a strong wind, and blessed is he who keeps his sights diligently on the objective. I am sorry to understand that some of the Welsh who arrived at Great Salt Lake last year are starting or have already started off for the gold mines, contrary to counsel, to die from the "yellow fever," as the lust for gold is called. Of the two choices it is better for the Saints to live and die faithful here and go to paradise than to lose their future glory by trying to gather and failing. I received a letter from Thomas Giles lately which caused me great comfort. Thank him for it for me, and I shall try to repay him before long by writing to him. I have had but one letter from you since I saw you, and the pleasure of seeing your name in your own hand on the pleasing gift of fruit stones. I have received about half of those which you sent, and thank you very much for them.

I haven't heard from Bro. Davis for a long time. What is the reason? And I have not received the *Udgorn* except the first volume, and a few issues after that nearly two years old, from H. Evans. Have nearly all my old colleagues died, or are they on their way here? My family is well and all the Welsh from what I hear. Greet the dear Saints there for me lovingly; may the gracious Lord bless them and you, and Bro. Davis, Pugh, etc. I, myself, bless you all. Amen.

I am yours, etc.

D. Jones.

Dear Brother Davis,

I received a comforting letter lately from my brother Edward in which he shows the spirit of a Saint and a longing desire to immigrate to Zion; and he earnestly beseeches me to assist him if I can. I wrote him back to ask you if you have on hand any money owing to me; and if so, be so kind as to present it to him, and his reception of it will be as good as money to me.

I am so short of money here that I have not had as much as one pound for more than a year! But I am grateful for sufficient food and peace to enjoy.

I depend on you, Brother Phillips and the faithful Saints there to do your best for me in this according to your customary kindness. Please convey thanks for me and for my wife to Margarett Jones for her delightful present of a little pair of shoes and stockings for our baby. They reached us when they were greatly needed, for leather is not to be had here for any price in the world, neither is it likely that any will be available until some is made here; I hear that some has been made in Salt Lake.

Thanks for your letters which you sent some time ago and for the books; I desire nothing more than to hear of the course of the gospel in dear Wales, and I would be very glad to hear more frequently. May wise God bless you all with charity, with wisdom and with eternal success is my sincere and daily prayer. My wife and my children are enjoying good health (thank goodness for that) and join with me in remembering you and your family, and Bro. Phillips and his family, beloved Pugh, together with all our acquaintances, especially all the Saints. Soon we shall meet you all here like wheat gathered to the barn before the coming of adversity.

Can you give to me news of my brother John? I have not heard from him since I left there, except one letter from his daughter Sarah about two years ago. Edward says that he is on his way here; I hope that he is. I rather expect to see the three of you here before I return there; yet that will be according to the mind and counsel of Him Who owns us all.

I hope to hear much from you before I start to the south in the fall to search out the Welsh Indians, after which I shall repay the news, most likely! I heard that you have published the Doctrine and Covenants, together with the Book of Mormon in Welsh. Oh, how glad I would be to see them. May their Author endow you with wisdom for the important work, say I. I must make an end now as you can see, by bidding farewell for a time.

Your brother, etc.,

D. Jones.

A Letter to Presidents W. S. Phillips and John Davis

(TD28)

Pottowatamie, June 22, 1852.

Dear Brothers Phillips and Davis,

I take the present opportunity to write to you from Pottowatamie. The Welsh branch has begun its journey toward the Great Salt Lake Valley, with some of the English and the French in the company. Fifty wagons make up the camp and are divided in five groups, that is, ten wagons in each group, and there is a captain over each ten wagons; also, a captain over the whole camp. I shall name those whom you know—Capt. D. Evans, Llanelli, the first; John Rees, blacksmith, formerly from near Pont Haiarn, Merthyr Tydfil, the second; H. Evans, former president of West Glamorgan, the third; Coward, the fourth; the fifth, you do not know him. William Beddoe, brickman, formerly from Pendaren, is the scribe of the camp, and Abel Evans is captain of the guards, and the writer is the servant of the whole camp. I have written three letters, and according to that which I heard from Bro. Evans, they have not reached their destination.

All the Saints are in good health, each one with his tent house as white as snow; and we would be glad if our brothers and sisters, many whom we know, were closer to us to get to see the truth of the word which is like this: "A country flowing with milk," etc. Much milk in our camp is thrown out as casually as is the bathwater used by three or four Merthyr colliers. We have more than we can use, and there is no one close by in need of it.

Rachel Rowlands, Hirwaun, is improving well; she and William's two daughters are in the camp on their journey to the Valley, together with Thomas Morris and Ann, my sister; thanks to you for sending them across. I shall make an end now; you shall have more of our story after we have crossed the river.

I am in haste,
William Morgan.

A Letter to Presidents W. S. Phillips and J. Davis

(TD29)

Bear River, 80 miles from Salt Lake City,
20 September 1852.

Dear Brothers Phillips and Davis—

According to my promise, I now take the opportunity of writing to you for the second time on this journey. We have had a comfortable journey all the way so far, and the weather has been unusually moderate with but little rain and no storms; and even though we crossed one mountain which was 7,700 feet above sea level, we saw not so much as one day of snow on our way. We did see a lot of black clouds rising with the wind, and we heard distant thunder as if the whole heavens above were gathering their forces to sweep us away; but they dared not harm us, because of that One Who has all authority, and who calls the stars by their names, and He whose command the winds obey. He parted them as if by His hand (i.e., the clouds) until they went past us on every side with us in the middle without our feeling their effects. And not just once or twice did this happen.

We are all well at present, and we had but little sickness on our journey. Four have died, i.e., William Dafydd, from Llanelli, and Thomas, his son. Also William, son of Sister Howells from Aberdare, who fell under his mother's wagon wheel which went over his chest. We administered to him through the ordinances of the Church of Jesus Christ, according to the scriptures, and the next night he was strolling around the camp. He fell sick again in a day or two, and Bro. Taylor and myself administered to him again, but he died in spite of everything and everyone. The other who died was Jennet, the daughter of Thomas and Anne Morris, from cancer. You shall have more of the account of our journey when we reach the Valley.

Last night we were in our camp on the bank of Sulphur Creek, two miles from here. We heard in the morning that our dear brother, Capt. D. Jones, was camped by the Bear River. It was not long, as you shall learn, after hearing the news, before the word "pack up and pick up" came out; and I know that nowhere on the journey was there a quicker response to any call. His name had lit a flame of love in the breast of everyone toward him so that nothing else could be heard through the camp but "Bro. Jones," and "let us go to meet him." It wasn't long before the wheels were turning. After traveling close to a mile, we saw a man of small stature walking quickly to meet us. We did not know who it was; but as we drew nearer to each other, to our joy who would it be but our dear Bro. Jones and his customary cheery smile. It is easier to imagine than to describe our meeting. After shaking hands, embracing, weeping and kissing, we went to the bank of the river where he had left his horse, having traveled from twenty to thirty miles during the night ahead of his company in order to meet us. We decided to spend a day in his friendship, to converse with each other about things pertaining to the kingdom of our God. Oh, brethren, how sweet the words poured over his lips. It is true that every word from his mouth was sweet earlier in Wales, but they were a thousand times sweeter here on the desolate mountains of America, between eight and nine thousand miles from Wales.

I must end this letter, for the camp is getting near, and Brothers Jeremy and Daniels are coming. Who can hold a pen when faithful brethren with whom I traveled thousands of miles in the bonds of love are getting near? Not I. There, the brothers and sisters are running; I cannot restrain myself any longer. Behold, everyone is coming back to the camp with his heart full of joy in full proof of the truthfulness of the words "how lovely is the dwelling of brothers together." We spent the rest of the day in brotherly love, at times singing, other times testifying of our determinations, listening to the teaching of the three brethren, until the day went past, and, if the truth be told, until twelve o'clock at night also. And though in the midst of the green willows we met, the Spirit of God was among us. We all took our leave so that each could fulfill his calling in full confidence that we would meet again in Zion. The camp is getting underway. Farewell for now, dear Brothers Phillips and Davis.

I am your brother in the bonds of the Gospel,
W. Morgan.

[William Morgan to William Phillips and John Davis]
(TD30)

Salt Lake City, June 25, 1852.
Dear Brothers Phillips and Davis,—

According to my promise in my last letter I take this opportunity to give some details of the account of our journey from the Bluffs to this lovely place. After taking our leave of Brothers Jones, Daniels, Jeremy and others, the ones I knew being more numerous than the ones I did not know, we continued our journey with our hearts rejoicing, reflecting on the conversations and the interesting and edifying counsels which we received from the aforementioned brethren, praying for our Father to bless all of them in their dangerous and goodly endeavors, on land and water and in the midst of our own nation. After arriving at Mountain Creek and traveling about three or four miles, we decided to rest through the night where there was plenty of grazing for the animals. The sun was about to hide its head in the west and the mantle of night was drawing nigh exhorting everyone except the watchmen to rest. We heard the noise of a wagon coming pell-mell from the city road; by then all were straining their eyes to see what was coming, and before long the lead watchmen shouted out, "Welsh from Salt Lake." There was no need to say it again, for the first word pierced through us all like an electric current. Everyone came near having a race to meet them. To our great joy who were they but Thomas Jones, Hirwaen; Morgan Hughes, Pontyates; and William, son of Evan Jones, Mill Street, Aberdare. They had come from thirty to forty miles to meet us with a load of fruits of the Valley, such as watermelons, mushmelons, potatoes, pickle cucumbers, grapes, etc., to welcome us. The watchmen came over to the camp, according to the language of the ancient Welsh, "without a sword unsheathed against them." They put their entire load under my care, and I had the honor of dividing the load among the brothers and sisters; and even though the divider normally gets the smallest share, I got plenty myself and everyone else, even though we had not tasted such delicacies all during the summer. We went no further than

the foot of the mountain the next day. The second day we crossed
the second mountain, as it is seen here; by the time we reached
the expanse which is between the second mountain and the first,
there was a multitude of the brethren awaiting us with the same
presents which we received from the other brethren. I shall name
some of them: John Parry, Newmarket and his son, Dl. Leigh,
Owen Roberts, Thomas James, Cadwaladr Owens, etc., too many
to name. We reached the city on the last day of September, all
healthy and our hearts thankful to our Father for the privilege. We
had traveled 1,130 miles, without a civilized man owning a furrow
of land except in two places, i.e., in Fort Laramie and Fort Bridger.
All except these two places is under the government of the
various Indian tribes and the buffaloes, thousands of them. It is
not unusual to see four or five hundred of them in one herd coming to the Platte River to get water. We killed five of them on our
journey; their meat is similar in its taste to Welsh beef. Salt is not
needed to keep it from smelling bad; drying it in the heat of the
sun serves the same purpose which the salt does over there, without
the salting. The Indians are kindly people if one behaves kindly
toward them. One day, totally unawares, I happened to come into
the midst of about three of four hundred of them, i.e., the Sioux.
As was my custom, I was on horseback riding in front of the camp
to look for the trail and for a comfortable place to have lunch; and
having gone ahead of the camp for about two miles, I saw two of
them coming as fast as their horses could carry them to meet me;
and as far as I was concerned I was like King Henry [*sic*] ready to
say, "Kingdom," not "for a horse," for I had a good one under
me, but "for being in camp." It was too late to turn back; it was
better to go forward, and it was not long before their Indian majesty
and myself met one another. He greeted me, "How do, Mormon
good." I thought by then that they were not as bad as I believed;
I went ahead between the two chieftains, who were in their official
and pompous dress, till we arrived at their camp which was about a
mile and a half from the place where we had met; their camp was
arranged in an astronomical manner in my opinion; their biggest
tent was in the middle, and a picture of the sun had been drawn
with something red, the same kind as is seen in the old country,
and the others with pictures which I did not understand. This

brought to my mind the words of the prophet, that "people worship the sun," etc., since they are totally ignorant of the "true and living God." They behaved toward me in an extremely gentlemanly fashion. Their chiefs spread their blankets on the ground, motioning for me to sit down to smoke what they called a "peace pipe," as I understood through the translator, Huntington. The manner of having a pipe handed around in each group is like the shilling jug in the taverns of the old country which is handed around to all the members of a group, and each one in his turn takes a drink. So it is with this pipe: the chief takes two or three puffs and then passes it to the next one and so on around the circle until the chief has it again. Refusing to sit down with them to smoke is a sign among them that the one who refuses is envious. Well, Brother Davis,* how will you react if you are called to the pipe? I am confident that Brother Phillips like myself has not forgotten and will take his turn. When the camp came we took up a collection from them, such as a spoonful or two of sugar, cakes, etc., and their majesty accepted our gifts. Then our camp got under way, with myself having shaken hands and spoken and received suggestions that I did not understand, and I followed after the camp. All that I understood of their speaking was "Good Mormon," and "swap pongo." Although the red boys, from what I could observe on the journey, were completely harmless, yet I do not say that they will not steal if they have the chance. But I can say this much, that after going past thousands of them, when some were sleeping in our camp, nothing was stolen from us nor was an insult ever given to any of us. And although the journey was long, I considered it nothing but enjoyment every step of the way; so it was to me, and so it is to everyone who is fond of observing the wonders of the desert and seeing something new every day.

Since I have spent one winter season in the city, perhaps you would like to hear a little of our history. The city is laid out in straight streets from north to south and the same from east to west; the land is square, or in "blocks" as they are called, with ten acres of land within each block. The town is between two and three miles

---

*Answer: I shall make the head of the pipe a chimney and not my mouth.—J. D.

long and about two miles wide. There are splendid buildings here: the Storehouse of the Church is about 190 feet long and three stories high and has been completed in a most excellent way; the Council House and the Social Hall are grand buildings, in addition to the other splendid buildings which are under construction. It is intended to put a hundred masons to work this summer on the wall which is to surround the Temple. The streets of the city are 130 feet wide with trees planted between the footwalks and the way for the vehicles, and there is water running with every street with places to turn it out according to the wishes of the inhabitants. The flat land on which the city is located is about 30 miles wide and 200 miles long with mountains surrounding it on every side; and there is snow on the mountaintops now, and I am told that it is there throughout the year; and there is a beautiful view to behold. The foot of the mountains is covered with plants and flowers, and their top is like white sheeting placed on a green table with the Salt Lake at their feet, in some places like a transparent glass. When the sun hides its face in the west it reflects on the snow, the leaves, the flowers and the water, and the sight is beautiful beyond description. Not much snow falls in the Valley; the idle animals can live through the winter on the flat land. The foundation of the Temple is almost finished; the cornerstone was placed last April, and it is thought now that the building will be ready within three years.

Here is a segment of a letter of Brother Jones to Bishop Hunter:

"Esteemed Bishop Hunter.—Many of my compatriots are coming across in the 13th company; I do not know their condition; perhaps their money and their provision are scarce. If so, when they reach the Valley, I shall be grateful to you for furnishing them their needs, through the hand of Brother Morgans [*sic*], and I shall pay you in Manti, San Pete Valley. I am, etc.,   D. Jones."

Brother Jones gave that letter to me on the banks of the Bear River, and I shall not soon forget his fatherly care over his fellow nation; and on behalf of myself and my camp I express warmest thanks to my brother and the hero Jones, although none of us was in need. I have been in Manti lately; Jane and the little girl were healthy, but Jane was expecting her baby any day. The Welsh who have come to the Valley from the beginning of the emigration until now are all alive and well except four, i.e., the wife of D. Phillips; Jane Morgan, Cardiff; Lucy, the wife of Captain Evans, Llanelli; and Mary Ann, the widow of George Davis, Rhymni; the last two died in childbirth, Jane from cancer, but I do not know what Sister Phillips's illness was, as she died before I came to the Valley. Everything is going along well in these valleys, and the land and the crops are abundant. Some wheat will be cut this week. If a diligent man comes here without one shilling in his pocket, in three years he will be self-sufficient if no misfortune befalls him. There is plenty of work on the Public Works for those who have no animals; and the wage for the laborers is 3 shillings 3 pence per day, and 12 shillings 6 pence per day for the masons. The price of flour in the Storehouse of the Church is 1 pound 5 shillings per hundred, and it does not rise or fall in price. Here is a better place for the workers of Merthyr Tydfil, is it not, together with those who have no animals? And the plants and flowers which spring from the earth say in their language, "Here is fruitful soil; till it and you shall have your daily bread." My paper is nearly full. My love to you, your wives and children, and to Brother Jones and all the Saints. Martha wishes to be remembered to you in the same way.

Your brother in Christ,
William Morgan.

Works Cited

Allen, James B., and Thomas G. Alexander, eds. *Manchester Mormons: The Journal of William Clayton, 1840 to 1842*. Santa Barbara and Salt Lake City: Peregrine Smith, 1974.

Appleby, William I. Journal. Housed in Library–Archives, Historical Division, The Church of Jesus Christ of Latter-day Saints, Salt Lake City; hereafter cited as LDS Church Archives.

Bowen, David D. "History of the Life of David D. Bowen." MS. LDS Church Archives.

Chambers, Rachel David. Biographical Sketch. Private collection.

Davies, John Johnson. "Historical Sketch of My Life." *Utah Historical Quarterly* 9 (1941): 155–67.

Davis, John. Preface to *Hanes ymfudiad y Saint i Galifornia* (An account of the Saints' emigration to California), iii–iv. Merthyr Tydfil: J. Davis, 1849.

[Davis, John.] J. D. "The Saints' Farewell." *Prophwyd y Jubili* (Prophet of the Jubilee), December 1848, 186.

————— to the Editor of *Seren Gomer* (Star of Gomer), 6 October 1848. Unpublished in private collection.

Elsom, Kendall A. "Asiatic Cholera." In *The Cyclopedia of Medicine, Surgery, Specialties*, 3:1410–11. Rev. ed. Philadelphia: F. A. Davis Company, 1966.

Hulme, William, to Orson Pratt, 28 April 1849. *Millennial Star*, 15 June 1849, 185–86.

Jaques, J., to Orson Pratt, 22 July 1856. *Millennial Star*, 30 August 1856, 553–57.

Jeremy, Sarah. Biographical Sketch. In *Heart Throbs of the West*, 11:8–9. Salt Lake City: Daughters of the Utah Pioneers, 1950.

Jeremy, Thomas. Journal. LDS Church Archives.

————— to John Davis, 18 April 1849. In *Hanes ymfudiad y Saint i Galifornia*, 21–24. Merthyr Tydfil: J. Davis, 1849.

————— to John Davis, 14 April 1850. *Udgorn Seion* (Zion's Trumpet), October 1850, 281–85.

————— to John Davis, 21 January 1852. *Udgorn Seion*, 8 May 1852, 142–45.

Jeremy, Thomas et al. "Last greeting of the emigrating Saints." *Udgorn Seion*, March 1849, 55–58.

Jones, Dan, to Orson Spencer, 29 September 1847. *Millennial Star*, 15 October 1847, 318–19.

_____. "Hail to California." *Prophwyd y Jubili*, October 1848, 158.

_____. "Counsels to the Emigrants to California." *Prophwyd y Jubili*, November 1848, 165–69. (The article is unsigned; authorship is obvious, however.)

_____ to John Davis, 18 April 1849, 5–21. In *Hanes ymfudiad y Saint i Galifornia*, 5–21. Merthyr Tydfil: J. Davis, 1849.

_____ to William Phillips, 30 April 1849. *Udgorn Seion*, June 1849, 122–23.

_____ to William Phillips, 13 July 1849. *Udgorn Seion*, September 1849, 179–82.

_____ to W. Morgan and W. Davies, 21 September 1849. In *Cyfarwyddiadau i'r ymfudwyr tua Dinas y Llyn Halen* (Directions to the emigrants to Salt Lake City), 2–6.

_____ to William Phillips, 12 October 1849. *Udgorn Seion*, April 1850, 105–10.

_____ to William Phillips, 20 November 1849. In *Tri llythyr oddiwrth Capt. D. Jones, ac un oddiwrth Mrs. Lewis (o Gydweli), o Ddinas y Llyn Halen* (Three letters from Capt. D. Jones, and one from Mrs. Lewis [from Kidwelly], from Salt Lake City), 1–3. Merthyr Tydfil: J. Davis, 1850.

_____ John Davis, 12 April 1850. In *Tri llythyr*, 4–5.

_____ to William Phillips, 12 April 1850. In *Tri llythyr*, 5–6.

_____ to William Phillips and John Davis, 10 September 1850. *Udgorn Seion*, 11 January 1851, 17–19.

_____ to William Phillips, March 1851. In *Llythyr oddiwrth Capt. D. Jones at Wm. Phillips, yn cynnwys newyddion o Seion* (A letter from Capt. D. Jones to Wm. Phillips, containing news from Zion), 1–8. Merthyr Tydfil: John Davis, 1851.

_____ to William Phillips, 1 May 1852. Private collection. All but the last one-fourth (which is a note to John Davis) published in *Udgorn Seion*, 4 September 1852, 287–90.

Jones, Noah. *Cwyn yr ymfudwr a'i ddau anerchiad* (Lament of the emigrant and his two greetings). Merthyr Tydfil: John Davis, n.d.

Jones, York F. *Lehi Willard Jones*. Salt Lake City: Woodruff Printing Co., [1972].

Lewis, Elizabeth to John Davis, 10 April 1850. *Tri llythyr*, 6–8.

_____ to John Davis, 1851. *Udgorn Seion*, 23 August 1851, 272–74.

Lewis, William. "Englynion." In *Cyfarwyddiadau i'r ymfudwyr*, 12.

Morgan, William, to William Phillips, 2 September 1849. *Udgorn Seion*, November 1849, 218–19.

_____ to William Phillips, 25 December 1849. *Udgorn Seion*, February 1850, 51–54.

_____ to William Phillips, 26 May 1850. *Udgorn Seion*, July 1850, 186–88.

_____ to William Phillips and John Davis, 19 July 1850. In *Cyfarwyddiadau i'r ymfudwyr* (Directions to the emigrants), 2, 6–10.

_____ to William Phillips and John Davis, 22 June 1852. *Udgorn Seion*, 7 August 1852, 259–60.

_____ to William Phillips and John Davis, 20 September 1852. *Udgorn Seion*, 8 January 1853, 32–33.

_____ to William Phillips and John Davis, 25 June 1853. *Udgorn Seion*, 27 August 1853, 143–47.

Nash, Isaac B. "The Life Story of Isaac B. Nash." MS. Arranged and copied from originals by his grandchildren, Mr. and Mrs. Lyn W. Nash.

Peters, David. Records. LDS Church Archives.

Phillips, William. "Emigration of the Saints to California." *Udgorn Seion*, March 1849, 59–61.

Pratt, David H., and Paul F. Smart. "Life on Board a Mormon Emigrant Ship." In *1980 World Conference on Records*, series 418, proceedings.

Scoville, Lucius N. to Church Headquarters, 8 June 1849. Journal History of the Church, 8 June 1849. LDS Church Archives.

Smith, George A., Ezra T. Benson, and Dan Jones to William Morgan and William Davis, 21 September 1849. In *Cyfarwyddiadau i'r ymfudwyr* (Directions to the emigrants), 2–6. Merthyr Tydfil: J. Davis, 1849.

Smith, George A. and William I. Appleby to Orson Hyde, 18 October 1849. *Millennial Star*, 15 April 1850, 125–27.

Spencer, Orson, to Orson Pratt, 10 April 1849. *Millennial Star*, 15 June 1849, 182–85.

Tullidge, Edward W. *The Women of Mormondom*. New York: N.p., 1877.

Warner, Jim, to John Keetle. In "List of Members . . . and Letters and Notes on the Warner and Kettle Families of Spanish Fork, Utah." Genealogical Department of The Church of Jesus Christ of Latter-day Saints, Salt Lake City.

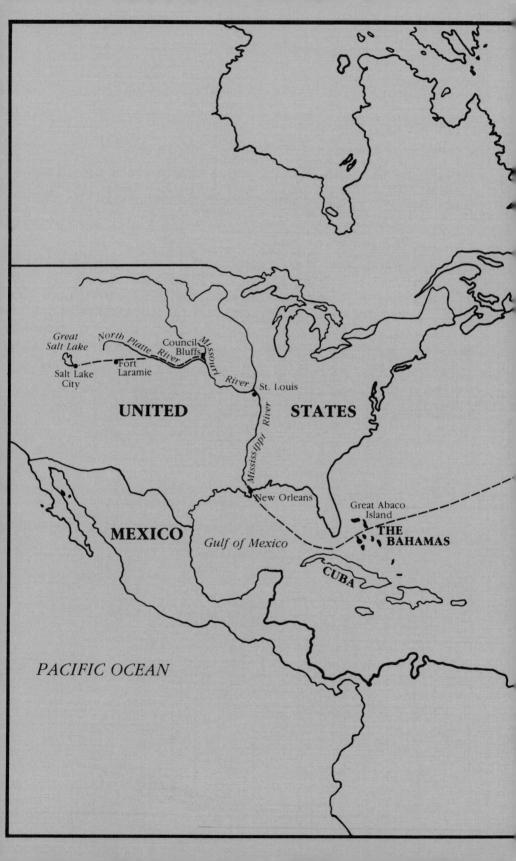